Mison 美森教育

丛书主编◎孙乐

剑桥领思备考
超核心系列

Linguaskill

Linguaskill
21天突破
剑桥领思 通用英语
超核心 词汇

编著◎孙乐

扫描二维码
免费听音频
免费下载网址
www.dutp.cn

大连理工大学出版社
Dalian University of Technology Press

图书在版编目（CIP）数据

21天突破剑桥领思通用英语超核心词汇 / 孙乐编著
. -- 大连：大连理工大学出版社，2023.12
（剑桥领思备考超核心系列丛书）
ISBN 978-7-5685-4664-5

Ⅰ.①2… Ⅱ.①孙… Ⅲ.①英语—词汇—自学参考
资料 Ⅳ.①H313

中国国家版本馆CIP数据核字（2023）第198005号

大连理工大学出版社出版
地址：大连市软件园路80号　邮政编码：116023
发行：0411-84708842　邮购：0411-84708943　传真：0411-84701466
E-mail：dutp@dutp.cn　　　URL：https://www.dutp.cn/
大连图腾彩色印刷有限公司印刷　　　大连理工大学出版社发行

幅面尺寸：145mm×208mm	印张：9	字数：308千字
2023年12月第1版		2023年12月第1次印刷

责任编辑：李玉霞　　　　　　　　　　　　　　责任校对：张晓燕
封面设计：美森教育

ISBN 978-7-5685-4664-5　　　　　　　　　　定　价：48.00元

本书如有印装质量问题，请与我社发行部联系更换。

前 言 ·················FOREWORD

一、剑桥领思考试简介

剑桥领思（Linguaskill）是由英国剑桥大学英语考评部研发的一项在线英语测评，它借助人工智能技术测试应试者的英语水平。剑桥领思以模块的形式，全面测试听、说、读、写四项英语技能。剑桥领思的特点是快速便捷，由于是在线考试，考生可以随时随地参加。同时，相比于传统考试，剑桥领思可以快速提供成绩，一般在考试完成后72小时内考生可以获得成绩报告。其考试成绩对标欧洲语言共同参考框架（CEFR），该框架是描述学习者语言能力的国际标准。由于其高效、准确、权威，目前剑桥领思已获得数千家国际组织机构的认可，在中国，认可剑桥领思成绩的组织机构包括但不限于中国石油天然气集团、中建国际建设、中国五矿集团、美的集团、中山华利集团、中国教育国际交流协会、山东省人名政府外事办公室、西交利物浦大学、宁波诺丁汉大学、昆山杜克大学等。

根据考生自身目标和想测试的英语种类，剑桥领思考试分为剑桥领思通用英语测评和剑桥领思职场英语测评两种。剑桥领思通用英语测评（以下简称"领思通用英语"）更侧重日常生活与学习等英语应用语境，测试的是日常生活英语。

二、本书编写目的

想要考取领思通用英语高分，掌握考试核心词汇是首要任务。本书可以帮助考生在短时间内攻克领思通用英语中的核心词汇，为考取高分打下坚实的基础。

三、本书核心特色

1. 21天学习计划，掌握840个考试核心词

本书的编者均为剑桥领思中国运营中心合作教师，且一线教学经验丰富。他们通过分析大量的领思通用英语试题，总结出书中的840个考试核心词，又将这840个核心词合理地分配在21天内，这样考生只需每天记忆40个。坚持21天后，便能掌握领思通用英语核心词。

2. 例句与搭配，加深词汇理解和运用

本书根据领思通用英语考试中词汇的考查特点，从大量领思通用英语试题中严格筛选出重点内容，对考试中出现的高频词和考点进行归纳和总结，提供了例句和常考搭配，让考生在学习时加深对词汇的理解，同时体会其在实际场景中如何运用。此外，每个词条也提供了派生词，帮助考生拓展词汇量。

3. 词根和联想记忆法，高效助记

本书中的绝大多数词汇提供了词根或者联想记忆法，借助词根规律、拆分单词以及谐音等方式帮助考生简化难词，高效记忆。

4. 复习方式多样，有效巩固提高

在课后复习环节，本书采用了扫码听写和单项选择两种形式，扫码听写主要考查单词读音，单项选择则是检验考生对单词词义的辨析和用法的掌握情况。

5. 英籍外教原声音频，扫码即听

本书的单词和例句由英籍外教录音，发音纯正，考生可以进行跟读，纠正单词发音。书中提供了二维码，扫码即可获取音频，方便考生随时随地听音。

在筹备及编写本套书的过程中，美森教育图书编撰委员会以下资深教师委员也参与了工作，分别是：孙乐、孙旭、李建荣、姚宝娇、杨李健、陈雪、孙晓丹、于京圣、姚宝丹、邢思毅、隋良东、景作鹏、皮姗姗、邢汝国、景文学、隋秀丽、景文菊、陈威、刘庆杰、孙连军、宋海蛟、周翼、潘宇、尹辉、张清川、孙成伟、辛连厚、吴馨玲、邵淑梅、侯殿东、朱汉民、王守斌、韩琦、崔林杰、杨丹、王海军等，在此一并表示感谢。

相信本书会成为广大领思通用英语考生备考路上的得力助手，陪伴你们一起考取领思高分。

美森教育

www.mison.cn

关注"剑桥领思考试"微信公众号
随时随地获取领思学习干货

致读者 •••••••••••••••••••••••••••• TO READERS

亲爱的本书读者：

在您正式开始学习这本书之前，请务必扫描下面的二维码观看本书的使用讲解视频，同时获取读者专享免费课程。

视频是本书作者团队的代表教师特意录制的，为大家介绍了本书的特点和结构，并精讲了高效使用本书的具体方法。

读者专享免费课程是给大家额外附赠的领思通用英语备考课（价值599元），该课程适用于所有备考领思通用英语的考生，为大家详细讲解备考重点，提供考试指导。

相信大家在看过视频和课程之后，能够有效提高学习效率，最终获得领思高分。

目 录 ·············· CONTENTS

Section 1　必考词汇

Section 2　高频词汇

Section 3　拓展词汇

Section 1
必考词汇

Day 1

扫码听音频

小试牛刀

浏览本单元所有单词，在你已掌握的单词前面打√。

☐ article	☐ course	☐ animal	☐ sport
☐ important	☐ local	☐ people	☐ time
☐ friend	☐ new	☐ always	☐ think
☐ different	☐ last	☐ say	☐ way
☐ even	☐ great	☐ know	☐ find
☐ look	☐ next	☐ quite	☐ school
☐ student	☐ job	☐ question	☐ film
☐ same	☐ young	☐ actually	☐ still
☐ learn	☐ ask	☐ old	☐ small
☐ however	☐ start	☐ special	☐ explain

词汇精讲

1. article [ˈɑːtɪkl] *n.* 文章，论文

例：The article truthfully reflects public opinion.

文章如实反映了公众的意见。

记：词根记忆 art组装，关节，技巧 + i + cle指小的物品→把各个小的部分连接起来→article文章

搭：article title 文章标题　an article about/on... 一篇关于……的文章

2. course [kɔːs] *n.* 课程；过程

例：The objective of the course is mainly to improve the quality of employees.

该课程的目标主要是提高员工的素养。

搭：elective course 选修课　course name 课程名称

3. animal [ˈænɪml] *n.* 动物

例：His responsibility is to inform people about the importance of protecting animals.

他的责任是告诉人们保护动物的重要性。

记：词根记忆 anim生命；精神；心神 + al表名词→有生命的东西→animal动物

搭：wild animal 野生动物　animal experiment 动物实验

4. sport [spɔːt] *n.* （某种）体育运动

例：I had never considered beach volleyball a sport before.

在此之前我从未把沙滩排球视为一项运动。

搭：team sport 团队运动　winter sport 冬季运动

派：sporty *adj.* 擅长运动的

5. important [ɪmˈpɔːtnt] *adj.* 重要的

例：It is important for a secretary to produce a detailed written report.

对于秘书来说写出一份详细备至的书面报告很重要。

记：词根记忆 im进入 + port拿，携带 + ant与……相关的→拿进来，后引申为重要的→important重要的

搭：play an important role in 在……方面起到作用　important event 大事件

派：importance *n.* 重要性　unimportant *adj.* 不重要的　importantly *adv.* 重要地，重要的是

6. local [ˈləʊkl] *adj.* 当地的，本地的　*n.* 本地居民；本地新闻

例：The local website set up a special section where people are encouraged to offer advice for building the city.

　　这家本地网站设立了专门的区域，鼓励人们为城市建设提供建议。

记：词根记忆 loc地方 + al ……的→local地方的；局部的

搭：local government 地方政府　local culture 本土文化

派：locality *n.* （特定的）地方，地区　locally *adv.* 局部地；在本地

7. people [ˈpiːpl] *n.* 人，人类；人们；民族

例：People are worried about the toxic gases that will be released from handling chemicals.

　　人们担心处理化工制品会释放出有毒气体。

记：词根记忆 popul人，后变形为people→people人们

搭：ordinary people 普通人，一般人　poor people 贫民，穷人

　　number of people 人数

8. time [taɪm] *n.* （可利用的）时间；（以分钟、小时、天等计量的）时间；次，回

例：In my spare time, I prefer to go fishing with my family at the stream rather than watching TV at home.

　　在空余时间，比起在家看电视，我更喜欢和家人在溪边垂钓。

搭：at the same time 与此同时　in time 及时　on time 准时

派：timeless *adj.* 永恒的

9. friend [frend] *n.* 朋友，友人

例：I intend to share the joy of victory with my friends.

　　我打算和我的朋友一起分享胜利的喜悦。

记：联想记忆 fr+i+e+nd夫人（fr）和我（i）的鹅（e）难得（nd）成了朋友。

搭：refer friends 介绍朋友；引见朋友　become friends 成为朋友

派：friendly *adj.* 友好的　friendless *adj.* 没有朋友的，无依无靠的

10. new [njuː] *adj.* 未用过的，崭新的；新兴的，新出现的

例：The new batch of goods was placed in the suburban warehouse.

　　新进的这批货物被置于了郊区的仓库。

记：联想记忆 门（n）后的鹅（e）长了新牙（w）。

搭：brand new 崭新，全新　new to... 对……不熟悉；对……没经验

派：newest *adj.* 最新的 newness *n.* 新奇；崭新

11. always [ˈɔːlweɪz] *adv.* 总是，每次都是；一直，长久以来

例：The government hall in this area is **always** decorated with flowers.

这个地区的政府大厅总是被鲜花所装饰。

搭：as always 一如往常 always ready 随时候命

12. think [θɪŋk] *v.* 认为，觉得；思考，考虑

例：She **thinks** it will be difficult to find an empty seat.

她认为找一个空位子会很困难。

搭：think over 仔细考虑 think through 彻底地想清楚 think twice 重新考虑；三思

派：thinkable *adj.* 可相信的；可考虑的 thinker *n.* 思考者；思想家

13. different [ˈdɪfrənt] *adj.* 不同的

例：My interest is in how employees react in **different** situations.

我的兴趣在于职员在不同情况下的反应。

记：词根记忆 differ相异 + ent表示具有……性质的→different不同的

搭：be different from 与……不同 dramatically different 截然不同的

派：differ *v.* 相异 difference *n.* 区别，差异

14. last [lɑːst] *adj.* 最近的，上一个的；最后的

例：When was the **last** time you went to the dentist?

你上一次去看牙医是什么时候？

搭：at last 最后 last but not least 最后但同样重要的 till the last 直到最后

派：lasting *adj.* 持久的，耐久的 lastly *adv.* 最后

15. say [seɪ] *v.* 说，讲；宣称；说明

例：I didn't know what else to **say**.

我不知道还能再说点什么。

搭：that is to say 那就是说 say for oneself 为自己辩解

16. way [weɪ] *n.* 方法，手段；道路，路线

例：This **way** is designed for team projects.

这方法是专为团队项目设计的。

搭：in a way 从某种程度上说 by the way 顺便问一下

17. even [ˈiːvn] *adv.* 甚至，即使；更加，愈加 *adj.* 平坦的，水平的

例：He can't **even** tie his shoelaces well.

他甚至连系鞋带这种事都做不好。

搭：even worse 更糟的是　even now 即使在现在；尽管这样

18. great [greɪt] *adj.* 大型的，巨大的；伟大的，著名的；美妙的

例：It was a great blow to Jenny when her uncle died.
　　珍妮的舅舅去世对她是个沉重的打击。

搭：great victory 大捷　great and small 大人物和小人物

派：greatly *adv.* 非常，大大地

19. know [nəʊ] *v.* 知道；懂得；熟悉

例：I know he hasn't left his job until last week.
　　我知道他直到上周才离职。

搭：in the know 知情的　know about 了解，知道……的情况

派：known *adj.* 已知的，有名的

20. find [faɪnd] *v.* 找到，找回；发现，发觉；（经过研究）找出，查明

例：It's hard to find a seat on the subway during the morning rush hour.
　　早高峰在地铁上很难找到座位。

搭：find out 找出，发现　find against 判决……有罪

派：findable *adj.* 可发现的　finding *n.* 发现，调查结果

21. look [lʊk] *v.* 看；看起来像　*n.* 表情，神色

例：He does not look fifty by any manner of means.
　　他看上去一点不像50岁的人。

搭：look after 照顾　look down on 轻视　look through 识破；浏览

派：looker *n.* 观看者，检查员

22. next [nekst] *adj.* 下一个的，接下来的；（时间）紧接着来到的，下次的；紧邻的

例：Now we'll turn to the next item on the list.
　　现在我们来讨论清单上的下一项议程。

搭：next year 明年　next step 下一步

23. quite [kwaɪt] *adv.* 相当，很；非常，十分

例：The author's point of view is quite evident in all of his works.
　　作者的观点在他所有的作品中都表达得很明显。

搭：quite other 完全不同的　quite something 非同寻常

24. school [skuːl] *n.* （中、小）学校；（大学的）系，学院

例：Her family lives five kilometers away from her school.

她家住在离学校五千米的地方。

记：**联想记忆** s+ch+ool蛇(s)吃(ch)两个鸡蛋一根油条(ool)去学校。

搭：of the old school 老派的　after school 下课后，放学后

派：schooling *n.* 学校教育

25. student [ˈstjuːdnt] *n.* 学生

例：She is a student in an academy of foreign language.

她是一所外语学院的学生。

记：**词根记忆** stud（y）学习，研读 + ent表示人→student学生

搭：associate student 旁听生　commuting student 走读生

26. job [dʒɒb] *n.* 工作，职业；任务；职责，责任

例：It's part of my job to know how business contracts are signed.

我工作的一部分是了解商务合同是如何签订的。

搭：job assignment 工作分配　on the job 在工作，在忙着

派：jobless *adj.* 失业的，无业的

27. question [ˈkwestʃən] *n.* 问题，疑问；试题，题目

例：He gave a quick answer to the teacher's question.

他对老师的提问做出了迅速的回答。

记：**词根记忆** quest搜寻，探寻 + ion表示行为，状态，结果→搜寻答案→question

问题

搭：raise a question 提出问题　put the question 提付表决

派：questioner *n.* 质问者，发问者　questionnaire *n.* 调查问卷

28. film [fɪlm] *n.* 电影，影片；胶卷，底片；薄膜，薄层

例：That film creates an atmosphere of terror.

那部影片营造出恐怖的气氛。

搭：shoot a film 拍摄一个镜头；拍摄电影　see a film 看电影

29. same [seɪm] *adj.* 同一的，一模一样的，没有变化的

例：It is very monotonous for Thomas to do the same task every day.

对于托马斯来说，每天做同样的工作是很单调的。

搭：stay the same 保持不变，保持一致　same again 同样的再来一份

all the same 还是，依然

30. young [jʌŋ] *adj.* 幼小的，年轻的；存在不久的，新成立的
　　 n. 年轻人

例：Many young people like to follow the popular trend blindly.
　　许多年轻人喜欢盲目地追随大众潮流。

记：词根记忆 由词根jun年轻演变而来→young年轻的

搭：young and old 老老少少；不分老少　young people 年轻人

31. actually ['æktʃuəli] *adv.* 实际上，事实上

例：Actually, my biggest regret is that I gave up being a lawyer.
　　实际上，我最大的遗憾就是放弃了从事律师这项工作。

记：来自actual（*adj.* 实际的，真实的）

派：actual *adj.* 实际的，真实的　actuality *n.* 现状，现实

32. still [stɪl] *adv.* 还，依旧；仍然，还是（会或可能）　*adj.* 静止的，不动的；宁静的，寂静的

例：There is still hope for Margaret to become the secretary of the company.
　　玛格丽特仍有希望当这家公司的秘书。

搭：still and all 不过，毕竟　stand still 静止不动

派：stillness *n.* 静止，沉静

33. learn [lɜːn] *v.* 学习，学会；得知，获悉

例：He suggested that I should learn from my previous failure.
　　他建议我应该从以前的失败中吸取教训。

搭：learn from 从……中吸取教训　learn of 获悉

派：learned *adj.* 博学的；学术性的　learning *n.* 学习；知识，学问

34. ask [ɑːsk] *v.* 询问，打听；要求，请求

例：May I ask if you are fond of surfing at sea?
　　请问你喜欢在海上冲浪吗？

搭：ask for help 寻求帮助　ask after 探问，问候

35. old [əʊld] *adj.* 年老的，年纪大的；古老的，历史悠久的；陈旧的；从前的　*n.* 老年人

例：The old man stood under the street lamp at the corner looked familiar.
　　站在街角路灯下的那个老人看上去很面熟。

搭：as of old 一如既往，照旧　old soldier 老兵；富有经验的人　old school 守旧派

派：oldness *n.* 年老；陈腐　older *adj.* 年长的；较旧的

36. small [smɔːl] *adj.* 小型的；（数量）少的；小规模的

例：The bedroom has two small single beds and a wardrobe.

卧室里陈列着两张小型单人床和一个立式衣柜。

搭：small talk 闲聊，聊天　small part 少部分；细小零件

派：smallish *adj.* 较小的，略小的　smallness *n.* 贫乏；小气

37. however [haʊˈevə (r)] *adv.* 然而，可是，不过；无论如何；（用于表示惊讶）究竟怎样

例：However，things did not go as we expected.

然而，事情并没有像我们预料的那样发展。

记：词根记忆 how怎样，如何 + ever究竟，到底→however（用于表示惊讶）究竟怎样

搭：however much 无论多少

38. start [stɑːt] *v.* 开始（做某事）；使发生，开始

例：The cooperation between them started from two years ago.

他们之间的合作是从两年前开始的。

搭：start with 以……开始　from start to finish 自始至终

39. special [ˈspeʃl] *adj.* 特殊的，特别的

例：Take special care tonight because the street lamp is broken.

今晚要特别小心，因为路灯坏了。

记：词根记忆 spec看，察 + ial表示属性→一眼就能看到的→special特别的

搭：special interest 特殊兴趣　on special 以特价出售

派：specialist *n.* 专家　specialized *adj.* 专业的，专门的

40. explain [ɪkˈspleɪn] *v.* 解释，说明

例：Please give me a chance to explain.

请给我个机会让我解释一下。

记：词根记忆 ex外 + plain平坦的→使变平坦，使变清晰→explain解释

搭：explain oneself 为自己辩解；说明自己意图　explain away 通过解释消除

派：explainable *adj.* 可解释的　explanation *n.* 解释，说明

巩固练习

1. 扫码听写（根据所听音频写出本单元对应单词）

（1）_____	（2）_____	（3）_____	（4）_____
（5）_____	（6）_____	（7）_____	（8）_____
（9）_____	（10）_____	（11）_____	（12）_____
（13）_____	（14）_____	（15）_____	（16）_____
（17）_____	（18）_____	（19）_____	（20）_____
（21）_____	（22）_____	（23）_____	（24）_____
（25）_____	（26）_____	（27）_____	（28）_____
（29）_____	（30）_____	（31）_____	（32）_____
（33）_____	（34）_____	（35）_____	（36）_____
（37）_____	（38）_____	（39）_____	（40）_____

2. 实战演练（选出最符合句意的选项）

（1）She felt that it would be difficult to finish the _____ the department had set for her by the end of the week.

    （A）bonus   （B）task

    （C）job   （D）sign

（2）Handheld computers come in _____ shapes and colors.

    （A）only   （B）any

    （C）same   （D）various

（3）After the teacher's explanation，I finally _____ this difficult math problem.

    （A）understood   （B）thought

    （C）knew   （D）taught

（4）The department store decided to have a _____ sale on the stock at the end of this month.

    （A）unique   （B）particular

    （C）special   （D）especial

（5）The cost is _____ much higher than we initially expected.

    （A）normally   （B）loudly

    （C）actually   （D）significantly

(6) After being single for many years, John finally found his ideal _____.

    (A) mate   (B) parents

    (C) relative   (D) friend

(7) The player's answer to the _____ satisfied the head coach.

    (A) issue   (B) list

    (C) question   (D) schedule

(8) The principal could not _____ the source of the school's teaching qualifications.

    (A) explore   (B) describe

    (C) subscribe   (D) explain

(9) How _____ the forest look under the sunset! The scene left a deep impression on me.

    (A) utter   (B) great

    (C) ugly   (D) simple

(10) The doctor advised him to take medication _____ to suppress the disease.

    (A) thoroughly   (B) always

    (C) seldom   (D) regularly

Day 2

扫码听音频

小试牛刀

浏览本单元所有单词，在你已掌握的单词前面打√。

☐ city	☐ leave	☐ home	☐ live
☐ difficult	☐ idea	☐ long	☐ visit
☐ recently	☐ restaurant	☐ child	☐ sure
☐ interesting	☐ buy	☐ food	☐ free
☐ enjoy	☐ review	☐ useful	☐ website
☐ famous	☐ read	☐ music	☐ social
☐ play	☐ life	☐ family	☐ meet
☐ appropriate	☐ popular	☐ possible	☐ try
☐ talk	☐ magazine	☐ language	☐ exactly
☐ available	☐ opinion	☐ several	☐ travel

词汇精讲

1. city ['sɪti] *n.* 城市，都市

例：Most of Europe's population is concentrated in cities.

欧洲大部分人口都集中在城市里。

搭：industrial city 工业城市　host city 主办城市

派：citizen *n.* 市民，公民　citizenship *n.* 公民权利；公民身份

2. leave [liːv] *v.* 离开（某人或某处）　*n.* 假期，休假；准许，许可

例：We learned from the Internet that the ship for New York will leave on Friday.

我们从网上得知驶往纽约的轮船将于星期五启程。

搭：leave for 动身去　leave aside 不考虑

派：leaver *n.* 离开者（常指学校毕业生）

3. home [həʊm] *n.* 家，住宅；（可买卖的）房子，寓所

例：He drives home from work at six every evening.

他每天晚上六点下班开车回家。

搭：set up home 成家；建立家园　feel at home 感到宾至如归

派：homely *adj.* 普通的，朴实无华的　homeless *adj.* 无家可归的

4. live [lɪv] *v.* 居住；生活在；生存，活着　*adj.* 活的，有生命的

例：Many young people in big cities choose to live in singles apartments.

大城市中许多年轻人都选择居住在单身公寓中。

搭：live by 靠……过活　live up to 到达，符合，不辜负

派：lively *adj.* 活泼的，生机勃勃的　living *adj.* 活着的，活的

5. difficult ['dɪfɪkəlt] *adj.* 困难的，费力的

例：I find it difficult to sketch out his views briefly.

我发现把他的观点简要概述出来是很困难的。

记：词根记忆 dif远离 + fic做 + ult→离得远所以不好做→difficult困难的

搭：difficult situation 困境；困厄　be difficult of 难于，不易

派：difficulty *n.* 困难

6. idea [aɪ'dɪə] *n.* 想法，主意；观点，看法，概念

例：It was my idea to hold a celebration party at the seaside this weekend.

这个周末在海边举行庆祝晚会是我的主意。

搭：have no idea of 完全不知道　fixed idea 固定观点

派：ideal *adj.* 理想的，最佳的 idealistic *adj.* 理想主义的

7. long [lɒŋ] *adj.* 长的；长久的，长期的；漫长的 *v.* 渴望

例：It may take a long time to address the shortage of talent.

要解决人才不足的问题可能要花很长时间。

记：联想记忆 龙（long）是长的。

搭：before long 不久 as long as 只要；和…一样长

派：longevity *n.* 寿命；长寿 longitude *n.* 经度，经线

8. visit ['vɪzɪt] *v. & n.* 参观，游览；拜访，做客

例：The places of interest I want to visit are located in the United States.

我想要去参观的名胜古迹位于美国。

记：词根记忆 vis看 + it→来看某人或某地→visit拜访

搭：pay a visit 进行访问 personal visit 个人访问

派：visitor *n.* 访问者，参观者；（网站的）浏览者

9. recently ['riːsntli] *adv.* 最近，不久前

例：The government has loosened its grip on tobacco recently.

最近政府对烟草的控制已经变松了。

记：来自recent（*adj.* 最近的）

搭：until recently 直到最近

派：recent *adj.* 最近的，最新的

10. restaurant ['restrɒnt] *n.* 餐馆，饭店

例：Jackson chooses to have lunch at this Chinese restaurant this noon.

今天中午杰克逊选择在这家中餐厅吃午餐。

记：词根记忆 restaur = restore恢复 + ant表示地点→restaurant饭店（使人恢复能量的地方）

搭：chain restaurant 连锁餐饮店

派：restaurateur *n.* 餐馆老板

11. child [tʃaɪld] *n.* 儿童，小孩

例：He tried to comfort the depressed child.

他试着去安慰那个情绪低落的孩子。

搭：raise a child 养育孩子；抚养孩子 child welfare 儿童福利；保育

派：childhood *n.* 童年 childish *adj.* 幼稚的

12. sure ［ʃʊə（r）］ adj. 确信，有把握，肯定；一定

例：The knowledge on the book is not sure all correct.

书上的知识不一定都正确。

搭：make sure 查明；确定 for sure 确切地

派：surely adv. 无疑，肯定

13. interesting ［ˈɪntrəstɪŋ］ adj. 有趣的，有吸引力的

例：This comic book has many interesting illustrations.

这本漫画书有很多有趣的插图。

搭：interesting point 兴趣点 look interesting 好像很有趣

派：interest n. 兴趣，关注 interested adj. 感兴趣的，关心的

14. buy ［baɪ］ v. 购买，买得到

例：It takes a large sum of money to buy a house.

买一所房子要花一大笔钱。

搭：buy up 全部买进 buy off 收买，贿赂

派：buyer n. 买主，采购员

15. food ［fuːd］ n. 食物，食品

例：Food is very crucial to keep the organs of the human body running.

食物对于维持人体各器官的运行来说非常重要。

搭：fast food 快餐 pet food 宠物食品

派：foodie n. 美食家

16. free ［friː］ adj. 免费的；自由的 v. 解放，释放

例：The US has been avoiding free trade issues with China.

美国一直逃避关于中国的自由贸易问题。

搭：for free 免费的 free sb. from 使某人摆脱……，使某人免除……

派：freely adv. 自由地 freedom n. 自由

17. enjoy ［ɪnˈdʒɔɪ］ v. 享受，欣赏，喜爱；过得愉快，玩得开心

例：The seals seemed to enjoy the good care of their keepers.

海豹似乎很享受饲养员们的精心照顾。

搭：enjoy oneself 过得快乐 enjoy doing 乐于做……，喜欢做……

派：enjoyable adj. 令人愉快的，有乐趣的 enjoyment n. 乐趣，乐事

18. review [rɪ'vjuː] *n.* 审查，检查；书评，评论文章 *v.* 仔细研究，审视；回顾，反思

例：The financial budget will be reviewed by the relevant departments in July.

财务预算等到七月份再由相关部门进行研究。

记：词根记忆 re—再，重新 + view 查看，观察→重新观察→review检查

搭：under review 在检查中 book review 书评

派：reviewer *n.* 评论者，评论家

19. useful ['juːsfl] *adj.* 有用的，有益的

例：This book is a storehouse of useful information and data.

这本书里汇集了大量有用的资料和数据。

搭：useful life 使用寿命；有效期

派：useable *adj.* 可用的 useless *adj.* 无用的，无价值的

20. website ['websaɪt] *n.* 网站

例：For detailed information about our products，please visit our website.

若需了解产品的具体信息，请访问我们的网站。

记：词根记忆 web网，网状物 + site 地点→website网站

搭：official website 官方网站 personal website 个人网站

派：web 网，网状物

21. famous ['feɪməs] *adj.* 著名的，出名的

例：The famous musician will go to Europe to give a concert recently.

那名著名音乐家近日将前往欧洲举办演奏会。

记：词根记忆 fam说 + ous有……，充满……（很多人都说的，即著名的）→famous著名的

搭：be famous for 以……著名

派：famously *adv.* 著名地

22. read [riːd] *v.* 阅读，读懂；朗读

例：It is a good study habit to take notes when you read an article.

阅读文章时做笔记是个好的学习习惯。

搭：read aloud 朗读 read for 攻读

派：reading *n.* 读物，阅读材料 reader *n.* 读者，爱读书的人

23. music ['mjuːzɪk] *n.* 音乐，乐曲；乐谱

例：His devotion to music is plain to see.

他对音乐的挚爱是显而易见的。

搭：pop music 流行音乐　music teacher 音乐老师

派：musical *adj.* 音乐的，配乐的　musician *n.* 音乐家

24. social [ˈsəʊʃl] *adj.* 社会的；社交的，交际的

例：Social change is always blocked by vested interests.

社会变革总是会遭受既得利益者的重重阻挠。

记：词根记忆 soc联合 + ial表示相关→联合需要交际→social社交的

搭：social network 社会网络；社交网络　social grace 社交礼仪

派：socialize *v.* 交往，交际　socially *adv.* 在社会上；在社交方面

25. play [pleɪ] *v.* （尤指儿童）玩，玩耍；参加（游戏、比赛等）；演奏（乐器或乐曲）

例：When he was a child, he often **played** with his friends under the big tree in front of his house.

他小时候经常和小伙伴们在他家门前的大树下嬉戏。

搭：play an important role 起到重要作用　play the piano 弹钢琴

派：player *n.* 运动员，选手　playful *adj.* 开玩笑的；幽默的

26. life [laɪf] *n.* 生活，人生；寿命，一生；生命，性命

例：With the development of society, the pace of **life** is becoming faster and faster.

随着社会的发展，生活的节奏正变得越来越快。

搭：daily life 日常生活　lead a life 过着……的生活

派：lifeless *adj.* 无生命的，死气沉沉的　lifelike *adj.* 逼真的

27. family [ˈfæməli] *n.* 家，家庭；家属，亲属；家族

例：The **family** environment has a great influence on children's character.

家庭环境对儿童性格影响很大。

记：联想记忆 family = father and mother I love you（爸爸和妈妈我爱你们）的首字母

搭：family name 姓氏　family tree 家谱

28. meet [miːt] *v.* （与……）见面，遇见；结识，被引见（给某人）；满足

例：I **met** her in a shop on the high street today.

今天我在商业街的一家店铺遇见了她。

搭：meet with 符合；偶然遇见　meet requirement 满足要求，达到要求

派：meeting *n.* 会议，集会

29. appropriate [əˈprəʊpriət] *adj.* 合适的，相称的

例：His impudent style is not appropriate to the occasion.

他鲁莽的风格不适合这个场合。

记：词根记忆 ap朝向，加强 + propri所有权，自己的 + ate表示……状态的→appropriate合适的

搭：be appropriate to/for 适于，合乎

派：appropriately *adv.* 适当地，恰当地 appropriateness *n.* 适当，适合

30. popular [ˈpɒpjələ (r)] *adj.* 流行的，受欢迎的；普遍的

例：Football is recognized as the most popular sport in the world.

足球是公认的全球范围内最受欢迎的体育运动。

记：词根记忆 popul人 + ar与……有关的→与许多人都有关的→popular大众的，受欢迎的

搭：be popular with 受……欢迎

派：popularity *n.* 流行，普及 popularly *adv.* 流行地，通俗地

31. possible [ˈpɒsəbl] *adj.* 可能的，可能做到的；可能发生的，可能存在的

例：I'll do everything possible to help you.

我会尽一切可能帮助你。

记：词根记忆 poss能力 + ible可……的；能……的→possible可能的

搭：as ... as possible 尽可能；愈……愈好 if possible 如有可能

派：possibly *adv.* 可能，或许 possibility *n.* 可能性

32. try [traɪ] *v.* 试图，努力；试用，试做，试验 *n.* 尝试，试图

例：The politician tried to ease the conflict between the people and the government.

那名政治家试图缓解民众与政府间的矛盾。

搭：give it a try 试一试 try again 再来一次

33. talk [tɔːk] *v.* 交谈，谈话；谈论（某个话题） *n.* 谈话，交谈；（专题）报告，演讲

例：It was a rare opportunity for him to talk to his superiors.

与上级交谈对他而言机会难得。

搭：have a talk with 与……谈话 small talk 闲聊；聊天

派：talkative *adj.* 健谈的

34. magazine [ˌmæɡəˈziːn] *n.* 杂志，期刊

例：This magazine has the highest annual sales volume.

这本杂志的年销量高居榜首。

搭：weekly magazine 周刊　magazine editor 杂志编辑

35. language [ˈlæŋɡwɪdʒ] *n.* 语言；语言文字

例：Language is the vehicle of human thought.

语言是人类表达思想的工具。

搭：foreign language 外语；外文　body language 肢体语言，身体语言

派：lingual *adj.* 语言的　bilingual *adj.* （人）熟悉两种语言的，能说两种语言的

36. exactly [ɪɡˈzæktli] *adv.* 精确地，确切地；（用于强调）恰好，完全

例：He explained to me exactly the solution to the problem.

他确切地向我讲解了这个问题的解决办法。

记：来自 exact（*adj.* 准确地，确切的）

搭：not exactly 根本不；不完全

派：exact *adj.* 确切的，精确的；严谨的　exactness *n.* 正确

37. available [əˈveɪləbl] *adj.* 可用的，可获得的；有空的，有闲暇的

例：With the summer holidays approaching, there are not many rooms available.

由于暑假将近，空余的客房已经为数不多了。

记：词根记忆 a朝向 + vail价值，力量 + able可……的，能……的→可带来价值的 →available可获得的

搭：be available for 可用于……的；对……有效的

派：avail *n.* 效用，利益　availability *n.* 可用性

38. opinion [əˈpɪnjən] *n.* 意见，看法；（群体的）观点，信仰

例：Please don't give your opinion freely about something you don't know.

对于自己不清楚的事情请不要随意地发表意见。

搭：in my opinion 依我看来，在我看来　public opinion 民意；公众舆论

派：opinionate *adj.* 基于观点的；固执己见的

39. several [ˈsevrəl] *adj.* 几个的，若干的

例：Several employees had their pay docked for being late for work.

有几名员工因为上班迟到被扣了工资。

记：词根记忆 sever分开，分割 + al形容词后缀→分开的东西→几个的，若干的

搭：several days 几天　several times 几次

40. travel [ˈtrævl] *v.* （尤指长途）旅行；走动，移动

例：Donald prefers to **travel** by ship rather than by air.

唐纳德宁可乘轮船也不愿乘飞机旅行。

搭：travel agency 旅行社　air travel 航空旅行

派：traveler *n.* 旅游者，旅客

扫码听音频

巩固练习

1. 扫码听写（根据所听音频写出本单元对应单词）

(1) _____	(2) _____	(3) _____	(4) _____
(5) _____	(6) _____	(7) _____	(8) _____
(9) _____	(10) _____	(11) _____	(12) _____
(13) _____	(14) _____	(15) _____	(16) _____
(17) _____	(18) _____	(19) _____	(20) _____
(21) _____	(22) _____	(23) _____	(24) _____
(25) _____	(26) _____	(27) _____	(28) _____
(29) _____	(30) _____	(31) _____	(32) _____
(33) _____	(34) _____	(35) _____	(36) _____
(37) _____	(38) _____	(39) _____	(40) _____

2. 实战演练（选出最符合句意的选项）

(1) After quitting their jobs in the city，they chose to _____ in the pleasant countryside.

　　(A) settle 　　　　　　　　(B) search

　　(C) count 　　　　　　　　(D) live

(2) New evidence has _____ come to light on the case.

　　(A) meanwhile 　　　　　　(B) recently

　　(C) lately 　　　　　　　　(D) past

(3) The crew prepared adequate _____ for the voyage.

　　(A) food 　　　　　　　　　(B) meal

　　(C) provisions 　　　　　　(D) dishes

(4) His rudeness has long been _____ in the community.

    (A) respectable   (B) famous

    (C) notorious   (D) reasonable

(5) Simple and plain clothes are _____ for this solemn occasion.

    (A) appropriate   (B) grateful

    (C) proper   (D) responsible

(6) The _____ has booked an apartment on the eighth floor of the building.

    (A) couple   (B) parents

    (C) family   (D) home

(7) The two-week _____ to Australia excited the college students.

    (A) flight   (B) trip

    (C) travel   (D) service

(8) His judgments on the current situation are _____ in line with the facts.

    (A) exactly   (B) normally

    (C) precisely   (D) accordingly

(9) This website is only _____ by the authorized personnel.

    (A) available   (B) delightful

    (C) visible   (D) accessible

(10) The kidnappers _____ the child after receiving the ransom.

    (A) saved   (B) released

    (C) sent   (D) liberated

Day 3

扫码听音频

小试牛刀

浏览本单元所有单词，在你已掌握的单词前面打√。

☐ receive	☐ company	☐ easy	☐ decide
☐ quickly	☐ country	☐ eat	☐ shop
☐ choose	☐ expensive	☐ problem	☐ keep
☐ information	☐ advice	☐ happy	☐ listen
☐ name	☐ kind	☐ busy	☐ love
☐ international	☐ right	☐ world	☐ wild
☐ change	☐ future	☐ experience	☐ suggest
☐ beautiful	☐ style	☐ exciting	☐ pay
☐ watch	☐ hotel	☐ move	☐ public
☐ happen	☐ ready	☐ improve	☐ main

词汇精讲

1. receive [rɪˈsiːv] *v.* 得到，收到；遭受，经受（特定待遇）

例：He received a package from France this morning.

他今天早上收到了一个来自法国的包裹。

记：词根记忆 re—再 + ceive拿，抓，握住→一再拿到→receive收到

搭：receive a letter from收到某人的来信 receive into 接受，接纳

派：receiver *n.* （电话）听筒

2. company [ˈkʌmpəni] *n.* 公司；陪伴，同伴

例：The new product became a major publicity target for the company.

这款新产品成了公司的主要宣传目标。

记：词根记忆 com—起 + pan面包 + y名词词尾→一起分享面包→company陪伴、公司

搭：listed company 上市公司 in company with 与……一起

派：companion *n.* 陪伴

3. easy [ˈiːzi] *adj.* 容易的，不费力的；舒适的，自如的

例：It's not easy to quit smoking in the short term.

想要在短期戒烟并非易事。

搭：take it easy 放轻松 easy to use 使用方便

派：easily *adv.* 容易地

4. decide [dɪˈsaɪd] *v.* 决定；判定

例：The professor decided to do a chemistry experiment with the students today.

教授决定今天和学生们一起做化学实验。

记：词根记忆 de加强 + cid切；杀 + e→切下去→decide下决心

搭：decide to do sth. 决定做某事 decide on 决定；选定

派：decision *n.* 决定

5. quickly [ˈkwɪkli] *adv.* 快速地；很快，马上

例：The maid cleaned the whole villa quickly.

女仆很快地打扫了整幢别墅。

搭：as quickly as possible 尽快

派：quick *adj.* 迅速的，快的

6. country ['kʌntri] *n.* 国，国家；乡下，乡村

例：The **country** issued massive national debts to continue the war.

为了继续战争，该国发行了大量国债。

记：**词根记忆** 由contra而来，表示相对→原指位于对面的土地，后引申为国家→country国家

搭：mother country 祖国 developed country 发达国家

7. eat [i:t] *v.* 吃，吃饭；侵蚀，损耗

例：To keep fit，he doesn't **eat** much fried food.

为了保持身体健康，他不怎么吃油炸食品。

搭：eat lunch 吃午餐 eat out 下馆子吃饭

派：eatery *n.* 餐馆

8. shop [ʃɒp] *n.* 商店，店铺

例：Our **shop** will be open for business next Friday.

本店将于下周五营业。

搭：coffee shop 咖啡店 shop assistant 售货员

派：shopping *n.* 购物 shopper *n.* 顾客

9. choose [tʃu:z] *v.* 选择，挑选

例：He will **choose** between employment at home and studying abroad.

他将在国内就业和出国留学之间做出选择。

搭：choose from 挑选，从……中选择

派：choice *n.* 选择 chosen *adj.* 挑选出来的，精选的

10. expensive [ɪk'spensɪv] *adj.* 昂贵的

例：That car is too **expensive** for him as an office worker.

那辆轿车对于他这个上班族而言太过昂贵了。

记：**联想记忆** ex（一休）+ pen（钢笔）+ sive（近似"five"）→一休的钢笔非常昂贵，价值五块钱。

派：inexpensive *adj.* 便宜的，廉价的

11. problem ['prɒbləm] *n.* 问题，难题，困难

例：The **problem** is how we can break through the technical difficulties of chips.

问题是我们如何能突破芯片的技术难题。

搭：no problem 没问题 pose a problem 造成问题

派：problematic *adj.* 成问题的，有困难的

12. keep [kiːp] v. 保持，处于；继续，重复

例：It is necessary to **keep** a good mood in busy work.

在繁忙的工作中需要保持一个良好的心情。

搭：keep doing 继续做某事　keep away 不接近；使离开

派：keeper *n.* 监护人；饲养员

13. information [ˌɪnfəˈmeɪʃn] *n.* 消息，资料，情报；数据，信息

例：For further **information**, please contact with my agent.

要进一步了解情况，请与我的经纪人联系。

记：词根记忆 inform通知，告知，影响 + ation表示状态→information信息，消息

搭：information age 信息时代　transfer information 传递信息

派：informative *adj.* 提供有用信息的；增长见闻的

14. advice [ədˈvaɪs] *n.* 忠告，劝告，建议

例：He put forward some constructive **advice** for the development of the school.

他为学校的发展提出了一些建设性的建议。

搭：good advice 好建议　sound advice 忠告

派：advise *v.* 劝告，建议

15. happy [ˈhæpi] *adj.* 快乐的；幸福的，使人高兴的

例：Mark looked **happy** after his promotion as director.

升职总监后马克看上去很快乐。

搭：be happy with 对……感到满意　feel happy 感到高兴

派：happiness *n.* 幸福，快乐

16. listen [ˈlɪsn] *v.* 听，倾听；听从，听信

例：Learning to **listen** is more important than being able to speak well.

学会倾听比能言善辩更重要。

搭：listen to music 听音乐　listen carefully 仔细听

派：listener *n.* 听者；收听广播节目的人

17. name [neɪm] *n.* 名字，名称；名声，名誉　*v.* 任命，委任

例：The client's **name** was printed on the business card.

客户的名字被印在了名片上。

搭：in the name of 以……的名义　sign one's name 签名

派：namely *adv.* 即，也就是　named *adj.* 命名的；指定的

18. kind [kaɪnd] *n.* 种类 *adj.* 宽容的，体贴的，亲切友好的

例：What kind of drink do you like best?

你最喜欢喝哪种饮料？

搭：kind of 有点儿 all kinds 形形色色，各种各样

派：kindly *adv.* 亲切地；温和地

19. busy [ˈbɪzi] *adj.* 繁忙的，忙碌的；热闹的

例：I'm too busy now to practice playing the piano.

我现在太忙，没有时间练习弹钢琴了。

搭：be busy with忙于干某事

派：busily *adv.* 忙碌地，起劲地

20. love [lʌv] *v.* 爱恋（某人）；关爱（尤指家人或密友）；热爱（国家、组织等）；*n.* 喜爱，关爱；爱情，恋爱

例：He swore at the wedding that he would love her forever.

他在婚礼上发誓将永远爱她。

搭：fall in love with 爱上 love letter 情书

派：lover *n.* 爱人 lovely *adj.* 可爱的，迷人的

21. international [ˌɪntəˈnæʃnəl] *adj.* 国际的

例：Beijing is expected to build a major international airport within five years.

北京预计在五年内建一座大型国际机场。

记：词根记忆 inter中间 + national国家的→international国与国之间的，即国际的

搭：international trade 国际贸易 international market 国际市场

派：national *adj.* 国家的，全国的

22. right [raɪt] *adj.* 正确的；（意见，判断）对的；右边的，右侧的 *n.* 权利；正当；公正

例：The solution he gave was found to be right.

人们发现他给出的解决办法是正确的。

记：词根记忆 rig对的 + ht→right正确的

搭：right away 马上 in one's own right 凭借自己的能力

派：righteous *adj.* 正直的，公正的

23. world [wɜːld] *n.* 世界

例：China has always played a positive role in the world economy.

中国一直在世界经济中发挥积极作用。

搭：around the world 世界各地　in the world 在世界上；到底

派：worldly *adj.* 世俗的；世间的

24. wild [waɪld] *adj.* （动植物）野生的；（土地）无人烟的，未开垦的

例：Going to the forest to track **wild** animals is a daily job for scientific research team members.

去森林追踪野生动物是科考队员的日常工作。

搭：wild animal 野生动物　be wild about 热衷于

派：wildly *adv.* 野蛮地；狂暴地　wilderness *n.* 未开发的地区，荒野

25. change [tʃeɪndʒ] *v.* 改变，变化；更换，替换　*n.* 变化，变革

例：The doctor felt that it was necessary for the patient to **change** his diet.

医生觉得那位病人改变一下饮食结构是有必要的。

搭：change into 把……变成；换衣　climate change 气候变化

派：changeable *adj.* 可改变的，可被改变的

26. future [ˈfjuːtʃə (r)] *n.* 未来，将来；前途，前景　*adj.* 将来的，未来的

例：He has made a detailed plan of his **future** career.

他已经对自己未来的事业有了周详的计划。

记：词根记忆 fu + ture行为，行为的结果→future未来

搭：in the future 在将来

派：futurist *n.* 未来主义者

27. experience [ɪkˈspɪəriəns] *n.* 经历，往事；经验，阅历　*v.* 经历，遭遇

例：That precious **experience** will be etched in my memory.

那次宝贵的经历将铭刻在我的记忆中。

记：词根记忆 ex出 + peri通过；尝试 + ence性质；状态；行为→尝试出来的东西→experience经验

搭：work experience 工作经验　lack the experience 缺乏经验

派：experienced *adj.* 熟练的，有经验的

28. suggest [səˈdʒest] *v.* 提议，建议；显示，表明；暗示，暗指

例：Arthur **suggested** that Merlin go to a hospital in the capital to treat her diabetes.

亚瑟建议梅林去首都的医院治疗她的糖尿病。

记：词根记忆 sug由下向上 + gest携带，运输→悄悄向上传递信息→suggest暗示，表明

搭：suggest doing 建议做…… suggest itself to 浮现在脑海里

派：suggestion *n.* 建议，意见

29. beautiful [ˈbjuːtɪfl] *adj.* 美丽的，漂亮的；令人愉悦的，美妙的

例：The lovely little girl has beautiful curly silver hair.
这个可爱的小女孩长着漂亮的银色卷发。

记：词根记忆 beauti(=beauty)美丽 + ful形容词后缀→beautiful漂亮的

搭：beautiful view 美丽的景色

派：beauty *n.* 美貌；美女

30. style [staɪl] *n.* 方式，作风；款式，样式

例：This evening dress is very popular in the fashion market for its simple style.
这件晚礼服以简约的风格而在时装市场很受欢迎。

记：词根记忆 styl（stig变形，表示独特标志）+ e→一个人的独特标志→style风格

搭：come into style 变得时髦

派：stylish *adj.* 时髦的，流行的

31. exciting [ɪkˈsaɪtɪŋ] *adj.* 令人兴奋的，令人激动的

例：Our solar water heater is an exciting new invention.
我们的太阳能热水器是一项激动人心的新发明。

记：词根记忆 excit（e）使兴奋 + ing ……的→exciting令人兴奋的

派：excite *v.* 使兴奋，使激动 excited *adj.* 激动的

32. pay [peɪ] *v.* 支付，付；偿还，缴纳 *n.* 工资，薪水

例：He would like to pay the shopkeeper $100 for the backpack.
他愿意付店主100美元来买这个背包。

搭：pay for 付款；偿还 pay off 还清；取得成功

派：payment *n.* 支付款项，支付额

33. watch [wɒtʃ] *v.* 看，注视；观看（电视节目等）；监视 *n.* 手表；观察；监视

例：Does Kevin often watch television in the evening?
凯文常常在晚上看电视吗？

搭：watch out 小心 keep watch for 留意

派：watcher *n.* 观察者；看守人

34. hotel [həʊˈtel] *n.* 旅馆，酒店

例：It's a twenty-minute walk from the **hotel** to the post office.

从旅馆到邮局走路需要二十分钟。

记：**词根记忆** hot词根意为招待，接待 + el表示与……相关的地方→hotel名词，酒店

搭：luxury hotel 豪华宾馆

35. move [muːv] *v.* （使）改变位置，（使）移动 *n.* 措施，行动；移动；活动

例：I barely had the strength to **move** my fingers.

我连移动手指的力气都几乎没有了。

搭：move on 继续，前进 move in 搬进新居

派：movement *n.* 运动

36. public [ˈpʌblɪk] *adj.* 公众的，大众的；公共的，公用的 *n.* 公众，大众

例：The failure of the new policy made the **public** more dissatisfied with the government.

新政策的失利使得大众对政府更加不满。

记：**词根记忆** publ词根意为公众 + -ic形容词词尾→public民众

搭：public place 公共场所 in public 当众

派：publication *n.* 出版，发行 publicly *adv.* 公开地；公然地

37. happen [ˈhæpən] *v.* 发生；使遭遇；碰巧

例：I dread to think what will **happen** if she finds out the truth.

我不敢去想她知道真相后会怎么样。

搭：happen to be 碰巧是；恰巧是 happen upon 偶然发现；偶然碰见

派：happening *n.* 事件，意外发生的事

38. ready [ˈredi] *adj.* 准备好；可方便使用的，现成的 *v.* 做好……的准备

例：He is not **ready** to leave school and go out into the society.

他还没有准备好离开学校进入社会。

搭：be ready for 为……做好准备 keep ready 备妥

派：readiness *n.* 准备就绪状态

39. improve [ɪmˈpruːv] v. 改进，改善；康复，健康好转

例：The company has devoted all its attention to finding ways to improve the quality of service.

该公司一直致力于寻找改善服务质量的方法。

记：词根记忆 im使得 + prov好的，优势 + e→improve改进，改善

搭：improve efficiency 提高效率 improve on 对……加以改进

派：improvement n. 改善；改进之处

40. main [meɪn] adj. 主要的，最重要的

例：The main character of the play is a calm and strong-willed man.

这部戏的主角是一个沉着冷静、意志坚强的人。

搭：main dish 主菜 main factor 主要因素

派：mainly adv. 主要地，首要地

扫码听音频

巩固练习

1. 扫码听写（根据所听音频写出本单元对应单词）

(1) _____	(2) _____	(3) _____	(4) _____
(5) _____	(6) _____	(7) _____	(8) _____
(9) _____	(10) _____	(11) _____	(12) _____
(13) _____	(14) _____	(15) _____	(16) _____
(17) _____	(18) _____	(19) _____	(20) _____
(21) _____	(22) _____	(23) _____	(24) _____
(25) _____	(26) _____	(27) _____	(28) _____
(29) _____	(30) _____	(31) _____	(32) _____
(33) _____	(34) _____	(35) _____	(36) _____
(37) _____	(38) _____	(39) _____	(40) _____

2. 实战演练（选出最符合句意的选项）

(1) Jonathan was _____ as the new chief executive by the board of directors.

　(A) named 　　　　　　　(B) designed

　(C) arranged 　　　　　　(D) ensured

(2) Please take action as soon as possible after _____ the letter to reduce the loss.

　(A) seeing 　　　　　　　(B) accepting

(C) receiving   (D) watching

(3) He eventually _____ the diamond ring as a token of affection for his girlfriend.

(A) laid   (B) selected

(C) ensured   (D) chose

(4) In spite of what he looks like now, he was a _____ gentleman when he was young.

(A) timid   (B) beautiful

(C) handsome   (D) faithful

(5) The Paul brothers are _____ in applying for land from the government to set up their own factory.

(A) indulged   (B) favoured

(C) prided   (D) engaged

(6) To become an astronaut, candidates have to _____ a lot of pain and challenges.

(A) remind   (B) forget

(C) experience   (D) realize

(7) It is very important to master the relevant _____ of this fighter jet for our country's military technology.

(A) data   (B) progress

(C) information   (D) sample

(8) He happened to _____ the conversation between the president and his secretary.

(A) search   (B) seek

(C) listen   (D) overhear

(9) The judges thought his dance _____ was too wild for the programme.

(A) reflection   (B) style

(C) fashion   (D) reason

(10) It is a _____ act to pick up someone's wallet and hand it over to the police.

(A) crafty   (B) grand

(C) kind   (D) simple

Day 4

扫码听音频

小试牛刀

浏览本单元所有单词，在你已掌握的单词前面打√。

☐ provide	☐ point	☐ successful	☐ skill
☐ recommend	☐ team	☐ send	☐ bring
☐ hour	☐ follow	☐ wait	☐ writer
☐ money	☐ mean	☐ teach	☐ stop
☐ build	☐ answer	☐ include	☐ month
☐ remember	☐ night	☐ plan	☐ water
☐ grow	☐ reason	☐ collect	☐ agree
☐ competition	☐ believe	☐ computer	☐ photo
☐ win	☐ club	☐ allow	☐ minute
☐ weekend	☐ book	☐ number	☐ park

词汇精讲

1. provide [prə'vaɪd] v. 提供，供给；配备，准备好

例：The manufacturer will provide us with all the commodities we need.

制造商将为我们提供所需要的全部商品。

记：词根记忆 pro前 + vid看 + e→预先看见→provide提供；供应

搭：provide with 给……提供；以……装备　provide for 为……做准备

派：provider n. 供应商；养家者

2. point [pɔɪnt] n. 观点，看法；要点，重点；分数，得分　v. 指，指向；对准，瞄准

例：He was completely negative about my point.

他对我的观点完全持否定态度。

搭：point out 指出　point of view 观点

派：pointless adj. 无意义的，无目标的

3. successful [sək'sesfl] adj. 容易的，不费力的；舒适的，自如的

例：A successful entrepreneur must have a long-term perspective.

一名成功的企业家必须有长远的眼光。

记：词根记忆 success成功 + ful表示富有……的→successful有成效的；获得成功的

搭：successful rate 成功率

派：success n. 成功　successfully adv. 成功地

4. skill [skɪl] n. 技巧，技艺；（特定的）技术，技能

例：The workers admire the engineer's superb skills immensely.

工人们对工程师的高超技艺钦佩不已。

搭：basic skill 基本技能　practical skill 实用技能

派：skilled adj. 熟练的，有技能的

5. recommend [ˌrekə'mend] v. 建议，劝告；推荐，介绍

例：He recommends buying ingredients at the mall in the square near Central Street.

他建议在中央街附近广场的购物中心购买食材。

记：词根记忆 re一再 + com共同 + mend修改→一再想要共同修改→recommend劝告

搭：recommend for 推荐；由于……而称赞　recommend doing sth. 建议做某事

派：recommendation *n.* 推荐

6. team [tiːm] *n.* （游戏或体育运动的）队，小组；工作队，工作组

例：The Chinese **team** defeated the strong opponent after many difficulties.

中国队经过重重困难后战胜了强大的对手。

搭：team spirit 团队精神；合作精神　team work 配合，协力

7. send [send] *v.* 邮寄，发送；传达，告知；派遣

例：Please **send** me your product catalogue of the electric tube.

请给我寄贵公司的电子管产品目录。

搭：send out 发送；派遣　send in 递送；呈报

派：sender *n.* 寄件人；发送人

8. bring [brɪŋ] *v.* 拿来，带来；引起，使产生

例：Please **bring** scissors and tape to school tomorrow.

请明天带剪刀和胶带来学校。

搭：bring about 引起　bring up 提出；教育；养育

9. hour [ˈaʊə (r)] *n.* 小时；（办公等的）固定时间；某个时间

例：He spends an **hour** on his way to work every day.

他每天要花一个小时在上班路上。

搭：an hour 一小时　rush hour 上下班高峰时间

派：hourly *adj.* 每小时的；按小时计算的

10. follow [ˈfɒləʊ] *v.* 跟着，跟随；遵循，听从

例：After a few steps forward, he motioned for his new friend to **follow** him.

他向前走了几步后，示意新朋友跟上他的步伐。

搭：follow me 跟我来　as follow 依下列各项

派：following *adj.* 之后的，接下来的

11. wait [weɪt] *v.* 等候；盼望，期待

例：We **waited** for her downstairs for a long time yesterday.

我们昨天在楼下等了她很长时间。

搭：wait for 等候；等待　wait and see 观望

派：waiter *n.* 服务员

12. writer [ˈraɪtə (r)] *n.* （职业的）作家，作者

例：She is a **writer** of international repute.

她是一位享有国际声誉的作家。

搭：freelance writer 自由撰稿人，自由作家

派：write v. 写作，编写 written adj. 书面的

13. money [ˈmʌni] n. 钱，钞票，货币

例：No matter in any country, buying a house can cost a lot of money for young people.

不管在哪个国家，买房对于年轻人来说都要花一大笔钱。

搭：earn/make money 赚钱 in the money 很有钱

派：monetary adj. 货币的，金融的

14. mean [miːn] v. 意味着；表示……的意思，作……的解释 adj. 吝啬的，小气的；不善良的，刻薄的

例：Refusal means giving up your parents' inheritance.

拒绝意味着你将放弃你父母的遗产。

搭：mean much to sb. 对某人很重要

派：meaning n. 意思 means n. 方法，手段

15. teach [tiːtʃ] v. 教授，讲授；教，训练

例：Can you teach me how to maintain a fishing rod?

你能教我怎么保养钓竿吗？

搭：teach oneself 自学 teach sb. a lesson 教训某人，给某人一个教训

派：teaching n. 教学工作 teacher n. 老师

16. stop [stɒp] v.（使）停止，结束；（使）中断 n. 停止，终止；车站

例：The truck finally stopped in front of the warehouse.

那辆卡车最终在仓库前停下。

搭：stop to do 停下来去做某事 stop doing 停止做某事

派：stopper n. 塞子；阻塞物 stoppage n.（因抗议进行的）停工，罢工

17. build [bɪld] v. 建造，修建；发展，建立

例：It takes a lot of labor to build a reservoir.

修筑一座水库要花费许多劳动力。

搭：build up 增进，加强 build on 把……建立在……上；以……为基础

派：building n. 建筑物

18. answer [ˈɑːnsə (r)] *v.* 回答，答复；回复；接电话 *n.* 回答；答案；解决办法

例：His **answer** is no more than a simple summary of the textbook.
他的答案不过是对课本的简单概括。

搭：answer questions 回答问题 in answer to 回答；应……要求

派：answerable *adj.* 应负责任的；可回答的

19. include [ɪnˈkluːd] *v.* 包含；把……列为一部分，把……算入

例：The symptoms of a cold **include** sneezing，runny nose，and coughing.
感冒的症状包括打喷嚏、流鼻涕和咳嗽。

派：included *adj.* 包括在内的 including *prep.* 包含，包括

20. month [mʌnθ] *n.* 月，月份

例：Mr. James was forced to spend three **months** in France because of the pandemic.
由于疫情，詹姆斯先生被迫在法国滞留了三个月。

搭：last month 上个月 next month 下个月 per month 每月

派：monthly *adj.* 每月的，每月一次的

21. remember [rɪˈmembə (r)] *v.* 回想起，记得；记起

例：**Remember** to clean the classroom before you leave school.
离开学校之前记得把教室打扫干净。

记：词根记忆 re再次，重新 + mem回忆，记忆 + ber→remember记得

搭：remember of 记得 remember to do 记得做某事

派：remembrance *n.* 纪念，怀念

22. night [naɪt] *n.* 夜间，夜晚

例：It was the sort of **night** when beasts might appear.
这种夜晚正是野兽出没的时候。

搭：at night 在夜里 good night 晚安 day and night 夜以继日

派：nightly *adj.* 每晚的，每夜的

23. plan [plæn] *n.* & *v.* 计划；打算

例：His **plan** was denied by the supervisor.
他的计划被领导否定了。

搭：plan to do 计划做某事 plan for 为……做计划

派：planner *n.* 计划者，规划师

24. water [ˈwɔːtə(r)] n. 水，雨水；水域　v. 给……浇水，灌溉

例：Every country has a responsibility to ensure water quality.

每个国家都有责任确保水质。

搭：water pollution 水污染　water resource 水资源　fresh water 淡水

派：waterless adj. 无水的，干的　watered adj. 掺水的；洒有水的

25. grow [grəʊ] v. 长大，成长；发展；增加；变得；种植

例：She started her own business and watched it grow into a successful venture.

她创办了自己的公司，并看着它成长为一个成功的企业。

搭：grow up 成长；逐渐形成　grow old 变老

派：growth n. 成长，生长　grown adj. 长大的，成年的

26. reason [ˈriːzn] n. 原因，理由；道理，情理　v. 推理，逻辑思考

例：In order to dispel his doubts, I explained to him the reason for doing so.

为了打消他的疑惑，我向他解释了这么做的理由。

搭：the reason of ……的原因　main reason 主要原因

派：reasonable adj. 有道理的，合情理的　reasonably adv. 尚可，过得去；理性地

27. collect [kəˈlekt] v. 聚集，聚积；收集，采集；收藏

例：The old kettle has collected a large amount of scale.

那个旧水壶已经聚积了大量水垢。

记：词根记忆 col共同＋lect选择；收集→选择后放在一起→collect收集

搭：collect up 把某物归拢到一起　collect for 为……筹钱

派：collection n. 收藏品，收集物

28. agree [əˈgriː] v. 同意，赞成；答应，接受

例：Henry agreed Benjamin to borrow money from the bank to solve the shortage of funds.

亨利同意本杰明向银行借款以解决资金短缺的问题。

搭：agree to do sth. 同意做某事　agree on/upon 对……取得一致意见

　　agree with 同意……的意见

派：agreement n. 协议，协定　agreeable adj. 可接受的

29. competition [ˌkɒmpəˈtɪʃn] n. 竞争；比赛，竞赛

例：The competition for young people to get into top universities is fierce.

年轻人想进一流大学的竞争是很激烈的。

记：词根记忆 compet（e）竞争＋ition表示行为，状态→competition竞争

搭：fierce competition 激烈的竞争　unfair competition 不公平竞争

派：competitive *adj.* 有竞争力的　compete *v.* 竞争，对抗

30. believe [bɪˈliːv] *v.* 相信；认为

例：Despite the adverse circumstances，the lawyer still **believed** that his client was innocent.

尽管情况不利，律师仍然相信他的委托人是无辜的。

记：**联想记忆** be（是）+ lieve（=love爱）→爱是相信

搭：believe in 信仰；信任　believe it or not 信不信由你

派：belief *n.* 相信，信心

31. computer [kəmˈpjuːtə(r)] *n.* 计算机；电脑

例：**Computer** science is a very popular subject for students.

计算机科学是一门非常受学生欢迎的学科。

记：**词根记忆** comput(e) 计算 + er表示能做某事的物→computer计算机

搭：computer game 电脑游戏　computer science 计算机科学

派：compute *v.* 计算，估算

32. photo [ˈfəʊtəʊ] *n.* 照片

例：It is forbidden to take **photos** in the nature reserve.

在自然保护区内禁止拍照。

搭：take a photo 拍照　photo album 相册

33. win [wɪn] *v.* （在战斗、比赛、游戏等中）赢，获胜

例：We **won** the battle with tenacious will.

我们以顽强的意志在这次战斗中获胜了。

搭：win back 重获　win the game 赢得比赛

派：winner *n.* 优胜者　winning *adj.* 获胜的；吸引人的

34. club [klʌb] *n.* 俱乐部，社团；活动室

例：College students should join **clubs** on a voluntary basis.

大学生加入社团应以自愿为原则。

搭：football club 足球俱乐部　in the club 在俱乐部里

35. allow [əˈlaʊ] *v.* 允许，准许；接受，认可

例：Please **allow** me to introduce this representative to you.

请允许我向各位介绍一下这位代表。

搭：allow sb. to do sth. 允许某人做某事

派：allowable *adj.* 容许的，可减免的（税收部分） allowance *n.* 津贴；零用钱；允许

36. minute [ˈmɪnɪt] *n.* 分，分钟；片刻，瞬间

例：There are still five **minutes** left before their agreed time.
距离他们约定的时间还有五分钟。

记：词根记忆 mini小的，少的 + ute→时间的一个小单位→minute分钟，微小的

搭：last minute 最后一刻；紧急关头 in a minute 一会儿

派：minutely *adv.* 详细地；精密地

37. weekend [ˌwiːkˈend] *n.* 周末

例：He decided to take a break from work and go camping with his family at the **weekend**.
他决定暂时放下工作，周末和家人一起去野营。

记：词根记忆 week周，星期 + end末尾→weekend周末

搭：at the weekend 在周末 last weekend 上周末

派：week *n.* 周，星期 weekday *n.* 普通日；工作日

38. book [bʊk] *n.* 书，书籍；本子，簿册 *v.* 预订，预约

例：This **book** inspired her to write her next work.
这本书给予了她写下一部作品的灵感。

记：联想记忆 书有600（boo）课（k）。

搭：by the book 按章办事 an open book 尽人皆知的事实

39. number [ˈnʌmbə(r)] *n.* 数字；电话号码；编号，序数；总量，数量

例：The **numbers** produced by the calculation make accountants very worried.
计算出来的数字让会计师们非常担心。

记：词根记忆 num数字，数量 + b + er做……的事物→number数字

搭：a number of 一些 the number of ……的数量

派：numerous *adj.* 众多的

40. park [pɑːk] *n.* 公园；专用区；园区 *v.* 停车，泊车

例：The city council plans to build a **park** in this area.
城市委员会计划在这个地区建一座公园。

搭：amusement park 游乐园 national park 国家公园

派：parking *n.* 停车，停车处

巩固练习

1. 扫码听写（根据所听音频写出本单元对应单词）

(1) _____ (2) _____ (3) _____ (4) _____

(5) _____ (6) _____ (7) _____ (8) _____

(9) _____ (10) _____ (11) _____ (12) _____

(13) _____ (14) _____ (15) _____ (16) _____

(17) _____ (18) _____ (19) _____ (20) _____

(21) _____ (22) _____ (23) _____ (24) _____

(25) _____ (26) _____ (27) _____ (28) _____

(29) _____ (30) _____ (31) _____ (32) _____

(33) _____ (34) _____ (35) _____ (36) _____

(37) _____ (38) _____ (39) _____ (40) _____

2. 实战演练（选出最符合句意的选项）

(1) The failure to _____ Europe was a lifelong regret for Napoleon.

　　(A) fight　　　　　　　　(B) persuade

　　(C) prevail　　　　　　　(D) conquer

(2) Policy changes may _____ new development opportunities for companies.

　　(A) answer　　　　　　　(B) provide

　　(C) supply　　　　　　　(D) respect

(3) What kind of _____ would you change if you want to visit Spain?

　　(A) paper　　　　　　　(B) currency

　　(C) label　　　　　　　(D) money

(4) The government _____ him to build a factory in the industrial park.

　　(A) permitted　　　　　　(B) allowed

　　(C) followed　　　　　　(D) brought

(5) The official does not _____ of the government's economic policy.

　　(A) understand　　　　　(B) agree

　　(C) approve　　　　　　(D) accept

(6) The company _____ the experienced employee and put him in charge of the safe.

　　(A) worried　　　　　　(B) believed

(C) trusted　　　　　　　　(D) disliked

(7) She ＿＿＿＿＿ to the telegram sent by the client quickly.

(A) replied　　　　　　　　(B) answered

(C) sent　　　　　　　　　(D) made

(8) Many old people have retained the habit of listening to ＿＿＿＿＿.

(A) computer　　　　　　　(B) projector

(C) camera　　　　　　　　(D) radio

(9) The campus speech ＿＿＿＿＿was won by the Faculty of Arts.

(A) concept　　　　　　　　(B) contest

(C) faith　　　　　　　　　(D) match

(10) She can always create new ＿＿＿＿＿for her inefficiency.

(A) chances　　　　　　　　(B) talents

(C) reasons　　　　　　　　(D) excuses

Day 5

小试牛刀

浏览本单元所有单词，在你已掌握的单词前面打√。

☐ sell	☐ discuss	☐ finish	☐ staff
☐ achieve	☐ art	☐ fly	☐ create
☐ event	☐ interview	☐ spell	☐ expect
☐ project	☐ relax	☐ increase	☐ letter
☐ space	☐ publish	☐ sleep	☐ ticket
☐ customer	☐ centre	☐ share	☐ worry
☐ office	☐ technology	☐ activity	☐ example
☐ equipment	☐ camera	☐ system	☐ concert
☐ party	☐ announcement	☐ message	☐ notice
☐ business	☐ view	☐ summer	☐ bear

词汇精讲

1. sell [sel] v. 出售，售卖

例：The new smartphone model is expected to sell out quickly.

新款智能手机预计很快就会售罄。

搭：sell out 卖光　sell off 廉价出售

派：sellable *adj.* 适于销售的，可销售的　sale *n.* 出售，销售

2. discuss [dɪˈskʌs] v. 讨论，谈论；详述，论述

例：It's no use to discuss the content of contract with Henry.

跟亨利讨论合同的内容是没有用的。

记：词根记忆 dis分散 + cuss摇动→分散敲击（问题）→discuss讨论

搭：discuss with 商洽；与……谈论

派：discussion *n.* 讨论；论述；辩论

3. finish [ˈfɪnɪʃ] v. 完成，结束

例：He finished the work the company assigned him before the deadline.

他在截止日之前完成了公司给他安排的工作。

记：词根记忆 fin边界 + ish表示做……→到了边界→finish完成，结束

搭：finish doing 完成做某事　finish line 终点线

派：finished *adj.* 结束了的，完成了的

4. staff [stɑːf] n. 全体员工，全体雇员；手杖，拐杖

例：The staff of the company is skeptical about the new president's ability.

公司全体员工对新总裁的能力表示怀疑。

搭：sales staff 销售人员　office staff 上班族

派：staffing *n.* 人员配置

5. achieve [əˈtʃiːv] v. （经努力）达到，取得，实现

例：Mary has finally achieved her goal of joining a foreign company.

玛丽终于实现了她入职外企的目标。

记：词根记忆 a朝向 + chiev头 + e→朝着老大的目标努力→achieve达到

搭：achieve one's goal 实现目标　achieve success 取得成功

派：achievement *n.* 成绩；成就

6. art [ɑːt] n. 美术，艺术；艺术品

例：He devoted his whole life to the study and creation of art.

他将自己的一生都奉献给了艺术研究与创作。

记：词根记忆 ar组装，关节，技巧 + t→工艺，技巧→art艺术，美术

搭：art school 艺术学校　art circle 艺术圈，艺术界

派：artist *n.* 艺术家　artistic *adj.* 艺术的

7. fly ［flaɪ］ *v.* 飞，飞翔；（飞机、航天器等）飞行，航行

例：It is impossible for man to fly in the air without the help of tools.

人不借助工具是不可能飞在空中的。

搭：fly a kite 放风筝　fly high 有雄心大志；情绪高涨

派：flyer *n.* 传单；飞鸟；飞行物

8. create ［kriˈeɪt］ *v.* 创造，创建；设计，创作

例：I fear that I may create a bad impression by behaving improperly.

我担心我的行为不当会给人留下不好的印象。

记：词根记忆 creat生产，生长 + e→create创造，发明

搭：create value 创造价值

派：creation *n.* 作品，创作　creative *adj.* 有创造力的，有想象力的

9. event ［ɪˈvent］ *n.* 事件，大事；社交场合，公开活动

例：This event marked the beginning of the French Revolution.

这个事件标志着法国大革命的开端。

搭：in that event 那样的话　at all events 不管怎样，无论如何

派：eventful *adj.* 充满大事的，多变故的

10. interview ［ˈɪntəvjuː］ *v. & n.* 面试，面谈；采访，访问

例：The purpose of the interview is to help the candidate find the job they want.

面试的目的是帮助应聘者找到心仪的工作。

记：词根记忆 inter互相 + view看→互相看→interview面试，采访

搭：job interview 求职面试　telephone interview 电话面试

派：interviewer *n.* 采访者；面试官　interviewee *n.* 被采访者；接受面试者

11. spell ［spel］ *v.* 拼写，拼出（单词）；拼作，拼成　*n.* 一段时间；咒语，符咒

例：This word is too difficult for pupils to spell.

这个单词对于小学生来说太难拼了。

搭：spell out 详加说明

派：spelling *n.* 拼写，拼写能力

12. expect [ɪkˈspekt] *v.* 期待；预计；要求，指望

例：They all expect what Christmas presents they will receive this year.

他们都期待着今年会收到什么圣诞礼物。

记：词根记忆 ex出，向外 + pect由spect而来，表示看→向外看→expect期待

搭：expect sb. to do sth. 期待某人做某事

派：expectation *n.* 期待，预期

13. project [ˈprɒdʒekt] *n.* 项目，计划；（学校的）课题，研究项目
　　　　　[prəˈdʒekt] *v.* 预计，推算；投射，投影

例：The student's research project was supported by the college.

这个学生的研究课题得到了学院的支持。

记：词根记忆 pro向前 + ject投掷→提前被投掷出来的是计划，项目→project计划

搭：hope project 希望工程　research project 研究项目

派：projector *n.* 放映机，投影仪

14. relax [rɪˈlæks] *v.* 休息，（使）放松；放心；镇定

例：The key to adjusting your mind is to learn to relax yourself.

调整心态的重点在于学会放松自我。

记：词根记忆 re重新 + lax松→重新松开→relax放松

搭：relax oneself 放松自己

派：relaxed *adj.* 放松的，轻松的　relaxing *adj.* 令人轻松的，愉快的

15. increase [ɪnˈkriːs] *v.* 增加，增强，增大

例：They decided to increase the amount of investment in the animation industry.

他们决定增加对动画产业的投资金额。

记：词根记忆 in在……之上 + creas生长 + e→increase增加；增大

搭：increase by 增加了……　increase to 增加到……

派：increasing *adj.* 越来越多的，渐增的

16. letter [ˈletə(r)] *n.* 信，信函；字母

例：I just received your letter from abroad yesterday.

我昨天刚收到你从国外寄来的信。

搭：write a letter 写信　send a letter 寄信

17. space [speɪs] *n.* 空间；空隙；太空

例：The large television takes up too much space.

那台大电视太占地方了。

记：词根记忆 spac空间 + e→space空间；太空

搭：in the space 在太空 time and space 时间和空间

18. publish [ˈpʌblɪʃ] v. 出版，发行（书等）；（作家等）发表（自己的作品）；公布

例：He plans to publish a novel about adventures in the jungle.

他计划出版一部有关丛林冒险的小说。

记：词根记忆 publ人+ ish表示"做"……→使公众化，引申为出版→publish出版，发行

搭：publish a book 出版书籍 publish an article 发表文章

派：publisher n. 出版商 publishing n. 出版业

19. sleep [sliːp] v. 睡，睡觉 n. 睡眠，睡觉

例：Students should sleep at least eight hours per day to ensure the quality of their study.

学生们每天至少要睡八小时才能保证学习质量。

搭：go to sleep 入睡 sleep in 睡过头；迟起床

派：sleepy adj. 困倦的

20. ticket [ˈtɪkɪt] n. 票，入场券

例：The ticket revenue has earned the organizers a lot of money.

门票收入让球赛主办方赚得盆满钵满。

记：词根记忆 tick标记 + et名词后缀，表示"小组"→ticket票，入场券

搭：air ticket 机票 ticket price 票价

派：ticketing n. 售票；票务

21. customer [ˈkʌstəmə (r)] n. 顾客

例：This customer hopes that the store can provide a reasonable response to product quality issues.

这位顾客希望店铺就产品质量问题给出合理答复。

记：词根记忆 custom习惯，风俗 + er与……相关的人→原指海关官员，后指顾客→customer顾客

搭：customer service 客户服务；售后服务 customer loyalty 顾客忠诚度

22. centre [ˈsentə (r)] n. （地理位置）中间，中心点

例：Victory Square is located in the centre of the city.

胜利广场坐落于市中心。

搭：in the centre of 在……的中心

派：central *adj.* 中央的，中心的

23. share [ʃeə (r)] *v.* 分享；共享，合用；分担（责任），分摊（费用） *n.* 股份，股票；份额

例：Thomas is so stingy that he won't even share snacks with his friends.

托马斯真是太小气了，连零食都不愿与朋友分享。

搭：share sth. with sb. 与某人分享某物　market share 市场占有率

派：sharing *adj.* 慷慨的，无私的

24. worry ['wʌri] *v.* & *n.* 担心，发愁

例：Don't worry about the money. I'll contact the bank to apply for a loan.

钱的事不要担心。我会与银行联系申请贷款。

搭：worry about 焦虑……；担心……

派：worried *adj.* 担心的，发愁的　worriment *n.* 烦恼，苦恼

25. office ['ɒfɪs] *n.* 办公室；办公楼，办事处

例：His style of behaviour caused dissatisfaction among the others in the office.

他的行事风格使办公室里的其他人感到不满。

记：词根记忆 of工作（由opus而来）+ fic做，造 + e→引申工作的地方→office办公室

搭：in the office 在办公室里　office clerk 职员

派：official *adj.* 正式的，官方的　officially *adv.* 正式地，官方地

26. technology [tek'nɒlədʒi] *n.* 科技，技术

例：This technology can be applied to agricultural irrigation.

这项技术能应用于农业灌溉领域。

记：词根记忆 techn技术 + o + logy学（科）→technology科技，技术；工艺

搭：information technology 信息技术　advanced technology 先进技术

派：technological *adj.* 技术的，科技的

27. activity [æk'tɪvəti] *n.* 活动；活跃状况

例：Special activity is designed in the department store to meet the needs of customers.

百货公司为满足顾客的需要而设计了特殊的活动。

记：词根记忆 act 做；驱使 + ivity 表状态→activity活动

搭：physical activity 体育活动；体力活动　economic activity 经济活动

派：active *adj.* 积极主动的；好动的

28. example [ɪɡˈzɑːmpl] *n.* 例子，例证；榜样，楷模

例：One **example** will suffice to explain this chemical change.
举一个例子解释这个化学变化就够了。

记：词根记忆 ex向外 + ample拿→拿出来的东西，样品，后引申为例子→example 例子

搭：for example 比方说 set an example 做出榜样

29. equipment [ɪˈkwɪpmənt] *n.* 设备；用具

例：Can you give a detailed description of the **equipment**?
你能详细描述一下这台设备吗？

记：词根记忆 equip装配 + ment名词词尾，表示行为，状态→equipment设备，用具

搭：medical equipment 医疗器械 sports equipment 运动器材

派：equip *v.* 装备，配备 equipped *adj.* 装备齐全的

30. camera [ˈkæmərə] *n.* 照相机，摄影机

例：You need a **camera** to record good moments while traveling.
旅行时要想记录美好瞬间的话需要一台相机。

记：联想记忆 ca擦 me我 ra热爱→擦（ca）我（me）热爱（ra）的照相机（camera）。

搭：digital camera 数码相机 video camera 摄影机

31. system [ˈsɪstəm] *n.* （协同工作的）系统；体制，制度

例：Logging into the university course selection **system** is very difficult every time.
每次登录大学选课系统都很难。

记：词根记忆 sy（n）共同一起 + st站立 + em→一起站立→system协同工作的系统

搭：control system 控制系统 information system 信息系统

派：systematic *adj.* 有系统的；有条理的

32. concert [ˈkɒnsət] *n.* 音乐会，演奏会

例：The world tour **concert** lasted three hours.
这场全球巡演音乐会持续了三个小时。

记：词根记忆 con共同一起 + cert使和谐→共同和谐→concert音乐会，演奏会

搭：give a concert 开音乐会 concert hall 音乐厅

33. party ['pɑːti] *n.* 聚会，派对；政党，党派；（契约或争论的）当事人，一方

例：To celebrate the harvest, Arizona ranchers decided to throw a party.

为了庆祝丰收，亚利桑那州的农场主们决定举办一场派对。

搭：hold a party 开聚会；举行宴会　birthday party 生日派对

34. announcement [əˈnaʊnsmənt] *n.* 公告；（报纸上的）布告；宣布

例：The government's announcement is seen as a step toward settlling the strike.

政府的公告已被视为迈向解决罢工的一步。

记：词根记忆 announce宣布 + ment表行为、状态、过程→announcement宣布

搭：make an announcement 通知；发表声明

派：announce *v.* 宣布，公布

35. message [ˈmesɪdʒ] *n.* 口信，消息

例：I passed Jenny's message on to her mother.

我把珍妮的口信带给她母亲了。

搭：short message 短讯　message from 来自……的消息

派：messenger *n.* 送信人

36. notice [ˈnəʊtɪs] *n.* 通告，布告；注意，察觉　*v.* 意识到；注意，留意

例：The boss asked his secretary to post the notice on the wall of the canteen.

老板让秘书把那条通告贴在食堂墙上。

记：词根记忆 not标记，值得注意的 + ice表示情况，状态→notice觉察，注意

搭：take notice of 注意到　without notice没有事先通知

派：noticeable *adj.* 显而易见的，明显的

37. business [ˈbɪznəs] *n.* 商业，生意；公司，企业；事情；私事

例：The business conference provided valuable opportunities for professionals in the industry.

该商业会议为业内专业人士提供了宝贵的机会。

记：联想记忆 bus公交车+ in里面+ e（一只鹅）+ ss（两条蛇）→一只鹅和两条蛇在公交车里谈生意

搭：business card 名片　in business 经商；在经营

38. view [vjuː] *n.* 风景，景色；观点，看法；景象；视野

例：There is a beautiful view of the lake from the forest.

从森林中可看到湖泊的美丽景色。

搭：point of view 观点　in view of 鉴于

派：viewer *n.* 观察者；观众

39. summer [ˈsʌmə (r)] *n.* 夏天，夏季

例：Summer is the hottest season of the year.

　　夏天是一年里最热的季节。

搭：in summer 在夏天；在夏季　summer vacation 暑假

派：summery *adj.* 夏天的

40. bear [beə (r)] *n.* 熊　*v.* 承受，容忍；承担，担负（责任）

例：Black bears live in the humid forests of Asia and America.

　　黑熊栖息在亚洲和美洲的潮湿森林地带。

搭：bear in mind 记住　bear oneself 举止，表现

派：bearable *adj.* 可忍受的

扫码听音频

巩固练习

1. 扫码听写（根据所听音频写出本单元对应单词）

(1) _____ (2) _____ (3) _____ (4) _____

(5) _____ (6) _____ (7) _____ (8) _____

(9) _____ (10) _____ (11) _____ (12) _____

(13) _____ (14) _____ (15) _____ (16) _____

(17) _____ (18) _____ (19) _____ (20) _____

(21) _____ (22) _____ (23) _____ (24) _____

(25) _____ (26) _____ (27) _____ (28) _____

(29) _____ (30) _____ (31) _____ (32) _____

(33) _____ (34) _____ (35) _____ (36) _____

(37) _____ (38) _____ (39) _____ (40) _____

2. 实战演练（选出最符合句意的选项）

(1) His contract with the club will _____ at the end of the year.

　　(A) close　　　　　　　　(B) oversee

　　(C) finish　　　　　　　 (D) terminate

（2）It took the congress five hours to _____ an agreement.

    （A）object　　　　　　　　　　（B）reach

    （C）achieve　　　　　　　　　（D）sign

（3）The practical purpose of social reform is to _____ an incentive for economic development.

    （A）invent　　　　　　　　　　（B）advise

    （C）create　　　　　　　　　　（D）lend

（4）It was an _____ when I hit you in practice today.

    （A）accident　　　　　　　　　（B）example

    （C）expectation　　　　　　　　（D）incident

（5）Studying carefully after class will definitely _____ your rates of passing the exam.

    （A）expand　　　　　　　　　　（B）increase

    （C）loosen　　　　　　　　　　（D）enlarge

（6）How can we make _____ for so much furniture?

    （A）line　　　　　　　　　　　（B）space

    （C）seat　　　　　　　　　　　（D）time

（7）I accidentally _____ Nora taking a cab to the shopping mall.

    （A）heard　　　　　　　　　　（B）smelled

    （C）noticed　　　　　　　　　（D）recorded

（8）It is impossible for a professor to _____ everyone's name in the elective course.

    （A）read　　　　　　　　　　　（B）choose

    （C）change　　　　　　　　　　（D）remember

（9）The _____ of England inspired Shakespeare to write his greatest poetry.

    （A）scenery　　　　　　　　　（B）emptiness

    （C）fantasy　　　　　　　　　（D）scene

（10）I feel highly honoured to be invited to the state _____.

    （A）event　　　　　　　　　　（B）banquet

    （C）activity　　　　　　　　　（D）party

Day 6

小试牛刀

浏览本单元所有单词，在你已掌握的单词前面打√。

☐ bed	☐ advantage	☐ birthday	☐ member
☐ order	☐ service	☐ guide	☐ table
☐ task	☐ programme	☐ research	☐ clothes
☐ weather	☐ sea	☐ garden	☐ history
☐ media	☐ museum	☐ flight	☐ ship
☐ condition	☐ story	☐ light	☐ beach
☐ guest	☐ advertisement	☐ conference	☐ culture
☐ diagram	☐ level	☐ report	☐ sign
☐ result	☐ environment	☐ challenge	☐ attitude
☐ mountain	☐ career	☐ wind	☐ text

词汇精讲

1. bed [bed] *n.* 床，床铺；底部，基座

例：She likes to decorate the double bed in her home with bright sheets.

她喜欢用鲜艳的被单布置家里的双人床。

搭：go to bed 上床睡觉 in bed 在床上；卧床

派：bedding *n.* 床上用品

2. advantage [əd'vɑːntɪdʒ] *n.* 有利条件，优势；优点；利益

例：He turned the bad situation to his advantage.

他把糟糕的局势转化成了利己的形势。

记：词根记忆 ad从 + vantage优势→从某处获得优势→advantage优势

搭：the advantage of ……的优点 take advantage of 利用

派：disadvantage *n.* 不利条件，劣势

3. birthday ['bɜːθdeɪ] *n.* 生日，诞辰

例：He gave his girlfriend an expensive handbag as a birthday present.

他送给女朋友一个昂贵的手提包作为生日礼物。

搭：birthday party 生日宴会 birthday present 生日礼物

派：birth *v.* 出生，诞生

4. member ['membə(r)] *n.* 成员，一分子；会员

例：Wilson is an active member of the school basketball club.

威尔逊是学校篮球俱乐部的一名活跃成员。

搭：family member 家庭成员 party member 党员

派：membership *n.* 会员资格

5. order ['ɔːdə(r)] *n.* 命令，指示；顺序，次序；订单 *v.* 命令，指示

例：Obeying the orders of the commander is very important in the army.

服从长官的命令在军队中是很重要的。

记：词根记忆 ord秩序，等级 + er→order顺序

搭：obey the order 听从命令 in order 整齐，秩序井然

派：orderly *adj.* 有条理的，整齐的

6. service ['sɜːvɪs] *n.* 接待，服务；服役

例：The hotel chain is famous for its excellent service.

这家连锁旅馆以其优质的服务而闻名。

记：词根记忆 serv服务 + ice表示情况，状态，性质→service服务

搭：of service 有帮助的　render a service 效劳

派：serve v. 服务　server n. 服务器

7. guide [gaɪd] v. 带领，引导　n. 指南，手册；导游，向导；准则

例：He guided the group through the lane towards the tourist spot.

　　他带着旅游团穿过小路奔向旅游景点。

搭：tour guide 导游人员

派：guidance n. 指导，指引

8. table ['teɪbl] n. 桌子；表格

例：The broken glass was hidden under the table by the child.

　　打碎的玻璃杯被那个小孩藏在了桌子下面。

搭：at table 在吃饭时；正在吃饭　clear the table 收拾桌子　on the table 公开地；
　　在桌子上

9. task [tɑːsk] n. 工作，任务

例：His main task is to introduce the products to the dealers at the exhibition.

　　他的主要任务就是在展会上对经销商介绍产品。

搭：team task 团队任务　basic task 基本任务

派：tasking n. 任务派遣

10. programme ['prəʊɡræm] n. 计划，方案；（电视或广播的）节目

例：What's the programme on TV for this weekend?

　　这周末电视上有什么节目？

搭：programme control 程序控制　programme schedule 节目表

派：programmer n. 程序员　programmable adj. 可编程的

11. research [rɪ's3ːtʃ] n. & v. 研究，探讨

例：Research indicates that men are sometimes more prone to impulse spending than
　　women.

　　研究表明，男性有时比女性更容易冲动消费。

记：词根记忆 re—再，再次 + search搜查，搜寻→再次搜查→research研究

搭：scientific research 科学研究　research result 研究结果，研究成果

派：researcher n. 研究人员　search v. 搜查，搜寻

12. clothes [kləʊðz] n.衣服，衣物

例：Their clothes were neatly folded in the wardrobe.

他们的衣服整齐地叠在衣柜里。

搭：clothes shop 服装店

派：cloth n. 布料 clothing n. 衣服（总称）

13. weather [ˈweðə (r)] n. 天气，气象

例：The hot weather has spoiled the food we bought yesterday.

炎热的天气使我们昨天买的食物变质了。

搭：weather forecast 天气预报 weather station 气象站

14. sea [siː] n. 海，海洋

例：The sea trip was a novel experience for their family.

海上旅行对于他们一家人来说是一次新奇的体验。

搭：sea level 海平面 at sea 在海上；茫然

15. garden [ˈɡɑːdn] n. 花园，菜园，果园；庭园

例：The garden was filled with vibrant flowers and lush greenery.

花园里长满了生机勃勃的鲜花和郁郁葱葱的草木。

记：联想记忆 哥哥（g）和他的爱人（ar）在花园（garden）里等（den）你。

搭：in the garden 在花园里

派：gardening n. 园艺 gardener n. 园丁

16. history [ˈhɪstri] n. 历史；历史课，历史学；个人经历，履历

例：He chose to teach American history at the state university last year.

去年他选择去州立大学教美国历史。

搭：in the history 在历史上 long history 历史悠久

派：historical adj. （有关）历史的；历史学的

17. media [ˈmiːdiə] n. 媒体，传媒

例：A keen politician should be aware of the role of the media.

一个精明的政治家应该意识到媒体的作用。

记：词根记忆 medi中间 + a →中间的（媒介）→media新闻媒体

搭：social media 社交媒体 new media 新媒体

18. museum [mjuˈziːəm] n. 博物馆

例：Many artists' masterpieces are collected in this museum.

许多艺术家的杰作都被收藏在这座博物馆里。

记：词根记忆 muse沉思 + um场所→museum博物馆

搭：city museum 城市博物馆　historical museum 历史博物馆

19. flight [flaɪt] n. 航班，班机；飞行

例：The flight from Beijing to Seattle had to be canceled because of the weather.
北京飞往西雅图的航班由于天气原因被迫取消。

记：联想记忆 本次航班（flight）要飞（fly）向 + 光明（light）。

搭：flight number 航班号　flight attendant 空中乘务员

派：flightless adj. （鸟等）不能飞的

20. ship [ʃɪp] n. （大）船，舰　v. （用船、飞机）运送，运输

例：The ship was detained for violating the laws of the host country.
那艘船因违反所在国法律而被扣押。

搭：by ship 坐轮船，乘船　board a ship 登船

派：shipment n. 运输，运送

21. condition [kən'dɪʃn] n. 状况，状态；条件，环境

例：Doctors suggest that Tara be told about her health condition.
医生们主张应告诉塔拉她的健康状况。

记：词根记忆 con与……一起 + dit说，讲 + ion表示行为，状态→讲述情况→condition状况，条件

搭：actual condition 实际情况　working condition 工作环境

派：conditional adj. 有条件的，有前提的

22. story ['stɔːri] n. （真实或虚构的）故事；叙述

例：The story reminds me of what happened in the village when I was a child.
这个故事使我想起了小时候村子里发生的事。

搭：tell a story 讲故事；说谎　love story 爱情故事

23. light [laɪt] n. 光，光线；日光，阳光　adj. 浅色的，淡色的；轻的

例：It is well known that light travels the fastest in the universe.
众所周知，宇宙中光的传播速度最快。

搭：traffic light 红绿灯　bring to light 揭示，揭露

派：lighting n. 照明　lighter n. 打火机

24. beach [biːtʃ] n. 海滩，沙滩，海滨

例：Lying on the beach in the sun is a pleasure to him.

躺在沙滩上晒太阳对他来说是一种乐趣。

搭：on the beach 在海滩上　beach volleyball 沙滩排球

25. guest [gest] *n.* 客人；特邀嘉宾

例：The hostess prepared delicious meals for the guests.

女主人为客人准备好了可口的饭菜。

搭：honored guest 贵宾　guest room 客房

26. advertisement [əd'vɜːtɪsmənt] *n.* 广告

例：In order to find his lost gold watch，he decided to place an advertisement in the local newspaper.

为了找到他丢失的金表，他决定在当地报社登个广告。

记：词根记忆 advertise为……做广告 + ment指物的状态→advertisement广告

搭：television advertisement 电视广告

派：advertise *v.* 为……做广告　advertising *n.* 广告活动，广告业

27. conference ['kɒnfərəns] *n.* （大型、正式的）会议，研讨会

例：The agent scheduled the press conference for next Friday.

代理人把记者招待会安排在下周五举行。

记：词根记忆 confer商讨，协商 + ence表示行为，状态→conference会议

搭：press conference 记者招待会　conference hall 会议厅

28. culture ['kʌltʃə (r)] *n.* 文化，文明

例：Chinese culture has been respected and loved by people all over the world in recent years.

中华文化近年来受到全球人民的尊重与喜爱。

记：词根记忆 cult照料，耕作 + ure表示行为，结果→原指耕耘、培养，后引申为文化→culture文化

搭：culture industry 文化产业　traditional culture 传统文化

29. diagram ['daɪəgræm] *n.* 图表，图解

例：The head of the department gave me a diagram of the generator installation.

部门负责人给了我一张发电机安装图解。

记：词根记忆 dia在……中间 + gram写→diagram图解；示意图

搭：bar diagram 柱形图；条形图

派：diagrammatic *adj.* 图解的；概略的

30. level ['levl] *n.* 标准，水平；数量，程度；层次，级别

例：The company's goal this year is to push production efficiency to a higher level.

今年公司的目标是将生产效率推向更高的水平。

搭：level of ……的水平；……的等级　basic level 基本水平

31. report [rɪ'pɔːt] *n.&v.* 报告，汇报

例：She was asked to write a report on the company's financial performance.

她被要求写一份关于公司财务状况的报告。

记：词根记忆 re向后 + port携带→将信息带回去→report汇报

搭：write a report 写报告　report on 就……做报告

派：reporter *n.* 记者

32. sign [saɪn] *n.* 指示牌，标志；迹象；手势　*v.* 签名，署名

例：The traffic sign means that there is a school nearby.

那个交通标志的意思是附近有学校。

搭：traffic sign 交通标志　sign in 签到；签收

派：signature *n.* 签名，署名

33. result [rɪ'zʌlt] *n.* 结果，后果　*v.* 发生，产生；导致，造成

例：Violet was very satisfied with the result of the game.

维奥莱特对比赛的结果非常满意。

记：词根记忆 re往回 + sult跳→拿到结果跳回去→→result结果

搭：as a result 因此；结果是　result in 导致；引起

34. environment [ɪn'vaɪrənmənt] *n.* 自然环境，生态环境

例：Protecting the environment is the duty of Chinese citizens.

保护环境是中国公民应尽的义务。

记：词根记忆 en向里面 + viron圆圈，闭环 + ment表示体系，机构→environment 环境

搭：environment protection 环境保护　ecological environment 生态环境

派：environmental *adj.* 自然环境的，生态环境的　environmentalist *n.* 环保主义者

35. challenge ['tʃæləndʒ] *n.&v.* 挑战；质疑，质询

例：Raising enough money is a big challenge for this small firm.

筹集足够的资金对于这家小公司来说是个巨大的挑战。

记：**联想记忆** cha=插，leng=冷，e=鹅 联想：插（cha）+ 冷（leng）+ 鹅（e）是困难的挑战（challenge）。

搭：meet the challenge 迎接挑战

派：challenger *n.* 挑战者　challenging *adj.* 具有挑战性的

36. attitude [ˈætɪtjuːd] *n.* 态度，看法

例：Forcing young people to vote will give them a hasty attitude.

逼迫年轻人投票会使他们抱有一种草率的态度。

记：词根记忆 att（apt）适合，适应＋i＋tude名词词尾→attitude态度

搭：attitude toward 对……的态度　positive attitude 积极态度

37. mountain [ˈmaʊntən] *n.* 高山，山岳；许多，大量

例：The mountain top is covered with thick fog.

浓雾覆盖着山顶。

记：词根记忆 mount山＋ain表示与……有关的→mountain高山，山岳

搭：climb the mountain 爬山　mountain area 山区

38. career [kəˈrɪə (r)] *n.* 职业，事业；职业生涯

例：Making such silly mistakes can be a big blow to your career.

犯这种低级错误会对你的事业造成沉重打击。

记：词根记忆 car马车＋eer→马车走过的路，引申为经历，生涯→career职业，事业

搭：career development 职业发展　make a career 在事业上有所成就

39. wind [wɪnd] *n.* 风，气流；风向　[waɪnd] *v.* 弯曲前进，蜿蜒而行

例：The use of wind energy is mainly concentrated in the northwest of our country.

风能的使用主要集中在我国西北地区。

搭：wind power风力　against the wind顶风，逆风　wind energy风能

派：windy *adj.* 多风的，风大的

40. text [tekst] *n.* 正文，文本；课本，教材；短信

例：An examination with the text will show us whether the translation is accurate.

查看一下文本就知道译文是否准确。

记：词根记忆 text编织→笔者一字一句编织成文→text文本

搭：full text 全文　original text 原文

派：textual *adj.* 本文的；按原文的

巩固练习

1. 扫码听写（根据所听音频写出本单元对应单词）

(1) ＿＿＿＿＿＿ (2) ＿＿＿＿＿＿ (3) ＿＿＿＿＿＿ (4) ＿＿＿＿＿＿

(5) ＿＿＿＿＿＿ (6) ＿＿＿＿＿＿ (7) ＿＿＿＿＿＿ (8) ＿＿＿＿＿＿

(9) ＿＿＿＿＿＿ (10) ＿＿＿＿＿＿ (11) ＿＿＿＿＿＿ (12) ＿＿＿＿＿＿

(13) ＿＿＿＿＿＿ (14) ＿＿＿＿＿＿ (15) ＿＿＿＿＿＿ (16) ＿＿＿＿＿＿

(17) ＿＿＿＿＿＿ (18) ＿＿＿＿＿＿ (19) ＿＿＿＿＿＿ (20) ＿＿＿＿＿＿

(21) ＿＿＿＿＿＿ (22) ＿＿＿＿＿＿ (23) ＿＿＿＿＿＿ (24) ＿＿＿＿＿＿

(25) ＿＿＿＿＿＿ (26) ＿＿＿＿＿＿ (27) ＿＿＿＿＿＿ (28) ＿＿＿＿＿＿

(29) ＿＿＿＿＿＿ (30) ＿＿＿＿＿＿ (31) ＿＿＿＿＿＿ (32) ＿＿＿＿＿＿

(33) ＿＿＿＿＿＿ (34) ＿＿＿＿＿＿ (35) ＿＿＿＿＿＿ (36) ＿＿＿＿＿＿

(37) ＿＿＿＿＿＿ (38) ＿＿＿＿＿＿ (39) ＿＿＿＿＿＿ (40) ＿＿＿＿＿＿

2. 实战演练（选出最符合句意的选项）

(1) The ＿＿＿＿＿＿ covers about 70 percent of the earth's total area.

  (A) sky   (B) sea

  (C) land   (D) ocean

(2) The patient's health ＿＿＿＿＿＿ has been greatly improved by the doctor's efforts.

  (A) circumstance   (B) condition

  (C) situation   (D) environment

(3) This indifferent ＿＿＿＿＿＿ towards politics is common among American voters.

  (A) attitude   (B) altitude

  (C) position   (D) market

(4) The ＿＿＿＿＿＿ of reckless action is to make mistakes that you will regret for the rest of your life.

  (A) reason   (B) result

  (C) consequence   (D) start

(5) The school requires students to wear ＿＿＿＿＿＿ at the flag-raising ceremony.

  (A) shoes   (B) uniform

  (C) clothes   (D) socks

(6) The horror ＿＿＿＿＿＿ of the film was really hard for me to accept.

  (A) definition   (B) level

(C) rank   (D) class

(7) He was going to ask for the famous actor's _____ after the excellent performance.

    (A) sign   (B) name

    (C) gender   (D) autograph

(8) The Romans brought _____ to many of the lands they conquered.

    (A) culture   (B) peace

    (C) civilization   (D) happiness

(9) The hot and humid _____ in Brazil is not suitable for long-term residence by East Asians.

    (A) climate   (B) temperature

    (C) weather   (D) wind

(10) The police made a thorough _____ of the crime scene.

    (A) investigation   (B) survey

    (C) report   (D) research

Section 2
高频词汇

Day 7

小试牛刀

浏览本单元所有单词，在你已掌握的单词前面打√。

☐ perfect	☐ especially	☐ certainly	☐ short
☐ strong	☐ practical	☐ high	☐ keen
☐ quiet	☐ eventually	☐ definitely	☐ generally
☐ unusual	☐ lucky	☐ cold	☐ natural
☐ fast	☐ obviously	☐ currently	☐ suddenly
☐ academic	☐ extra	☐ late	☐ polar
☐ hot	☐ immediately	☐ comfortable	☐ properly
☐ welcome	☐ common	☐ present	☐ mobile
☐ proud	☐ professional	☐ suitable	☐ modern
☐ similar	☐ friendly	☐ top	☐ wide

词汇精讲

1. perfect [ˈpɜːfɪkt] *adj.* 完美的，理想的；无瑕的，完好的；最佳的，绝配的

例：The herd mentality is a perfect example of this phenomenon.

从众心理就是这种现象的一个完美例子。

记：词根记忆 per完全的 + fect做→完全做好的，即完美的→perfect完美的

搭：perfect competition 完全竞争 perfect oneself in 精通；熟练

派：perfectly *adv.* 完美地 perfection *n.* 完美，完善

2. especially [ɪˈspeʃəli] *adv.* 尤其，特别；专门，特地

例：Thompson is especially impressed with Chinese cuisine.

汤普森对中国菜的印象尤其深刻。

记：来自especial（*adj.* 特殊的，特别的）

派：especial *adj.* 特殊的，特别的

3. certainly [ˈsɜːtnli] *adv.* 无疑，确定；当然（用于回答）

例：Certainly, balanced diet is crucial to keep fit.

毫无疑问，均衡饮食对于保持健康至关重要。

记：来自certain（*adj.* 肯定的，确定的）

搭：certainly not 当然不是；一定不会

派：certain *adj.* 必然的，必定的

4. short [ʃɔːt] *adj.* （长度或距离）短的，矮的；短暂的，短期的；简短的；短缺的

例：Because of that movie, short skirts have become popular with many women recently.

由于那部电影，短裙近期受到众多女性青睐。

搭：in short 简言之；总之 be short of 缺乏；不足

派：shortly *adv.* 不久，很快 shortage *n.* 短缺，不足

5. strong [strɒŋ] *adj.* 强壮的，健壮的；坚固的，结实的；坚定的；坚强的

例：One of the recruitment requirements for construction workers is to be strong.

建筑工人的招聘要求之一是要强壮。

搭：strong wind 大风 be strong in 擅长

派：strongly *adv.* 强有力地；坚强地 strength *n.* 力量；力气

6. practical [ˈpræktɪkl] *adj.* 实际的，实用的；（计划、方法等）切实可行的；（人）务实的

例：This job requires the applicant to master relevant **practical** skills.

这份工作要求应聘者掌握相关的实用技能。

记：词根记忆 practic（e）做法，实践 + al 与……有关→practical实际的，实践的

搭：practical value 实际价值 practical application 实际应用

派：practice *n.* 实践，实际操作

7. high [haɪ] *adj.* 高的；富含……的；重要的；先进的，高级的

例：Goods of **high** quality are few and far between these days.

高品质的商品现在不多见。

搭：high school 高中 high quality 高品质 high temperature 高温

派：highly *adv.* 极其，非常；高度地，高水平地

8. keen [kiːn] *adj.* 渴望的，热衷的；热情的，热心的；思维敏捷的，敏锐的

例：At the same time，New York was **keen** to strengthen its dominance in the financial world.

与此同时，纽约热衷于加强其在金融界的统治地位。

搭：be keen on 喜爱；渴望

派：keenly *adv.* 敏锐地；强烈地 keenness *n.* 敏锐；锐利

9. quiet [ˈkwaɪət] *adj.* 安静的，宁静的；不出声的；沉默寡言的，文静的

例：The blue old castle is located in a **quiet** forest.

这座蓝色的古堡坐落在一片宁静的森林中。

搭：keep quiet 保持安静 peace and quiet 安静；宁静

派：quietly *adv.* 轻轻地，安静地 quietness *n.* 平静，安静

10. eventually [ɪˈventʃuəli] *adv.* 最终，结果

例：We **eventually** arrived at the port.

我们最终到达了港口。

派：eventual *adj.* 最终的，结局的

11. definitely [ˈdefɪnətli] *adv.* 肯定地，当然；明确地，确定地

例：This tourist site is **definitely** worth visiting.

这个旅游景点绝对值得参观。

记：来自definite（*adj.* 肯定的）

搭：definitely not 决不；绝对不

派：definite *adj.* 清晰的；确定的

12. generally [ˈdʒenrəli] *adv.* 通常，普遍地；笼统地，大概

例：**Generally** speaking, Europeans are not used to eating spicy food.

一般来说，欧洲人不习惯吃辛辣的食物。

记：词根记忆 来自general=gener种类，通用＋al与……相关的→general一般性的；普通的

搭：generally speaking 一般而言

派：general *adj.* 总体的，普遍的

13. unusual [ʌnˈjuːʒuəl] *adj.* 不寻常的，罕见的；与众不同的，独特的

例：Snow is an **unusual** sight in the equatorial region.

下雪在赤道地区是一种罕见的景象。

记：词根记忆 un不＋usual通常的→unusual异乎寻常的

派：unusually *adv.* 异乎寻常地，显著地　usual *adj.* 通常的，惯常的

14. lucky [ˈlʌki] *adj.* 幸运的，走运的

例：Derma is very **lucky** to have someone as attentive as you to help him.

德玛有你这样细心的人帮助他真是幸运至极。

搭：lucky dog 幸运儿　lucky day 幸运日

派：luckily *adv.* 幸运地　luck *n.* 幸运　unlucky *adj.* 不幸的

15. cold [kəʊld] *adj.* 冷的，凉的；冷淡的，冷漠的　*n.* 感冒，伤风；寒冷，低温

例：This kind of corn can grow during a **cold** winter.

这种玉米能在寒冷的冬天生长。

搭：cold water 冷水；凉水　catch a cold 感冒

派：coldly *adv.* 冷淡地　coldness *n.* 寒冷；冷淡

16. natural [ˈnætʃrəl] *adj.* 天然的；正常的；意料之中的；天生的，本能的

例：Africa is rich in **natural** resources under the ground.

非洲地下蕴藏着丰富的天然资源。

记：词根记忆 nat本身的，自然的 + ure名词词尾（e略）+ al形容词词尾→natural 天然的

搭：natural science 自然科学　natural gas 天然气

派：nature *n.* 大自然，自然界　naturally *adv.* 自然地，天然地

17. fast [fɑːst] *adj.* 快的，迅速的；系牢的，紧缚的　*adv.* 快速地

例：This kind of **fast** food is not fit for my appetite.

这种快餐不合我的胃口。

搭：fast food 快餐　as fast as 和……一样快

派：fasten *v.* （使）牢固，（使）固定

18. obviously [ˈɒbviəsli] *adv.* （用于强调）显然，显而易见

例：**Obviously**，it is impossible to conclude the mission in ten days.

显然，在十天内结束这个任务是不可能的。

派：obvious *adj.* 明显的，显然的　obviousness *n.* 显而易见；显著性

19. currently [ˈkʌrəntli] *adv.* 现时，当前

例：Jefferson is **currently** in Paris on a business trip on behalf of the company.

杰斐逊目前正代表公司在巴黎出差。

派：current *adj.* 现在的；流通的，通用的

20. suddenly [ˈsʌdənli] *adv.* 突然地，出乎意料地

例：The scientist was **suddenly** stirred to excitement.

那名科学家突然激动起来。

派：sudden *adj.* 突然的　suddenness *n.* 意外；突然

21. academic [ˌækəˈdemɪk] *adj.* 学业的，学术的；学校的，学院的

例：Business administration is now a mature **academic** subject.

工商管理目前已是一门成熟的学科。

记：词根记忆 academ（y）学术 + ic 构成形容词→academic学业的，学术的

搭：academic research 学术研究　academic circle 学术界

派：academically *adv.* 学术上，专业上　academia *n.* 学术界

22. extra ['ekstrə] *adj.* 额外的；另外收费的

例：He was forced to pay an **extra** charge due to operational errors.

由于操作失误，他被迫支付了一笔额外费用。

搭：extra charge 额外费用；附加费 extra work 加班；额外工作

23. late [leɪt] *adj.* 晚的，迟的；晚期的，末期的；已故的 *adv.* 晚，迟

例：The **late** boy decided to take a taxi to school.

迟到的男孩决定坐出租车去学校。

搭：be late for 迟到；来不及……

派：lately *adv.* 近来，最近 latest *adj.* 最近的，最新的

24. polar ['pəʊlə (r)] *adj.* 极地的，来自极地的；截然不同的；磁极的

例：Most creatures do not live in **polar** regions.

大多数的生物不在极地地区生存。

搭：polar region 极地 polar circle 极圈

派：polarization *n.* 两极分化

25. hot [hɒt] *n.* 温度高的，烫的；辣的；热门的，流行的

例：Taking a **hot** bath in winter can make people feel relaxed.

在冬天洗个热水澡可以使人心情放松。

搭：hot pot 火锅 hot topic 热门话题

派：hotly *adv.* 激烈地；热心地；暑热地 hotness *n.* 热烈；热心

26. immediately [ɪˈmiːdiətli] *adv.* 立即，马上

例：The French government took action **immediately** to counter the devaluation.

法国政府立即采取行动来应对货币贬值。

记：来自immediate（*adj.* 立刻的，即时的）

派：immediate *adj.* 立刻的，即时的

27. comfortable ['kʌmftəbl] *adj.* 令人舒适的；感到舒服的，安逸的

例：The subtle smell of flowers in the room made her feel **comfortable**.

房间里淡雅的花香使她感到舒适。

记：词根记忆 comfort安慰，抚感＋able可……的→comfortable舒服的，安逸的

搭：feel comfortable 感觉舒适 comfortable temperature 舒适的温度

派：comfort *n.* 舒服，舒适 uncomfortable *adj.* 感到不舒服的

28. properly ['prɒpəli] *adv.* 正确地，适当地；得体地，恰当地

例：The heater in my apartment doesn't work **properly**.

我公寓里的供暖设施出了点毛病。

记：来自 proper（*adj.* 适合的）

搭：behave properly 行为正当

派：proper *adj.* 正确的；合适的 improperly *adv.* 不适当地

29. welcome ['welkəm] *v.* & *n.* 欢迎，迎接

例：We warmly **welcome** new members to join the club.

我们热烈欢迎新成员加入社团。

记：词根记忆 wel愿望，福利 + come来→希望来→welcome欢迎

搭：warm welcome 热烈欢迎 welcome ceremony 欢迎仪式

30. common ['kɒmən] *adj.* 共同的，共享的；常见的，普遍的

例：Increasing market share is a **common** goal for all companies.

提高市场占有份额是所有公司共同的目标。

记：词根记忆 com与……一起 + mon公共→common常见的

搭：common sense 常识 in common 共同的；共有的

派：commonly *adv.* 通常地 uncommon *adj.* 不寻常的，罕有的

31. present ['preznt] *n.* 现在，眼前；礼物，赠品 *adj.*（人）在场的，出席的 [prɪ'zent] *v.* 颁发，赠送；出示（证件等供检查）；正式提交

例：What do you think of the **present** international conflict?

你对目前的国际冲突有何看法？

搭：at present 目前，现在 present situation 现状

派：presence *n.* 出席，存在

32. mobile ['məʊbaɪl] *adj.* 活动的，可移动的；行动方便的

例：**Mobile** phones are still too expensive for many Africans to afford.

对许多非洲人来说，移动电话仍然太贵。

搭：mobile phone 手机，移动电话 mobile communication 移动式通信

派：mobilize *v.* 动员，组织 mobility *n.*（住处、社会阶层、职业方面的）流动能力

33. proud [praʊd] *adj.* 自豪的，得意的；傲慢的，自负的

例：What's one accomplishment you're most **proud** of?

你最引以为傲的成就是什么？

搭：be proud of 骄傲

派：proudly *adv.* 傲慢地，自负地

34. professional [prə'feʃənl] *adj.* 职业的，专业的

例：When I was 24 I became a professional engineer.

24岁时，我成为一名职业工程师。

记：词根记忆 profession职业 + al与……相关的→professional职业的，专业的

搭：professional knowledge 专业知识　professional design 专业设计

派：profession *n.* 职业

35. suitable ['su:təbl] *adj.* 适宜的，合适的

例：I've been looking for a suitable job since I got here three months ago.

我从三个月前到这儿起就一直在找一份合适的工作。

记：词根记忆 suit匹配 + able能……的→能相配的→suitable适宜的

搭：meet the challenge 迎接挑战

派：suit *v.* 匹配　suitably *adv.* 适当地，适宜地

36. modern ['mɒdn] *adj.* 近代的，现代的；现代化的；新式的；摩登的，时髦的

例：He expressed dissatisfaction with the laziness of modern young people.

他对现代年轻人的懒惰表示不满。

记：词根记忆 mod方法，方式 + ern……的→引申为现存的→modern现代的，新式的

搭：modern society 现代社会　modern technique 现代技术

派：modernism *n.* 现代主义　modernization *n.* 现代化

37. similar ['sɪmələ (r)] *adj.* 相像的，类似的

例：Customer complaint letters show a similar problem.

客户的投诉信也体现了类似的问题。

记：词根记忆 simil类似 + ar有关的→similar类似的

搭：be similar to 与……相似　in a similar way 按同样的方式

派：similarity *n.* 相似性，相似点

38. friendly ['frendli] *adj.* 亲切的，友善的

例：The friendly contacts between two peoples can improve the relations between China and Japan.

两国人民之间的友好交往可以改善中日关系。

搭：environment friendly 环保的　friendly service 友好的服务

派：friendliness *n.* 友谊

39. top [tɒp] *adj.* 顶端的，顶部的；（地位、程度或重要性）最高的
　　　　 n. 顶部，顶端

例：The paint on the top of the castle has peeled off over time.

　　随着时间的推移，城堡顶部的油漆已经脱落了。

搭：on the top of 在……之上　come out top 名列前茅

40. wide [waɪd] *adj.* 宽的，广阔的；广泛的

例：There are many wide roads in this area.

　　该地区有许多宽阔的公路。

搭：a wide range of 大范围的　wide application 应用广泛

派：wideness *n.* 宽度　widely *adv.* 普遍地，广泛地

扫码听音频

巩固练习

1. 扫码听写（根据所听音频写出本单元对应单词）

(1) ＿＿＿＿＿　(2) ＿＿＿＿＿　(3) ＿＿＿＿＿　(4) ＿＿＿＿＿

(5) ＿＿＿＿＿　(6) ＿＿＿＿＿　(7) ＿＿＿＿＿　(8) ＿＿＿＿＿

(9) ＿＿＿＿＿　(10) ＿＿＿＿＿　(11) ＿＿＿＿＿　(12) ＿＿＿＿＿

(13) ＿＿＿＿＿　(14) ＿＿＿＿＿　(15) ＿＿＿＿＿　(16) ＿＿＿＿＿

(17) ＿＿＿＿＿　(18) ＿＿＿＿＿　(19) ＿＿＿＿＿　(20) ＿＿＿＿＿

(21) ＿＿＿＿＿　(22) ＿＿＿＿＿　(23) ＿＿＿＿＿　(24) ＿＿＿＿＿

(25) ＿＿＿＿＿　(26) ＿＿＿＿＿　(27) ＿＿＿＿＿　(28) ＿＿＿＿＿

(29) ＿＿＿＿＿　(30) ＿＿＿＿＿　(31) ＿＿＿＿＿　(32) ＿＿＿＿＿

(33) ＿＿＿＿＿　(34) ＿＿＿＿＿　(35) ＿＿＿＿＿　(36) ＿＿＿＿＿

(37) ＿＿＿＿＿　(38) ＿＿＿＿＿　(39) ＿＿＿＿＿　(40) ＿＿＿＿＿

2. 实战演练（选出最符合句意的选项）

(1) A ＿＿＿＿＿ sense of duty made him insist on continuing the investigation.

　　(A) vigorous　　　　　　　　(B) large

　　(C) strong　　　　　　　　　(D) severe

(2) The game appeals to a wide range of people, _____ young people who are obsessed with games.

(A) suddenly   (B) specially

(C) certainly   (D) especially

(3) Although he is eighty years old, his mind is still _____ as a young man's.

(A) sharp   (B) stupid

(C) keen   (D) clever

(4) The tourism bureau expects August to be the _____ season for tourism this year.

(A) flourishing   (B) peak

(C) prospective   (D) top

(5) It was not _____ for us to go so far just to see the cherry blossom.

(A) comfortable   (B) useful

(C) practical   (D) personal

(6) We shall have to bring in _____ advisers to help us to cut the budget.

(A) professional   (B) successful

(C) reasonable   (D) desirable

(7) He is a _____ person and seldom takes the initiative to talk to strangers.

(A) calm   (B) irritable

(C) brave   (D) quiet

(8) Human are so _____ to think they can change the earth.

(A) confident   (B) arrogant

(C) proud   (D) humble

(9) This ointment is _____ for people with allergies.

(A) affordable   (B) valuable

(C) fit   (D) suitable

(10) The president _____ the heads of neighbouring countries at the airport.

(A) greeted   (B) accepted

(C) welcomed   (D) guided

Day 8

小试牛刀

浏览本单元所有单词，在你已掌握的单词前面打√。

□ personal	□ underwater	□ previous	□ unique
□ effective	□ cheap	□ fresh	□ daily
□ funny	□ incredible	□ simple	□ deep
□ regular	□ major	□ serious	□ basic
□ gym	□ commercial	□ extended	□ physical
□ brilliant	□ warm	□ afraid	□ digital
□ typical	□ enormous	□ positive	□ single
□ electronic	□ fair	□ boring	□ dry
□ grateful	□ independent	□ delicious	□ foreign
□ impossible	□ global	□ initial	□ low

词汇精讲

1. personal ['pɜːsənl] *adj.* 个人的，私人的；私密的，隐私的

例：You have no right to see my personal correspondence without permission.

未经允许，你无权看我的私人信件。

记：词根记忆 person人 + al与……相关的→personal私人的

搭：personal information 个人信息　personal computer 个人电脑

派：person *n.* 人　personally *adv.* 就个人而言；亲自地

2. underwater [ˌʌndə'wɔːtə (r)] *adj.* 在水中的；水面下的

例：If you get panic underwater, you just consume more oxygen.

在水下如果陷入慌乱的话，你只会消耗更多氧气。

记：词根记忆 under 在……下面 + water 水→underwater水面下的

搭：underwater world 水底世界　underwater swimming 潜泳

3. previous ['priːviəs] *adj.* 以前的，先前的；（时间或顺序上）稍前的

例：My previous experience might not be directly applicable to this position.

我以前的经验可能不直接适用于这个职位。

记：词根记忆 pre在前 + vi路径，道路 + ous与……有关的→走在前方的路上→previous先前的

搭：previous year 前一年

派：previously *adv.* 以前，先前

4. unique [ju'niːk] *adj.* 独一无二的，独特的

例：As we all know, everybody is made unique and different.

我们都知道，每个人都是独一无二的。

搭：unique feature 特色　unique style 独特的风格

派：uniqueness *n.* 独特性　uniquely *adv.* 独特地

5. effective [ɪ'fektɪv] *adj.* 产生预期结果的，有效的；实际的，事实上的

例：We have no idea how to take effective action.

我们不知道该如何采取有效的行动。

记：词根记忆 effect影响 + ive表示有……倾向的→effective有效的

搭：effective measure 有效措施　be effective on 对……有效应，对……起作用

派：effectiveness *n.* 有效性，效力 effectively *adv.* 有效地；实际上

6. cheap [tʃiːp] *adj.* 便宜的，廉价的；价低质劣的；小气的，吝啬的

例：Due to a shortage of cash，he had to choose a cheap hotel to stay.
他由于手头现金不足，不得不选择便宜的酒店来住。

搭：on the cheap 便宜地；低廉地 cheap labour 廉价劳动力

派：cheaply *adv.* 便宜地；廉价地

7. fresh [freʃ] *adj.* 新鲜的；新颖的；清新的，清爽的；（水）淡的，无盐的

例：The fresh ingredients selected by this restaurant come from the local farm.
这家饭店选取的新鲜食材来自本地的农场。

搭：fresh air 新鲜空气 fresh water 湖水，淡水

派：freshness *n.* 新鲜 freshly *adv.* 新近；精神饱满地

8. daily ['deɪli] *adj.* 每日的，日常的

例：The daily newspaper provides me with the latest updates on the business world.
这份日报向我提供商业界的最新消息。

搭：daily life 日常生活 daily necessity 日用品

派：day *n.* 一天

9. funny ['fʌni] *adj.* 滑稽的，有趣的；奇怪的，难以解释的

例：The clown's funny performance caused the audience to burst into laughter.
小丑滑稽的表演引得观众哄堂大笑。

搭：feel funny 感觉不舒服、不自在

派：fun *n.* 乐趣，享受

10. incredible [ɪn'kredəbl] *adj.* 不可思议的，难以置信的；了不起的，极好的

例：It seemed incredible that she had been there a week already.
真让人难以置信，她已经在那里待了一个星期了。

记：词根记忆 in不是，非 + credible可相信的→不可相信→incredible难以置信的，极好的

派：incredibly *adv.* 难以置信地；非常地 credible *adj.* 可信的，可靠的

11. simple ['sɪmpl] *adj.* 简单的，简明的；简朴的，朴素的；纯粹的，完全的

例：I don't think it's necessary to ask him such a simple question.
我觉得这么简单的问题没有必要问他。

记：词根记忆 sim相似 + pl折叠 + e→折叠一次得到相似的东西，引申为简单的→simple简单的

搭：simple life 简单生活 simple and easy 简易明了

派：simply *adv.* 仅仅，只，不过

12. deep [diːp] *adj.* 深的，厚的；纵深的，位于深处的

例：Deep breathing helps relieve stress and adjust your mind.
深呼吸有助于缓解压力，调整思维。

搭：deep breath 深呼吸 in deep 深陷其中，深深卷入（尤指麻烦）

派：depth *n.* 深度 deeply *adv.* 很，非常

13. regular ['reɡjələ (r)] *adj.* 定期的；有规律的；频繁的；惯常的，通常的 *n.* 常客，老主顾

例：She took her medicine on a regular basis as the doctor ordered.
她按照医生的吩咐定期服药。

记：词根记忆 reg统治 + ular与……有关→统治，引导使形成规范→regular有规律的

搭：regular meeting 例会 on a regular basis 定期地；经常地

派：regularly *adv.* 定期地，有规律地 regularity *n.* 规律性

14. major ['meɪdʒə (r)] *adj.* 重大的，主要的 *n.* 主修科目，专业

例：She played a major role in this comedy.
她在这部喜剧中扮演一个重要的角色。

记：词根记忆 maj大，伟大 + or→major主要的

搭：major factor 主要因素 major in 主修

派：majority *n.* 大多数

15. serious ['sɪəriəs] *adj.* 严重的，危急的；认真的，严肃的

例：Due to the developed heavy industry, the air pollution in this city is very serious.
这座城市由于重工业发达，空气污染很严重。

搭：be serious about 严肃；认真对待 serious damage 严重损害；严重损坏

派：seriously *adv.* 严重地，认真地 seriousness *n.* 严重性；严肃；认真

16. basic [ˈbeɪsɪk] *adj.* 最重要的，基本的；最简单的，初级的

例：People usually describe the basic appearance of the people they meet.

对于见过的人，人们通常都会描述其基本的外貌。

记：词根记忆 bas低，下；基础 + ic……的→basic基础的

搭：basic principle 基本原理　basic theory 基本理论

派：basically *adv.* 基本上，大体上

17. gym [dʒɪm] *n.* 体育馆，健身房；（尤指学校的）体育活动

例：The gym offers a variety of fitness classes, such as yoga, aerobics, and spinning.

健身房提供各种健身课程，如瑜伽、有氧运动和动感单车。

搭：gym shoe 健身鞋；球鞋　gym class 体育课；体育教室

派：gymnastics *n.* 体操；体育；体操运动

18. commercial [kəˈmɜːʃl] *adj.* 商业的，商务的　*n.* 电视广告

例：Ancient Rome announced permission for free commercial trade outside its own territory.

古罗马宣布允许本土以外的自由商业贸易。

记：词根记忆 commerc（e）商业 + ial属于……的→commercial商业的

搭：commercial bank 商业银行

派：commerce *n.* 贸易，商业　commercially *adv.* 商业上，从商业角度看

19. extended [ɪkˈstendɪd] *adj.* 延长了的，扩展了的；详尽的

例：He applied for an extended leave because of his long overtime work.

由于长期加班，他申请延长休假。

记：词根记忆 extend（使）扩展 + ed已……的，被……的→extended延长的

搭：extended family 大家庭　extended period 延长期

派：extend *v.* 延伸；扩大；延长

20. physical [ˈfɪzɪkl] *adj.* 身体的，肉体的；物质的，有形的；物理的，物理学的

例：Exercise helps both mental and physical health.

锻炼有助于身心健康。

记：词根记忆 phys自然 ＋ical 与……有关的→与自然有关的→physical身体的，物理的

搭：physical education 体育课　physical fitness 体育健身；身体素质

派：physics *n.* 物理学　physically *adv.* 身体上，肉体上

21. brilliant [ˈbrɪliənt] *adj.* 聪颖的；成功的，辉煌的；巧妙的；使人印象深的

例：It is so **brilliant** of him to handle the problem smoothly.
　　他能顺利地处理这个问题，真是太聪明了。

记：词根记忆 brilli发光 + ant形容词后缀→发光的，光辉的→brilliant辉煌的

搭：brilliant sunshine 灿烂的阳光　brilliant achievement 辉煌成就

派：brilliance *n.* 光辉，才华

22. warm [wɔːm] *adj.* 暖和的，温暖的；（衣服）保暖的，防寒的；友好的，热情的

例：Pigeons go to **warm** places for the winter every year.
　　鸽子每年都去温暖的地方过冬。

搭：warm up 变热；热身运动　in the warm 在暖和的地方

派：warmth *n.* 温暖，暖和；热情，友好　warmer *n.* 保温衣；保温器

23. afraid [əˈfreɪd] *adj.* 害怕的；担心的；遗憾的

例：Being **afraid** of new things is a normal psychological phenomenon.
　　害怕新事物是一种正常的心理现象。

记：词根记忆 affra（y）滋事，冲突 + id与……有关的→害怕冲突发生→演变为afraid害怕的

搭：be afraid of 害怕

24. digital [ˈdɪdʒɪtl] *adj.* 数字的，数码的

例：My father bought me a **digital** camera as a reward.
　　我父亲给我买了台数码相机作为奖励。

记：词根记忆 digit数字 + al表示……的→digital数字的

搭：digital signal 数字信号　digital image 数字图像

派：digitalization *n.* 数字化

25. typical [ˈtɪpɪkl] *adj.* 典型的，有代表性的；平常的

例：Rental housing is a **typical** residence for graduate students.
　　出租房是研究生的典型住所。

记：词根记忆 typ模范，模型 + ical→typical典型的

搭：be typical of 是……的典型特征

派：typically *adv.* 典型地　typicality *n.* 典型性

26. enormous [ɪ'nɔːməs] *adj.* 巨大的，极大的

例：Scientists predict that the potential of artificial intelligence is enormous.

科学家预测，人工智能的潜力是巨大的。

记：词根记忆 e从……出 + norm规范，范式 + ous→原指不符合范式，畸形→enormous巨大的

搭：enormous pressure 巨大的压力

派：enormously *adv.* 非常，极其

27. positive ['pɒzɪtɪv] *adj.* 乐观的，有信心的；积极的；赞成的，支持的

例：We should adopt a positive attitude to face the suffering in life.

我们应该采取积极的态度来面对生活中的苦难。

记：词根记忆 posit放置，确定，肯定 + ive 形容词词尾→positive乐观的，有信心的

搭：positive attitude 积极态度 positive effect 积极的效果

派：positively *adv.* 绝对地；乐观地

28. single ['sɪŋɡl] *adj.* 单一的，单个的；单身的，未婚的；各自的，分别的

例：The single rose on the table caught everyone's attention with its beauty.

桌上的一枝玫瑰以其美丽吸引了每个人的注意。

搭：single room 单人房 every single 每一个

派：singleness *n.* 单一；独身

29. electronic [ɪˌlek'trɒnɪk] *adj.* 电子的，电子学的

例：Passengers are required to turn off their electronic devices while on board.

乘客在飞机上必须关闭电子设备。

记：词根记忆 electr电 + on名词词尾，微粒子 + 后缀ic 表示……的→electronic电子的

搭：electronic equipment 电子设备 electronic commerce 电子商务

派：electrical *adj.* 电的，与电有关的 electricity *n.* 电，电流

30. fair [feə(r)] *adj.* 公平的；合理的；公正的 *n.* 集市；展销会

例：The judge's verdicts on both the plaintiff and the defendant were fair.

法官对原告和被告的判决都是公正的。

搭：fair competition 公平竞争 fair and square 正大光明地；不偏不倚地

派：fairness *n.* 公平　fairly *adv.* 相当地；公平地，公正地

31. boring [ˈbɔːrɪŋ] *adj.* 乏味的，无趣的，无聊的

例：The director emphasized that the task was prolix and boring.

主管强调这项任务冗长又无聊。

搭：so boring 真无聊

派：bored *adj.* 无聊的，厌倦的　bore *v.* 使厌烦，使讨厌

32. dry [draɪ] *adj.* 干的；干旱的，少雨的；（头发或皮肤）干燥的，干性的

例：Vegetables need to be stored in a cool and dry place.

蔬菜需要储存在凉爽干燥的地方。

搭：keep dry 保持干燥　dry out 变干；戒酒

派：dryer *n.* 烘干机；干燥剂，催干剂

33. grateful [ˈɡreɪtfl] *adj.* 感谢的，感激的

例：I am grateful for the support and guidance of my family during difficult times.

我很感激家人在困难时期给予我的支持和指导。

记：词根记忆 grate（= grat）令人高兴的；高雅 + ful ……的→grateful 感谢的；愉快的

搭：be grateful to 感谢；感激　be grateful for 为……而感谢

派：gratefully *adv.* 感激地；感谢地　gratefulness *n.* 感谢

34. independent [ˌɪndɪˈpendənt] *adj.* 自立的，自力更生的；自治的，独立的

例：Going away to college has made me much more independent.

离家上大学使我变得更加自立。

记：词根记忆 in不是，非 + dependent依赖的→不依赖别人的→independent独立的

搭：independent of 不依赖……的；不受……支配的　independent thinking 独立思考

派：dependent *adj.* 依赖的，依靠的　independently *adv.* 独立地，自立地

35. delicious [dɪˈlɪʃəs] *adj.* 美味的，芬芳的

例：The delicious dishes left the guests full of praise.

美味的菜肴让客人们赞不绝口。

记：词根记忆 de从 + lic诱惑，吸引 + ious具有……性质的→好吃的东西把人吸引过来→delicious美味的

搭：delicious food 美食

派：deliciousness *n.* 美味；怡人；芬芳　deliciously *adv.* 美味地

36. foreign [ˈfɒrən] *adj.* 外国的，来自国外的；外交的；涉外的

例：China has become less attractive to foreign investment in recent years.

中国近年来对外资的吸引力在逐渐下降。

记：词根记忆 fore门外 + ign→foreign外国的

搭：foreign language 外语　foreign exchange 外汇；国际汇兑

派：foreigner *n.* 外国人；外地人

37. impossible [ɪmˈpɒsəbl] *adj.* 不可能的，办不到的

例：It is almost impossible for him to tell the truth about the matter.

要他说出这件事的真相几乎是不可能的。

记：词根记忆 im不是，非 + possible可能的→impossible不可能的

搭：next to impossible 几乎不可能　not impossible 并非不可能

派：possible *adj.* 可能的　impossibly *adv.* 不可能地；难以置信地

38. global [ˈgləʊbl] *adj.* 全球的，全世界的；全面的，整体的；球形的

例：The excessive emissions of greenhouse gases have led to global warming.

温室气体的过量排放导致了全球变暖。

记：词根记忆 glob球 + al与……相关的→global球形的；全球的

搭：global warming 全球变暖　global economy 全球经济

派：globe *n.* 地球，世界　globalization *n.* 全球化

39. initial [ɪˈnɪʃl] *adj.* 开始的，最初的；（字母）位于词首的

例：The initial trial is scheduled for September this year.

最初的审判预定在今年九月进行。

记：词根记忆 in进入 + it强烈的感情开始+ ial属于……的→进入新领域总是一腔热血→initial最初的

搭：initial condition 初始条件；起始条件

派：initially *adv.* 开始，最初　initialize *v.* 初始化

40. low [ləʊ] *adj.* 低的，矮的；在底部的；低于通常/平均数值的；（地位阶层上）低微的　*n.* 低点；（人生的）低谷

例：If you exercise regularly, your chances of getting sick will be very low.

如果你经常锻炼，你生病的概率就会很低。

搭：low cost 低成本　low temperature 低温

派：lower *adj.* 下面的，下方的；*v.* 降低，减少

巩固练习

1. 扫码听写（根据所听音频写出本单元对应单词）

(1) _____ (2) _____ (3) _____ (4) _____

(5) _____ (6) _____ (7) _____ (8) _____

(9) _____ (10) _____ (11) _____ (12) _____

(13) _____ (14) _____ (15) _____ (16) _____

(17) _____ (18) _____ (19) _____ (20) _____

(21) _____ (22) _____ (23) _____ (24) _____

(25) _____ (26) _____ (27) _____ (28) _____

(29) _____ (30) _____ (31) _____ (32) _____

(33) _____ (34) _____ (35) _____ (36) _____

(37) _____ (38) _____ (39) _____ (40) _____

2. 实战演练（选出最符合句意的选项）

(1) They deliberately suppressed _____ media in order to conceal the scandal.

　　(A) useful　　　　　　　　(B) private

　　(C) commercial　　　　　　(D) personal

(2) The _____ prime minister expressed his views on the issue of terrorist attacks at the forum.

　　(A) later　　　　　　　　 (B) recent

　　(C) former　　　　　　　　(D) previous

(3) It is not _____ to other players to use appliances other than those prescribed in the competition.

　　(A) fair　　　　　　　　　(B) sincere

　　(C) possible　　　　　　　(D) comparable

(4) He is really _____ in accomplishing the complicated task at such a low cost.

　　(A) effective　　　　　　　(B) efficient

　　(C) diligent　　　　　　　 (D) stubborn

(5) Seeing the world in a _____ light will make you much less stressed.

　　(A) practical　　　　　　　(B) optimistic

　　(C) negative　　　　　　　(D) positive

(6) Professor Roger is a highly respected _____ teacher on campus.

(A) strange   (B) alien

(C) foreign   (D) radical

(7) Immortality is _____ for humanity in the 21st century.

  (A) impossible   (B) difficult

  (C) incredible   (D) boring

(8) The headmaster won the students' applause and laughter with his _____ speech.

   (A) humourous   (B) tedious

   (C) simple   (D) irritating

(9) _____ equipment will ignite new sparks to provide power for the car.

   (A) Coppery   (B) Electronic

   (C) Electrical   (D) Wooden

(10) It is predicted that this new product has _____ market potential.

   (A) promising   (B) enormous

   (C) regular   (D) typical

Day 9

小试牛刀

浏览本单元所有单词，在你已掌握的单词前面打√。

☐ manage	☐ prepare	☐ suppose	☐ apply
☐ encourage	☐ cook	☐ compare	☐ affect
☐ avoid	☐ celebrate	☐ surprise	☐ wear
☐ arrange	☐ break	☐ imagine	☐ return
☐ organize	☐ realize	☐ design	☐ express
☐ identify	☐ repair	☐ delay	☐ admire
☐ admit	☐ perform	☐ prevent	☐ prove
☐ borrow	☐ raise	☐ explore	☐ inform
☐ necessary	☐ dangerous	☐ average	☐ constant
☐ valuable	☐ noisy	☐ financial	☐ dark

词汇精讲

1. manage ['mænɪdʒ] v. 管理，处理；操纵，控制；设法做到

例：He was asked by his superiors to manage the project.

他被上级要求管理这项项目。

搭：manage to do sth. 设法做某事 manage system 管理体制

派：management n. 经营，管理

2. prepare [prɪ'peə (r)] v. 使做好准备，把……预备好；（为……）做好准备

例：The keepers prepare breakfast for the animals every day.

饲养员们每天都要为动物们准备早餐。

记：词根记忆 pre在……之前 + par准备 + e→prepare使做好准备

搭：prepare for 为……准备，使有准备 prepare goods 备货

派：prepared adj. 有准备的，准备好的 preparation n. 准备

3. suppose [sə'pəuz] v. 推断，猜想；假设，假定，设想

例：They supposed that Henry had cleaned the classroom.

他们猜想亨利已经打扫了教室。

记：词根记忆 sup（sub）在下 + pos放置→在某前提下放置一个想法→suppose推断

搭：suppose that 假如 to suppose 假定

派：supposed adj. 假定的；想象上的 supposable adj. 可假定的；想象得到的

4. apply [ə'plaɪ] v. 申请；施加，实施；应用，运用

例：He wanted to apply for the army in order to fulfill his childhood dream.

他为了实现儿时的梦想而想要申请参军。

记：词根记忆 ad（ap）去 + ply折叠→去折叠，去做某件事→apply申请

搭：apply for 申请，请求

派：applied adj. 应用的，实用的 application n. 正式申请

5. encourage [ɪn'kʌrɪdʒ] v. 鼓励，激励

例：The government encourages college students to start their own businesses.

政府鼓励大学生进行创业。

记：词根记忆 en使……做某事，使进入 + courage勇气→注入勇气→encourage鼓励

搭：encourage investment 鼓励投资

派：encouragement *n.* 鼓励　encouraging *adj.* 鼓舞人心的

6. cook [kʊk] *v.* 烹饪，烹调　*n.* 厨师

例：What is your favorite dish to cook?

你最喜欢做的菜是什么？

记：词根记忆 由词根coqu演变而来→cook做饭

搭：cook food 做饭

派：cooker *n.* 炊具，锅，厨灶

7. compare [kəm'peə (r)] *v.* 比较，对比；把……比作；（与……）相比

例：If you compare British English with American English, you will find many differences.

如果你把英式英语与美式英语进行比较，便会发现许多不同之处。

记：词根记忆 com共同 + par相等 + e→放在一起看是否相等→compare比较

搭：compare with 与……相比较　compare to 把……比作，比喻为

派：comparison *n.* 比较，对照

8. affect [ə'fekt] *v.* 影响；（疾病）侵袭，感染；（在感情上）深深打动

例：The southern region is easily affected by floods due to high precipitation in summer.

南方地区在夏天由于降水量大很容易受洪水影响。

记：词根记忆 af朝向 + fect做，造→对某人做某事以影响他→affect影响

搭：be affected by 受到……的影响

派：affection *n.* 喜爱，关爱；爱恋

9. avoid [ə'vɔɪd] *v.* 避免，防止；回避，避开

例：I tried to avoid eye contact in case she recognized me.

我尽量避免眼神接触以防被她认出来。

记：词根记忆 a分离，没有 + void空白→把空的东西分离出去，避免混淆→avoid避免

搭：avoid doing 避免做某事

派：avoidable *adj.* 可避免的　avoidance *n.* 避免，避开

10. celebrate ['selɪbreɪt] *v.* 庆祝，庆贺；赞扬，赞美

例：They **celebrated** their graduation in the school playground.

他们在学校操场庆祝自己的毕业。

记：词根记忆 celebr频繁，人多，拥挤 + ate表示……的状态，性质，特性→celebrate庆祝

搭：celebrate with 与……庆祝

派：celebration *n.* 庆祝活动 celebrated *adj.* 著名的，驰名的

11. surprise [sə'praɪz] *v.* 使某人吃惊；给某人惊喜

例：The policeman took the thief by **surprise** as he opened the door.

小偷开门时，警察出其不意地抓住了他。

记：词根记忆 sur在上方 + pris抓住 + e→突然性的抓住，自然就让人惊讶→surprise惊奇，惊讶

搭：in surprise 惊奇地 by surprise 出其不意地

派：surprised *adj.* 意外的，惊讶的 surprising *adj.* 令人惊讶的，出人意料的

12. wear [weə (r)] *v.* 穿（衣服），戴（首饰等）；蓄（须），留（发）

例：He chose to **wear** a white suit for tonight's charity party.

他为了参加今晚的慈善晚会选择穿白西装。

搭：wear out 被用坏；穿旧 wear off 逐渐消逝

派：wearable *adj.* 可穿戴的；穿戴舒适的

13. arrange [ə'reɪndʒ] *v.* 安排，筹备；整理，布置，排列

例：The secretary **arranged** for a car to take the client to the airport.

秘书安排了一辆汽车送客户去机场。

记：词根记忆 ar加强 + range行，列；顺序→成行→arrange排列

搭：arrange for 为……作安排 arrange shipment 安排发货

派：arrangement *n.* 安排，筹备；商定，约定

14. break [breɪk] *v.* （使）破，碎；折断；破坏；违反（规则、承诺或协议）

例：How did he **break** his leg while walking on flat ground?

他是怎么在平地行走时摔断腿的？

搭：break up 打碎；结束；解散 break out 爆发；突然发生

派：broken *adj.* 损坏的，破碎的

15. imagine [ɪ'mædʒɪn] v. 想象，设想；料想，认为

例：It's hard to imagine anyone in modern society who doesn't know how to use a mobile phone.

很难想象在现代社会还有人不会用手机。

记：词根记忆 imag想象 + ine表示抽象名词→imagine想象；设想

搭：imagine doing 想象做某事

派：imagination n. 想象力 imaginable adj. 可能的；可想象的

16. return [rɪ't3ːn] v. 回来，回去；归还，退还；回报，回应

例：He just returned from his hometown in the countryside yesterday.

他昨天刚从乡下老家探亲回来。

记：词根记忆 re 回；向后 + turn 转动→向后转→return返回

搭：return home 回家 in return 作为报答

17. organize ['ɔːgənaɪz] v. 组织，筹备

例：The speech contest was organized by the student union of the university.

这次演讲比赛是由校学生会组织的。

记：联想记忆 或者（or）说干（gan）活的是（iz）鹅（e），已经把它们"组织"（organize）起来了

搭：organize an attack 组织一次进攻 organize effectively 有效地组织

派：organization n. 组织；团体 organized adj. 有组织的

18. realize ['riːəlaɪz] v. 了解，意识到；实现（目标、梦想等）

例：After experiencing multiple failures, he finally realized his shortcomings.

经历了多次失败后，他终于意识到了自己的不足。

记：词根记忆 real现实 + ize动词词尾→realize使成为现实

搭：realize one's dream 实现梦想 realize the value 实现价值

派：realization n. 认识，领悟；（目标等的）实现

19. design [dɪ'zaɪn] v. 设计；制图；构思 n. 设计，布局，安排

例：In order to gain the attention of high society, she designed a gorgeous dress.

为了获得上流社会关注，她设计了一套华丽的连衣裙。

记：词根记忆 de向外 + sign标记→把自己的创意向外标记出来→design设计

搭：web design 网页设计 fashion design 时装设计

20. express [ɪk'spres] v. 表达，表露；表现，体现

例：It is important to express your views bravely in the workplace.

在职场中勇敢地表达自己的看法是很重要的。

记：词根记忆 ex出，向外 + press压力→向外释放压力，即表达→express表达，表示

搭：express oneself 表达自己的思想

派：expression *n.* 表达，表示；表情，神情 expressive *adj.* 富于表情的，富于表现力的

21. identify [aɪˈdentɪfaɪ] *v.* 认出，识别；查明，确认；发现；证明（身份）

例：The new technique has been used to identify the genes of rare creatures.
这项新技术已被用来鉴定珍稀生物的基因。

记：词根记忆 ident相同 + i + fy便成为……→使相同，引申为确认，辨认→identify鉴定，识别

搭：identify oneself 证明自己（的身份） identify with 与某人产生共鸣，谅解

派：identification *n.* 辨认，识别；确认，确定 identified *adj.* 被识别的；经鉴定的

22. repair [rɪˈpeə (r)] *v.* 修理，修补；补救，挽救（关系或声誉）

例：It will take a week to repair the broken bike.
修好那辆摔坏的自行车需要一周的时间。

记：词根记忆 re重新 + pair准备（由词根par演变而来）→复原→repair修理

搭：repair cost 修理费 repair work 修理作业

派：repaired *adj.* 修好的

23. delay [dɪˈleɪ] *v. & n.* 推迟，延期；延误，耽搁

例：What has caused the delay of the shipment?
是什么导致发货时间推迟的?

记：词根记忆 de分离；破坏 + lay（lax变形而来）放松→不能够去放松→delay推迟，延期

搭：without delay赶快，立刻

24. admire [ədˈmaɪə (r)] *v.* 钦佩，仰慕；欣赏，观赏

例：I admire this gentleman for his courage in coming forward.
我钦佩这位先生挺身而出的勇气。

记：词根记忆 ad朝向 + mir好奇 + e→好奇某物→引申为admire仰慕；欣赏

搭：be admire at 对……感到羡慕

派：admirable *adj.* 令人钦佩的 admiration *n.* 钦佩，赞美

25. admit [əd'mɪt] *v.* 承认；招认，招供；准许进入（某处）；接纳，接收（入学）

例：He admitted that he found a bill on the road.

他承认自己在路上捡到了一张钞票。

记：词根记忆 ad去，往 + mit发送→可以发送出去→admit准许进入；承认

搭：admit to 承认 admit of 容许，有……的可能

派：admitted *adj.* 公认的；被承认了的

26. perform [pə'fɔːm] *v.* 演出，表演；执行，履行（尤指复杂的任务）；运转

例：It is difficult to perform magic on the stage without being exposed.

在舞台上表演魔术而不被揭穿是一件很困难的事。

记：联想记忆 一个人（per）为了某个节目（for+m）进行表演（perform）。

搭：perform an operation 动手术；做手术

派：performance *n.* 表演，演出；表现 performer *n.* 表演者，演出者

27. prevent [prɪ'vent] *v.* 阻止，阻碍；防止，预防

例：They are introducing measures to prevent these kinds of things.

他们在出台一些措施防止这种事情的发生。

记：词根记忆 pre在前 + vent到，来→在到来之前阻止→prevent预防

搭：prevent...from阻止……做某事

派：prevention *n.* 预防，防止

28. prove [pruːv] *v.* 证实，证明；证明是，结果是

例：The prosecution needs sufficient evidence to prove the defendant's guilt.

检方需要有充分的证据证明被告有罪。

记：词根记忆 prov尝试，试用，测试 + e→测试以证明→prove证明是，原来是

搭：prove to be 结果是，证明为 prove yourself 证明你自己

派：proven *adj.* 被证明的，已证实的

29. borrow ['bɒrəʊ] *v.* 借，借入；（向……）借贷

例：Private business owners have to borrow money at outrageous interest rates.

私营企业主不得不以离谱的利率借钱。

搭：borrow money 借钱；借债 borrow from 向……借

派：borrowed *adj.* 借来的

30. raise [reɪz] *v.* 提升，举起；增加，提高（数量、水平等）；筹集，筹募；引起

例：It is the government's duty to do everything possible to **raise** the people's standard of living.

尽全力提高人民的生活水平是政府的责任。

搭：raise money 集资；筹款　raise doubts 引起怀疑

31. explore [ɪkˈsplɔː (r)] *v.* 考察，探索；探讨，探究

例：Scientists are applying to authorities to **explore** ancient tombs.

科学家们正在向有关部门申请探索古代墓穴。

记：词根记忆 ex向外 + plor叫喊 + e→原指猎人叫喊引出猎物，后引申为探索→explore探索

派：exploration *n.* 探测；探究　explorer *n.* 探险家；探测者

32. inform [ɪnˈfɔːm] *v.* 通知，告知

例：The news anchor **informed** the viewers about the latest developments.

新闻主播告知观众最新的事态发展。

记：词根记忆 in进入 + form形式，类型→引申为教导，教育，通知→inform通知，告知，影响

搭：inform sb. of sth. 告诉某人某事；通知某人某事　inform against 检举；告发

派：informed *adj.* 有知识的；了解情况的　informer *n.* 告密者；通知者

33. necessary [ˈnesəsəri] *adj.* 必要的，必需的；必然的，不可避免的

例：It is **necessary** for every company to formulate strict management regulations.

每个公司都有必要制定严格的管理规定。

记：词根记忆 ne不 + cess离开 + ary表示与……有关的→不能离开的，即不可缺少的→necessary必要的

搭：if necessary 如果必要的话　necessary for 所必需；对……是必要的

派：necessarily *adv.* 必定，必然　necessity *n.* 必需品，必需的事物

34. dangerous [ˈdeɪndʒərəs] *adj.* 危险的，有威胁的

例：It is **dangerous** to play mobile phone while crossing the road.

过马路时玩手机是很危险的。

记：词根记忆 danger危险 + ous有……性质的，关于……的→dangerous危险的

搭：dangerous situation 危险的处境　dangerous goods 危险物品

派：danger *n.* 危险

35. average [ˈævərɪdʒ] *adj.* 普通的，平常的；平均的；中等的，适中的

例：The average milk contains 125 grams of protein.

一般的牛奶含125克蛋白质。

搭：above the average 在一般水平以上　below the average 在一般水平以下

派：averagely *adv.* 平均地；一般地

36. constant [ˈkɒnstənt] *adj.* 持续不断的，经常发生的；恒定的，不变的

例：It takes peace of mind to accept the results of constant failures.

接受持续失败的结果需要平和的心态。

记：词根记忆 con与……一起 + st站立 + ant具有……性质的→与……站在一起→constant不变的

搭：constant temperature 恒温；定温　constant pressure 恒压

派：constantly *adv.* 总是，经常地，不断地

37. valuable [ˈvæljuəbl] *adj.* 值钱的，贵重的；有益的；宝贵的；重要的，珍贵的

例：The hotel has a room dedicated to the storage of valuable items.

旅馆有一个房间专门用来存放贵重物品。

记：词根记忆 valu（e）重要性 + able能……的，可……的→有重要性的→valuable宝贵的

搭：valuable experience 宝贵的经验　valuable information 有价值的情报

派：value *n.* 价值　valuably *adv.* 有价值地；昂贵地

38. noisy [ˈnɔɪzi] *adj.* 嘈杂的，充满噪音的；嗓门大的，聒噪的

例：Elderly people generally do not like noisy environments.

老年人一般不喜欢嘈杂吵闹的环境。

记：词根记忆 nois（e）名词，噪音 + y表示状态→noisy吵闹的，嘈杂的

搭：too noisy 太吵

派：noise *n.* 噪音，嘈杂声　noiseless *adj.* 无声的；寂静的

39. financial [faɪˈnænʃl] *adj.* 财政的，金融的

例：His company is deeply troubled by the financial crisis.

他的公司因金融危机而深陷困境。

记：词根记忆 financ(e)金融，财政 + ial表示属于……的→financial金融的，财政的

搭：financial center 金融中心　financial crisis 金融危机；财政危机

派：finance n. 财政，金融　financially adv. 财政上，金融上

40. dark [dɑ:k] *adj.* 黑暗的，昏暗的；深色的，暗色的；恐怖的，悲惨的；邪恶的，阴险的　*n.* 黑暗，暗处；暗色，阴影

例：He groped for the candle in the dark environment.

他在黑暗的环境下摸索着找到了蜡烛。

搭：in the dark 在黑暗中；不知道；秘密地

派：darken v.（使）变暗，变黑；（使）变得阴郁　darkness n. 黑暗；深色，暗色

巩固练习

1. 扫码听写（根据所听音频写出本单元对应单词）

(1) _____　(2) _____　(3) _____　(4) _____

(5) _____　(6) _____　(7) _____　(8) _____

(9) _____　(10) _____　(11) _____　(12) _____

(13) _____　(14) _____　(15) _____　(16) _____

(17) _____　(18) _____　(19) _____　(20) _____

(21) _____　(22) _____　(23) _____　(24) _____

(25) _____　(26) _____　(27) _____　(28) _____

(29) _____　(30) _____　(31) _____　(32) _____

(33) _____　(34) _____　(35) _____　(36) _____

(37) _____　(38) _____　(39) _____　(40) _____

2. 实战演练（选出最符合句意的选项）

(1) It's still too early for this young man to _____ his father's corporation.

　　(A) distribute　　　　　　(B) govern

　　(C) dominate　　　　　　(D) manage

(2) Scientists have _____ nanotechnology in experiments to cultivate plants that emit light.

　　(A) designed　　　　　　(B) applied

(C) used   (D) invented

(3) He was widely _____ to be the best chemical professor in the academic circles.

    (A) admitted   (B) seen

    (C) acknowledged   (D) supposed

(4) I was _____ by his excellent performance in the game.

    (A) impressed   (B) annoyed

    (C) affected   (D) disturbed

(5) After yesterday's embarrassment, Jackson tried to _____ meeting with Michael alone.

    (A) remember   (B) avoid

    (C) evade   (D) practice

(6) I can't _____ how much pain he went through to accomplish this mission.

    (A) take   (B) fantasize

    (C) imagine   (D) think

(7) _____ the elderly is a traditional virtue of the Chinese nation.

    (A) Accepting   (B) Admiring

    (C) Respecting   (D) Praising

(8) The reporter was probing into several _____ scandals of this firm.

    (A) political   (B) financial

    (C) fiscal   (D) monetary

(9) The surgeon has _____ thirteen operations in a row today.

    (A) performed   (B) prepared

    (C) executed   (D) started

(10) Choosing to take the elevator during a fire is extremely _____.

    (A) hazardous   (B) horrible

    (C) safe   (D) dangerous

Day 10

小试牛刀

浏览本单元所有单词，在你已掌握的单词前面打√。

☐ individual	☐ facility	☐ coffee	☐ massive
☐ street	☐ interest	☐ honest	☐ observe
☐ remote	☐ disappoint	☐ convince	☐ enrol
☐ establish	☐ hand	☐ escape	☐ kitchen
☐ strange	☐ temporary	☐ advanced	☐ product
☐ traditional	☐ mall	☐ critic	☐ persuade
☐ delivery	☐ record	☐ reduce	☐ recycle
☐ replace	☐ detail	☐ form	☐ mind
☐ model	☐ sculpture	☐ location	☐ belong
☐ demand	☐ song	☐ hate	☐ introduce

词汇精讲

1. individual [ˌɪndɪ'vɪdʒuəl] *adj.* 个人的；独特的；单独的，个别的 *n.* 个人，个体

例：These patterns can be modified to suit individual preferences.

这些样式可以加以更改，以适合个人的喜好。

记：词根记忆 in不是 + divid分离 + ual表示相关→不可分开的，后指个体的→individual个人的

搭：individual sport 个人运动

派：individually *adv.* 分别地，单独地；独特地，有个性地

2. facility [fə'sɪləti] *n.* 设施，设备；卫生间；天赋，才能

例：The hotel is known throughout Asia for its luxurious leisure facilities.

该酒店以豪华的休闲设施而闻名于亚洲。

记：词根记忆 fac制作 + il + ity表示状态，性质→让做事情简化的工具→facility设施；场所

搭：facility management 设施管理；设备管理 medical facility 医疗设施

派：facilitate *v.* 促进；帮助

3. coffee ['kɒfi] *n.* 咖啡；咖啡豆；咖啡色

例：He is used to drinking a cup of coffee every morning to refresh himself.

他习惯每天早上喝一杯咖啡提神。

搭：drink coffee 喝咖啡 coffee shop 咖啡店

4. massive ['mæsɪv] *adj.* 大而重的，结实的；非常严重的；大量的，大规模的

例：A massive rock blocked the way of the tourists into the mountain.

一块巨大的岩石堵住了游客们进山的道路。

记：词根记忆 mass大量，许多 + ive与……有关的→massive巨大的，非常严重的

搭：massive attack大举进攻 massive data 海量数据

派：mass *n.* 大量，许多 massively *adv.* 大量地；沉重地

5. street [striːt] *n.* 街道；道路

例：The star was witnessed wandering on the street by fans.

粉丝们亲眼看到了这个明星在街上闲逛。

搭：on the street 在街上 beat the street 巡街

6. interest [ˈɪntrəst] *n.* 兴趣，关注；吸引力，趣味；爱好；利息；利益   *v.* 使人感兴趣（娱乐，消遣），引起……的关注

例：His **interest** has shifted from painting to collecting stamps.

他的兴趣已经由绘画转移到集邮上来了。

记：词根记忆 inter在……之间 + est（esse变形而来）存在→在很多人之间都存在的→interest利益，兴趣

搭：have no interest 不感兴趣   interest rate 利率

派：interested *adj.* 感兴趣的，关心的   interesting *adj.* 有趣的

7. honest [ˈɒnɪst] *adj.* 诚实的，正直的；坦诚的，直率的；真诚的

例：James is known to be an **honest** and trustworthy man.

大家都知道詹姆斯是一个诚实可靠的人。

记：词根记忆 hones荣誉；尊严 + t→honest诚实的

搭：to be honest 老实说   be honest with 坦诚，对……诚实

派：honesty *n.* 诚实，正直   honestly *adv.* 真诚地；公正地

8. observe [əbˈzɜːv] *v.* 注意到，观察；注视，监视

例：It is his job to **observe** the change of substance in the test tube.

他的工作是观察试管中物质的变化。

记：词根记忆 ob在……前面 + serv照看，保护 + e→在……前面保护，即观察→observe观察

搭：observe sth. carefully 留心观察

派：observation *n.* 观察；监视   observer *n.* 观察者   observant *adj.* 善于观察的，观察力强的

9. remote [rɪˈməʊt] *adj.* 边远的，偏僻的；（距离上）遥远的；（时间上）久远的

例：She worked in poverty alleviation in a **remote** village ten years ago.

十年前，她在一个偏远的村庄从事扶贫工作。

记：词根记忆 re回 + mot移动 + e→remote偏远的

搭：remote region偏远地区   remote sensing 遥感

派：remoteness *n.* 遥远；偏僻   remotely *adv.* 遥远地；偏僻地

10. disappoint [ˌdɪsəˈpɔɪnt] *v.* 使失望；使破灭，使落空

例：Her indifferent attitude towards study **disappoints** her parents.

她对学习漠不关心的态度使她的父母失望。

记：词根记忆 dis相反 + appoint任命→并未任命，并未安排好→disappoint使失望

搭：disappoint at 对……感到失望

派：disappointed *adj.* 失望的，沮丧的；受挫折的 disappointing *adj.* 令人失望的；令人扫兴的

11. convince [kən'vɪns] *v.* 使确信，使信服；说服，劝服

例：It may be too tough to convince him of this theory.
要使他相信这个理论可能真的太困难了。

记：词根记忆 con共同 + vince征服→共同征服，引申为劝服→convince说服，劝服

搭：convince sb. of sth. 使某人相信某物

派：convinced *adj.* 确信；深信 convincing *adj.* 令人信服的；有说服力的

12. enrol [ɪn'rəʊl] *v.* （招生）登记入学；注册（课程）；（使）加入

例：The agency will soon be ready to enrol students for the new course.
该机构将很快准备为新课程招收学生。

记：词根记忆 en使进入 + rol（rot变形而来）轮子，圆→使进入圈子→enrol登记

搭：enroll in 参加；选课

派：enrollment *n.* 登记；入伍

13. establish [ɪ'stæblɪʃ] *v.* 建立，设立；证实，确定；发现，找出

例：The foreign language university was established thirty years ago.
这所外国语大学成立于三十年前。

记：词根记忆 e向外 + st站起来 + abl能够 + ish动词后缀→establish建立，设立

搭：establish as 确立为……；使成为…… establish a business 创业

派：established *adj.* 确定的；已制定的；已建立的 establishment *n.* 确立；制定；公司

14. hand [hænd] *n.* 手；（钟表的）指针；帮助，援手 *v.* 交，递；支持

例：The host warmly shook hands with each guest in the program.
节目中主持人热情地与每位嘉宾握手致意。

搭：green hand 新手；生手 give a hand 提供帮助 hand over 上交，交出

15. escape [ɪ'skeɪp] *v.* 逃跑，逃脱；逃避，摆脱 *n.* 逃跑，逃离

例：He fought his life to escape from the battlefield.
他拼上性命才从战场上逃了出来。

记：词根记忆 es（同ex）向外 + cape斗篷→脱掉斗篷→escape逃跑

搭：escape from 从……逃脱

16. kitchen ['kɪtʃɪn] *n.* 厨房；一套厨具

例：She cleaned all the tablewares in the **kitchen**.

她清洗了厨房里所有的餐具。

记：联想记忆 kit（成套工具）+ chen（沉）→厨房（kitchen）中成套工具（kit）很沉（chen）。

搭：kitchen table 餐桌　kitchen knife 菜刀，厨刀

17. strange [streɪndʒ] *adj.* 奇怪的，不寻常的；陌生的，不熟悉的

例：He was curious about the **strange** sound in the pond.

他对池塘里的奇怪声音很好奇。

搭：look strange 看起来奇怪　strange to say 说来奇怪

派：stranger *n.* 陌生人；外地人　strangely *adv.* 奇怪地；奇妙地

18. temporary ['temprəri] *adj.* 暂时的，临时的；短期的，短暂的

例：They had to move into **temporary** shelters due to the earthquake.

由于地震，他们不得不搬进临时避难所。

记：词根记忆 tempor时间或时间引起的现象 + ary物→有时间性的→temporary临时的

搭：temporary shelter 临时避难所

派：temporal *adj.* 暂时的；当时的　temporarily *adv.* 临时地

19. advanced [əd'vɑːnst] *adj.* 先进的；高级的，高等的

例：The existence of the **advanced** military equipment is kept secret from all countries.

先进军事装备的存在对所有国家都是保密的。

搭：advanced technology 先进技术　advanced education 高等教育

派：advance *v.* 发展；前进　advancement *n.* 前进，进步；提升

20. product ['prɒdʌkt] *n.* 产品，制品；（自然、化学或工业过程的）生成物

例：The company recently expanded its **product** line because of the favorable market response.

由于市场反响不错，该公司最近扩展了生产线。

记：词根记忆 pro向前 + duct引导→向前引导着，引申为生产→product产品，

制品

搭：product quality 产品质量　product development 产品开发；产品发展

派：production n. 成果；产品　productivity n. 生产力；生产率

21. traditional [trəˈdɪʃənl] adj. 传统的；因袭的，守旧的；（活动）惯例的

例：He has made improvements to the traditional business model.

他对传统的商业模式进行了改善。

记：词根记忆 tradition传统 + al与……相关的→traditional传统的，习俗的，惯例的

搭：traditional culture 传统文化　traditional festival 传统节日

派：tradition n. 惯例，传统　traditionally adv. 传统上；习惯上

22. mall [mɔːl] n. 购物中心，步行商业区

例：This city has already settled six large shopping malls this year.

这座城市今年一共有六家大型购物中心入驻。

搭：shopping mall 大商场，大型购物中心

23. critic [ˈkrɪtɪk] n. 批评家，评论员；批评者

例：Donald has been a food critic for many years.

唐纳德多年来一直是一名美食批评家。

搭：art critic 艺术评论家　film critic 影评家；影评人

派：criticize v.批评；评论　criticism n. 批评；考证

24. persuade [pəˈsweɪd] v. 说服，劝服；使相信，使信服

例：They tried to persuade me to give up this crazy idea.

他们试图说服我放弃这个疯狂的想法。

记：词根记忆 per彻底 + suad劝告 + e→彻底的劝告→persuade劝说；说服

搭：persuade sb. to do sth. 劝说某人做某事

派：persuasive adj. 有说服力的　persuasively adv. 令人信服地；口才好地

25. delivery [dɪˈlɪvəri] v. 递送，投递；递送物；分娩，生产

例：Delivery service is available from Monday to Saturday.

星期一至星期六提供送货服务。

记：词根记忆 deliver分发 + y行为→delivery运送

搭：time of delivery 交货时间；交货期

派：deliver v. 交付；发表　deliverable adj. 可以传送的；可交付使用的

26. record ['rekɔːd] *n.* 记录，记载；（某人过去的）记录，经历；最好成绩　[rɪ'kɔːd] *v.* 记录，记载；录制；（仪器）显示，标示

例：He managed to break the world record in the high jump.
他成功打破了跳高的世界纪录。

记：词根记忆 re再，重新 + cord心脏→使信息再次回到心里记住→record记录

搭：keep a record 保持纪录，做记录　world record 世界纪录

派：recorder *n.* 录音机；记录器

27. reduce [rɪ'djuːs] *v.* 减少，降低

例：They have been trying to reduce the company's production costs in recent years.
他们近年来一直在努力降低公司的生产成本。

记：词根记忆 re回 + duc引导 + e→使引导至较低的水平→reduce减少

搭：reduce pollution 降低污染　reduce waste 减少浪费

派：reduction *n.* 减少；下降

28. recycle [ˌriː'saɪkl] *v.* 回收利用，再利用

例：We got permission from the environmental department to recycle plastic products.
我们从环部部门获取了回收塑料制品的许可。

记：词根记忆 re再次 + cycl循环 + e→recycle回收利用

搭：recycle bag 环保袋　recycle bin 回收站；资源回收筒

派：recyclable *adj.* 可回收利用的；可再循环的

29. replace [rɪ'pleɪs] *v.* 取代；（用……）替换，（以……）接替；更换

例：Artificial intelligence is expected to replace many human occupations in the future.
人工智能有望在未来取代许多人类从事的岗位。

记：词根记忆 re重新，再次 + place位置→replace替代

搭：replace by 取代，以……代替　replace with 替换为；以……代替

派：replacement *n.* 更换　replaceable *adj.* 可替换的；可置换的

30. detail ['diːteɪl] *n.* 细节，细微之处；详情；（*pl.*）资料

例：The details of the operating steps of this machine have been recorded in the manual.
这台机器的操作步骤已详细记录在说明书中。

记：词根记忆 de破坏，完全地 + tail剪裁→detail引申为细节

搭：in detail 详细地；具体地　detail design 详细设计

派：detailed *adj.* 详细的，精细的

31. form [fɔːm] *v.* （使）（关系、习惯或想法）形成；构成，是……的组成部分；培养　*n.* 类别，种类；表格；形状，外形；体形

例：Cycling is a good **form** to exercise.

　　骑自行车是很好的锻炼方式。

搭：in the form of 以……的形式

派：formal *adj.* 正式的；拘谨的　formally *adv.* 正式地；形式上

32. mind [maɪnd] *n.* 头脑，大脑；智慧，思维方式　*v.* （请求允许或客气地请人做事）介意

例：My **mind** brought back the memories with him.

　　我想起了和他在一起的回忆。

搭：keep in mind 记住　state of mind 心理状态，思想状态

派：mindless *adj.* 愚蠢的；不小心的　mindful *adj.* 留心的；记住的；警觉的

33. model ['mɒdl] *n.* 模型；模式；（机器等的）型号；模范，典型；模特

例：The **model** plane in the shop window caught his eye.

　　摆在商店橱窗里的飞机模型吸引了他的目光。

记：词根记忆 mod方法，方式 + el器物→用来作为模式的器物，即模型→model模型，建模

搭：new model 新模型；新型号　business model 商业模式

34. sculpture ['skʌlptʃə (r)] *n.* 雕像，雕塑作品；雕刻艺术，雕塑艺术

例：**Sculpture** works can be seen everywhere in city art museums.

　　雕塑作品在城市美术博物馆里四处可见。

记：词根记忆 sculpt雕刻，雕塑 + ure名词后缀→sculpture雕像

搭：clay sculpture 泥塑　ice sculpture 冰雕

派：sculptor *n.* 雕刻家

35. location [ləʊ'keɪʃn] *n.* 地点，位置

例：What is the exact **location** of the train station?

　　火车站的确切位置在哪里？

搭：fault location 故障定位　strategic location 战略位置；关键部分

派：locate *v.* 定位；定居　locator *n.* 定位器，探测器

36. belong [bɪˈlɒŋ] *v.* 归……所有；是……的成员，属于（某团体或组织）

例：All minerals excavated from underground belong to the state.

从地下挖掘出的一切矿物均属国家所有。

记：词根记忆 be使…… + long长 → 使长久（拥有）→belong属于

搭：belong to 属于；附属；归属

派：belonging *n.* 所有物；行李；附属物

37. demand [dɪˈmɑːnd] *v.* 强烈要求；需要，需求　*n.* 坚决的要求；需求，需求量

例：I demand that the relevant departments give a reasonable explanation for this mistake.

我强烈要求相关部门对此次失误给出一个合理的解释。

记：词根记忆 de加强 + mand命令→demand强烈要求

搭：market demand 市场需求　supply and demand 供需

派：demanding *adj.* 苛求的；要求高的

38. song [sɒŋ] *n.* 歌，歌曲；歌唱，声乐

例：This song is widely recognized as one of the classics in the music industry.

这首歌被公认为是乐坛经典歌曲之一。

搭：sing a song 唱一首歌，唱支歌　folk song 民歌

派：songful *adj.* 旋律美妙的；充满歌声的；声乐的

39. hate [heɪt] *v.* 讨厌，厌恶，不喜欢；仇恨，憎恨

例：I hate being treated like a child by adults.

我讨厌被成年人当作孩子对待。

搭：hate doing 不喜欢做某事；讨厌做某事

派：hateful *adj.* 可憎的；可恨的　hatred *n.* 憎恨；怨恨

40. introduce [ˌɪntrəˈdjuːs] *v.* 介绍，引见；使初次了解，使尝试

例：Please allow me to introduce myself.

请允许我自我介绍一下。

记：词根记忆 intro在内 + duc引导 +e→在……之内引导，即介绍，引进→introduce介绍，引进

搭：introduce oneself 自我介绍　introduce into 把……引进，传入

派：introduction *n.* 介绍；引进；采用　introductory *adj.* 引导的，介绍的

扫码听音频

巩固练习

1. 扫码听写（根据所听音频写出本单元对应单词）

(1) _____	(2) _____	(3) _____	(4) _____
(5) _____	(6) _____	(7) _____	(8) _____
(9) _____	(10) _____	(11) _____	(12) _____
(13) _____	(14) _____	(15) _____	(16) _____
(17) _____	(18) _____	(19) _____	(20) _____
(21) _____	(22) _____	(23) _____	(24) _____
(25) _____	(26) _____	(27) _____	(28) _____
(29) _____	(30) _____	(31) _____	(32) _____
(33) _____	(34) _____	(35) _____	(36) _____
(37) _____	(38) _____	(39) _____	(40) _____

2. 实战演练（选出最符合句意的选项）

(1) Electricity and running water need to be introduced to _____ rural areas.

 (A) dirty   (B) familiar

 (C) remote   (D) distant

(2) He is an _____ man who hated to deceive others with a mean lie.

 (A) vile   (B) honest

 (C) calm   (D) creative

(3) Golden beaches are a _____ feature of the Maldives island landscape.

 (A) different   (B) individual

 (C) characteristic   (D) common

(4) It is impossible for criminals to _____ the severe punishment of the law.

 (A) quit   (B) leave

 (C) flee   (D) escape

(5) The investigator _____ over the evidence he had gathered to the police station.

 (A) sent   (B) passed

(C) handed   (D) submitted

(6) Because of the flash flood, the soldiers had to cut a _____ up the mountain to save time.

    (A) road   (B) path

    (C) tree   (D) grass

(7) The hostess went to the _____ to fetch napkins for her guests.

    (A) kitchen   (B) garage

    (C) toilet   (D) basement

(8) We should reject materials that cannot be _____ or degraded.

    (A) restored   (B) resigned

    (C) recycled   (D) responded

(9) It's _____ that the opera, which was supposed to open this weekend, has been cancelled.

    (A) eccentric   (B) delightful

    (C) interesting   (D) strange

(10) We can _____ another three advanced skills classes of 15 students each.

    (A) enlist   (B) attend

    (C) recruit   (D) enrol

Day 11

小试牛刀

浏览本单元所有单词，在你已掌握的单词前面打√。

☐ suffer	☐ teenager	☐ solve	☐ appeal
☐ manager	☐ actor	☐ island	☐ attempt
☐ attention	☐ aeroplane	☐ marry	☐ audience
☐ behaviour	☐ ring	☐ safety	☐ body
☐ adopt	☐ community	☐ employ	☐ fight
☐ graduate	☐ price	☐ power	☐ force
☐ complain	☐ determine	☐ control	☐ contact
☐ inspire	☐ driver	☐ material	☐ date
☐ hide	☐ invent	☐ reflect	☐ traffic
☐ qualify	☐ paint	☐ village	☐ register

词汇精讲

1. suffer ['sʌfə (r)] v. 经受，遭受（坏事）；（因疾病、痛苦、悲伤等）受苦，受折磨

例：Young people are bound to suffer setbacks in their quest for a life path.

年轻人在探索人生道路的过程中必然会遭受挫折。

记：词根记忆 suf由下向上 + fer承担，承载→承受重压→suffer遭受，经受

搭：suffer from 遭受；患病；忍受　suffer loss 遭受损失

派：suffering adj. 受苦的；患病的　sufferable adj. 可忍耐的；可容忍的

2. teenager ['tiːneɪdʒə (r)] n. 青少年，十几岁的孩子（13到19岁之间的孩子）

例：But when I was a teenager, war broke out and I was forced to leave my hometown.

但在我十几岁的时候，战争爆发了，我被迫离开了家乡。

记：词根记忆 teenage十几岁的 + er人→青少年

派：teenage adj. 青少年的；十几岁的

3. solve [sɒlv] v. 解决，处理；解释，解答

例：It will take a long time to solve this problem.

解决这个问题需要耗费很长时间。

记：词根记忆 solv松开 + e→（乱麻）松开→solve解决

搭：solve problems 解决问题；排忧解难

派：solution n. 解决方案　solved adj. 解决了的

4. appeal [ə'piːl] n. 呼吁，恳求；上诉，申诉；吸引力，感染力　v. 呼吁，恳求；上诉，申诉；有吸引力，引起兴趣

例：The host made a powerful appeal on the issue of moral decay.

主持人就道德败坏的问题提出了强有力的呼吁。

搭：appeal to 向……呼吁；诉诸；吸引　appeal for 恳求，请求

派：appealing adj. 吸引人的；动人的；引起兴趣的

5. manager ['mænɪdʒə (r)] n. （公司、部门等的）经理；（艺人或运动员的）经纪人

例：The department manager asked his subordinates to send the document to his computer.

部门经理让他的下属把文件发到他的电脑上。

搭：general manager 总经理 project manager 项目经理

派：management *n.* 经营，管理 manageable *adj.* 易管理的；易控制的

6. actor ['æktə (r)] *n.* 男演员

例：US President Reagan was an **actor** before entering politics.

美国总统里根在从政前曾经是一名演员。

记：词根记忆 act行动 + or与……相关的人→actor演员

搭：leading actor 主角，主要演员 voice actor 配音演员

派：actress *n.* 女演员

7. island ['aɪlənd] *n.* 岛，岛屿；岛状物

例：They chose to get married on an **island** in Southeast Asia.

他们选择在东南亚的一座海岛上举行婚礼。

记：联想记忆 岛（island）是（is）陆地（land）。

搭：on the island 在岛上

派：islander *n.* 岛上居民

8. attempt [ə'tempt] *v.* 努力，尝试 *n.* 试图，努力

例：The media **attempted** to shift people's attention to other aspects.

媒体试图将民众的注意力转移到别的方面。

记：词根记忆 at朝向，加强 + tempt尝试→attempt试图；尝试

搭：attempt to do 尝试去做 make an attempt 试图；尝试；企图

派：attempted *adj.* 企图的；未遂的

9. attention [ə'tenʃn] *n.* 注意；注意力

例：His fancy dress and weird expression caught my **attention**.

他那花哨的服饰和诡异的神色引起了我的注意。

记：词根记忆 at朝向 + tent（tend演化而来）+ion表示行为→紧绷大脑注意倾听→attention注意

搭：pay attention to 注意；重视；留心

派：attentive *adj.* 留意的，注意的 attentiveness *n.* 注意力

10. aeroplane ['eərəpleɪn] *n.* 飞机

例：The **aeroplane** lost its balance due to the turbulence in the air.

这架飞机由于经受了空中旋涡失去了平衡。

记：词根记忆 aero空气，大气 + plane飞机→aeroplane飞机

搭：aeroplane chess 飞行棋

11. marry ['mæri] v. 结婚，嫁，娶；把……嫁给，为……娶亲

例：I can't understand why she chose to **marry** William.

我无法理解她为什么选择与威廉结婚。

搭：marry into 经结婚成为……的一员 marry off 把……嫁出去

派：married *adj.* 已婚的，有配偶的 marriage *n.* 结婚；婚姻生活

12. audience ['ɔːdiəns] n. 观众，听众；读者

例：The **audience** was impressed by the host's excellent performance.

观众为主持人的精彩表现所折服。

记：词根记忆 aud听，听觉，声音 + i + ence表示行为，状态→audience

听众，观众

搭：target audience 目标受众；目标观众 audience rating收视率；视

听率

13. behaviour [bɪ'heɪvjə (r)] n. 行为，举止，态度

例：Individual **behaviour** patterns are often influenced by groups.

个人的行为模式往往受到团体的影响。

记：词根记忆 be使…… + hav拥有 + iour→ behaviour举止行为

搭：good behaviour 品行良好；得体的行为 consumer behaviour 消费行为

派：behavioural *adj.* 行为的；动作的

14. ring [rɪŋ] n. 戒指，指环；环状物；铃声，钟声；电话铃声 v. （给……）打电话；（电话）铃声响

例：This **ring** was prepared by him for his proposal.

这枚戒指是他为了求婚准备的。

搭：give someone a ring 给某人打电话 ring finger 无名指

派：ringing *adj.* 响亮的；明白的 ringed *adj.* 环状的；戴戒指的

15. safety ['seɪfti] n. 安全；安全性；安全场所，安全的地方

例：The **safety** of this car is an important concern for the transportation department.

该款汽车的安全性是交通部门的重要关注点。

记：词根记忆 salv（=safe）安全 + ty表示状态，性质→safety安全

搭：traffic safety 交通安全；行车安全 in safety 安全地；平安地

派：safe *adj.* 安全的；可靠的 safely *adv.* 安全地

16. body [ˈbɒdi] n. （人、动物的）身体；躯干；尸体；（书或文件的）正文

例：She was badly burned on the face and body.

她面部和身上严重烧伤。

搭：human body 人体 main body 主体，主要部分

派：bodily adv. 身体的；肉体的 bodied adj. 有形的；有躯体的

17. adopt [əˈdɒpt] v. 收养；采取，采纳，接受；正式通过

例：Susan adopted an orphan of her own accord after her divorce.

苏珊离婚后自愿收养了一个孤儿。

记：词根记忆 ad朝向 + opt选择→在一群里选择→adopt采纳；采用

搭：adopt various methods 采取不同办法

派：adopted adj. 被收养的；被采用的 adoptable adj. 可采用的；可收养的

18. community [kəˈmjuːnəti] n. 社区，社会

例：The robber was sentenced to one hundred hours of community service.

这个抢劫犯被判罚做社区服务一百个小时。

记：词根记忆 commun（e）群居团体、公社 + ity表示状态，性质→community 社区

搭：community service 社会服务 community health 社区卫生（健康）；公共卫生

派：commune v. 谈心，亲密交谈；密切联系 communal adj. 公共的

19. employ [ɪmˈplɔɪ] v. 雇佣某人；使用，利用

例：A number of people have been employed to deal with the backlog of work.

已雇来一些人处理积压的工作。

记：词根记忆 em在……里面 + ploy折叠一把……折叠入，使卷入→employ雇用，使用

搭：find employment 找工作 employment rate 就业率

派：employee n. 雇员 employer n. 雇主

20. fight [faɪt] v. 与……做斗争，坚决反对；努力争取，为……而斗争；打仗，作战；打架 n. 斗争；打斗，打架；争吵，争论

例：The government is trying to fight against the phenomenon of corruption.

政府正在努力与贪污腐败的现象做斗争。

搭：fight for 为……而战，而奋斗 fight against 对抗，反对；与……做斗争

派：fighting adj. 战斗的；好战的 fighter n. 战士，斗争者

21. graduate [ˈgrædʒuət] v. （从大学或中学）毕业；获得学位　n. 毕业生

例： She will **graduate** from the University of Washington this June.
　　她今年六月将从华盛顿大学毕业。

记： 联想记忆 grad步，级+ u+ ate做→到达某一个级别→graduate毕业

搭： graduate from 从……毕业　graduate student 研究生

派： graduation n. 毕业；毕业典礼

22. price [praɪs] n. 价格；代价

例： Oil **prices** have been falling recently because of increased production.
　　由于产量增加，石油价格近期不断下降。

搭： low price 低价；廉价　reasonable price 合理的价格　current price 时价；现行价格

派： priceless adj. 无价的；极贵重的

23. power [ˈpaʊə (r)] n. 力量，体能；权力，职权；能源，（尤指）电力；动力，功率

例： People often rely on the **power** of faith when they are in trouble.
　　人们在遇到困难时通常会依赖于信仰的力量。

搭： electric power 电力；电功率　in power 执政的；掌权的

派： powerful adj. 强大的；强有力的

24. force [fɔːs] n. 力，力量；暴力，武力　v. 强迫；用力推

例： Young people are a powerful **force** in any social activity.
　　年轻人在任何社会活动中都是一股强大的力量。

搭： by force 强迫地；靠武力

派： forced adj. 被迫的；强迫的　forceful adj. 强有力的；有说服力的；坚强的

25. complain [kəmˈpleɪn] v. 抱怨，投诉

例： Parents often **complain** about their children's poor grades.
　　父母经常抱怨自己家的孩子成绩差。

记： 词根记忆 com表强调 + plain捶胸顿足→complain抱怨

搭： complain about sth. 抱怨某事

派： complaint n. 抱怨；诉苦

26. determine [dɪˈtɜːmɪn] v. 决定，控制；查明，确定；下定决心

例： People's economic conditions **determine** their standard of living.

人们的经济条件决定他们的生活水平。

记：词根记忆 de从，分离 + termin界限 + e→画出界线以和······分开→determine
决定

搭：determine to do sth. 决心做某事；决定做某事

派：determined *adj.* 决定了的；坚决的 determination *n.* 决心；果断

27. control [kən'trəʊl] *v.* 控制，掌管；限制，限定；抑制，克制

例：The candidate declared that he would control inflation first if he took office.
这位候选人宣称如果自己上台会首先控制通货膨胀。

记：词根记忆 contro对抗 + rol圆→向反方向转动→control控制

搭：control system 控制系统 quality control 质量控制，质量管理

派：controllable *adj.* 可控制的；可管理的 controller *n.* 控制器

28. contact ['kɒntækt] *v.* 联系，联络；接触 *n.* 联系，联络；接触，触摸；联络人，熟人，社会关系

例：He was unable to contact Jackson by phone.
他未能通过打电话和杰克逊取得联系。

记：词根记忆 con与······一起 + tact接触→与······一起接触→contact联系，接触

搭：contact with 与······联系

29. inspire [ɪn'spaɪə (r)] *v.* 激励，鼓舞；赋予灵感，激发（想法）；使产生（感觉或情感）

例：Michael Jordan's achievements inspired a generation to follow their basketball
dreams.
迈克尔乔丹的成就激励了一代人追随自己的篮球梦。

记：词根记忆 in进入 + spir呼吸 + e→吸入活力，引申为鼓舞→inspire鼓舞，启发

搭：inspire sth. in sb. 使某人产生某种感情；激发某人的某种感情

派：inspiring *adj.* 鼓舞人心的 inspiration *n.* 灵感；鼓舞

30. driver ['draɪvə (r)] *n.* 司机，驾驶员

例：Drivers who drive under the influence of alcohol will be detained in accordance
with the law.
司机如果酒驾将会被依法拘留。

搭：taxi driver 出租车司机 bus driver 公交车司机

派：drive *v.* 驾驶 driven *adj.* 被动的，受到驱策的

31. material [mə'tɪərɪəl] *n.* 材料，原料；衣料，布料；素材 *adj.* 物质的，非精神上的

例：The main **materials** of this down jacket are cotton and nylon.

这件羽绒服的主要材料是棉和尼龙。

搭：raw material 原材料；原料

派：materially *adv.* 实质地；物质上；极大地

32. date [deɪt] *n.* 日期，日子；约会，幽会

例：When is the final **date** for the submission of essays?

提交论文的最后日期是什么时候？

搭：up to date 最新的；最近的 out of date 过时的；过期的

派：dated *adj.* 陈旧的；过时的

33. hide [haɪd] *v.* 把……藏起来，隐藏；躲藏，躲避；掩盖，隐瞒

例：He tried to **hide** his cellphone in his backpack to avoid the teacher's inspection.

他试图把手机藏进书包里以躲避老师的检查。

搭：hide from 隐瞒 hide and seek 捉迷藏

派：hidden *adj.* 隐藏的

34. invent [ɪn'vent] *v.* 发明，创造；编造，虚构

例：Edison **invented** the electric light in his laboratory in the 19th century.

爱迪生十九世纪在自家的实验室里发明了电灯。

记：词根记忆 in 使……＋ vent 来→使……出来 →invent发明出

搭：invent sth. 发明某物

派：invention *n.* 发明；发明物 inventor *n.* 发明家

35. reflect [rɪ'flekt] *v.* 反射（光、热或声音）；反映，照出（影像）；显示，表明；深思，反省

例：The clear surface of the lake **reflects** the harsh sunlight.

清澈的湖面反射着刺眼的阳光。

记：词根记忆 re回 ＋ flect弯曲→reflect反射

搭：reflect on 反省；思考

派：reflection *n.* 反射；沉思；映象 reflective *adj.* 反射的；反映的；沉思的

36. traffic ['træfɪk] *n.* 路上行驶的车辆，交通；（沿固定路线的）航行，行驶，飞行

例：Today, I was stopped at a **traffic** light when a mid-aged homeless woman asked me for change.

今天，当一个无家可归的中年妇女找我要零钱的时候我在红绿灯前停下了。

搭：traffic accident 交通事故　traffic jam 交通堵塞

37. qualify ['kwɒlɪfaɪ] v. 取得资格，达到标准；（使）具有资格，胜任；符合，可算作

例：The company does not qualify for a customs drawback.

该公司没有资格获得海关退税。

记：词根记忆 qual性质，特征 + ify动词词尾→qualify取得资格

搭：qualify for 合格；有……的资格　qualify as 取得……资格；作为……合适

派：qualified adj. 合格的；有资格的　qualification n. 资格；条件；限制

38. paint [peɪnt] n. 油漆，涂料；绘画颜料　v. （用颜料）绘画；（给……）上油漆，（给……）涂颜料

例：A drop of white paint dripped from the ceiling to the floor.

一滴白色的油漆从天花板滴落到地板上。

搭：oil paint 油彩；油性漆；油画颜料　spray paint 喷漆

派：painting n. 绘画；油画；着色　painter n. 画家；油漆匠

39. village ['vɪlɪdʒ] n. 乡村，村庄

例：The village is located in a valley to the south of Dongting Lake.

这个村庄坐落于洞庭湖以南的一个山谷中。

记：联想记忆 vill（a）别墅 + age 场所→别墅一般都在郊外→village村庄

搭：in the village 在村里　small village 小村庄

派：villager n. 乡村居民，村民

40. register ['redʒɪstə(r)] v. 登记，注册　n. 登记表，注册簿

例：Foreigners must register with the relevant authorities upon entering China.

外籍人士一进入中国就必须向有关部门进行登记。

记：联想记忆 re回，往后 + gist运输，携带 + er原指带回，后指记录以便有案可查→register登记，注册

搭：register for 注册；选课　cash register 收银机；现金出纳机

派：registered adj. 注册的；记名的　registration n. 登记；注册

巩固练习

1. 扫码听写（根据所听音频写出本单元对应单词）

(1) _____ (2) _____ (3) _____ (4) _____

(5) _____ (6) _____ (7) _____ (8) _____

(9) _____ (10) _____ (11) _____ (12) _____

(13) _____ (14) _____ (15) _____ (16) _____

(17) _____ (18) _____ (19) _____ (20) _____

(21) _____ (22) _____ (23) _____ (24) _____

(25) _____ (26) _____ (27) _____ (28) _____

(29) _____ (30) _____ (31) _____ (32) _____

(33) _____ (34) _____ (35) _____ (36) _____

(37) _____ (38) _____ (39) _____ (40) _____

2. 实战演练（选出最符合句意的选项）

(1) The police issued an _____ that the citizen should ensure their own safety when they meet robbery.

　(A) plan 　　　　　　　(B) appeal

　(C) demand 　　　　　(D) solution

(2) Many _____ choose to come to the scene to watch baseball games and cheer for the players.

　(A) audiences 　　　　(B) onlookers

　(C) spectators 　　　　(D) coaches

(3) Enterprises can obtain information about consumer _____ on the Internet through technological means.

　(A) attitude 　　　　　(B) manner

　(C) mood 　　　　　　(D) behaviour

(4) It is very important to teach children knowledge about traffic _____.

　(A) safety 　　　　　　(B) danger

　(C) language 　　　　　(D) mode

(5) Almost all countries _____ material control measures in time of war.

　(A) absorb 　　　　　　(B) introduce

　(C) adopt 　　　　　　(D) adapt

(6) The enemy's unrepentant attitude strengthened his resolve to _____ on.

    (A) fight   (B) put

    (C) take   (D) depend

(7) Harrison _____ that he had been treated unfairly in the shopping mall.

    (A) assigned   (B) complained

    (C) praised   (D) attempted

(8) The company shall bear the _____ incurred by the staff on business trips.

    (A) money   (B) price

    (C) tip   (D) fare

(9) He tried to _____ his emotions so as not to let his opponent seize his weakness.

    (A) rule   (B) remove

    (C) control   (D) dispose

(10) The army unit lost _____ with its headquarter because of radar failure.

    (A) code   (B) contact

    (C) communication   (D) signal

Day 12

小试牛刀

浏览本单元所有单词，在你已掌握的单词前面打√。

☐ communication	☐ owner	☐ series	☐ elementary
☐ option	☐ ability	☐ dish	☐ factor
☐ luggage	☐ leisure	☐ menu	☐ employee
☐ plant	☐ address	☐ door	☐ air
☐ degree	☐ pilot	☐ band	☐ exhibition
☐ position	☐ adult	☐ front	☐ treat
☐ mistake	☐ process	☐ colleague	☐ journalist
☐ river	☐ applicant	☐ goal	☐ lack
☐ passenger	☐ science	☐ collection	☐ issue
☐ star	☐ case	☐ image	☐ nature

词汇精讲

1. communication [kəˌmjuːnɪˈkeɪʃn] *n.* 交流，交际；信息，书信；通讯，交通联系

例：This **communication** is sent to you when you choose to receive marketing messages.

当您选择接收营销信息时，此通信将会发送给您。

记：词根记忆 com 与……一起 + mun 公共 + ic + ation 表示行为，结果→使信息共享→communication 通讯；交流

搭：communication with 与……交流；与……通讯 communication skill 沟通技巧

派：communicational *adj.* 通信的；通讯的

2. owner [ˈəʊnə (r)] *n.* 所有人，物主

例：Non-disabled car **owners** may be fined if they park here.

非残疾人的车主如果在这里停车可能会被罚款。

记：词根记忆 own 自己的 + er 某种人→owner 所有人，物主

搭：property owner 业主；产权人 part owner 部分所有者

3. series [ˈsɪəriːz] *n.* 连续，一系列（事件）

例：His weekly cooking **series** has given us hours of fun and entertainment over the years.

多年来，他每周的烹饪系列节目给我们带来了数小时的乐趣和娱乐。

记：发音记忆 series 写日子→他写下了一系列有关现在日子的事情→series 一系列

搭：series of 一系列；一连串 in series with 与……相连；与……串联

4. elementary [ˌelɪˈmentri] *adj.* 简单的，基本的；基础的，初级的；小学的

例：You will lose everything if you don't store the **elementary** knowledge in this field.

如果你不把这个领域的基本知识储存起来，你就会失去一切。

记：词根记忆 element 本源 + ary ……的 → elementary 初等的，基础的

搭：elementary school 小学 elementary geometry 初等几何

派：elemental *adj.* 基本的；主要的 element *n.* 元素；要素

5. option [ˈɒpʃn] *n.* 可选择的事物；选择，选择权；期权

例：It might be a good **option** to do some charity work.

做一些慈善工作可能是一个不错的选择。

记：词根记忆 opt选择 + ion表示物→option选择，选项

搭：the first option 最佳选择，第一选择　stock option 职工优先认股权

派：optional *adj.* 可选择的；非强制的

6. ability [ə'bɪləti] *n.* 能力，能够；才能，技能，本领

例：Humans are born with the ability to cry.

人类天生具有会哭泣的能力。

记：词根记忆 abili 能力 + ity ⋯⋯的状态，性质→ability能力，能够；才能

搭：learning ability 学习能力

7. dish [dɪʃ] *n.* 碟，盘；一盘食物；菜肴；碟状物，盘状物；
   v. 说⋯⋯的闲话；把（食物）装盘

例：Aunt Judy asked me for some dishes when she first went to my restaurant.

朱迪阿姨第一次来我的饭店时，向我点了一些菜。

搭：do the dishes 洗餐具；洗碗碟　dish out 给予，分发

8. factor ['fæktə (r)] *n.* 因素，要素；等级，系数

例：In my opinion，the pictures David takes of people are affected by different kinds of factors.

在我看来，大卫拍摄的人物照片受到各种因素的影响。

记：联想记忆 fact做 + or表示与⋯⋯有关的物→做事情需要的物→factor因素，要素

搭：factor in ⋯⋯的因素；将⋯⋯纳入　key factor 关键因素；主要因素

9. luggage ['lʌgɪdʒ] *n.* 行李；精神负担

例：Luggage must be ready for loading into the car after lunch.

行李必须准备好，以便午餐后装上汽车。

记：联想记忆 lug 用力拖 + g + age场所，物品→luggage行李；精神负担

搭：hand luggage 手提行李　left luggage 行李寄存

10. leisure ['leʒə (r)] *n.* 闲暇，业余时间；休闲活动　*adj.* 空闲
   的，有闲的；业余的

例：There are a lot of sports and leisure clubs in the college.

这所大学有许多运动和休闲俱乐部。

记：联想记忆 leis允许 + ure表示行为，结果→时间允许做自己的事→leisure闲暇，空闲

搭：leisure time 业余时间 at leisure 从容地；悠闲地

11. menu [ˈmenju:] *n.* 菜单；饭菜，菜肴；（电脑屏幕上的）菜单，功能选择单

例：While there are no free meals, the cafe offers an affordable menu.
虽然没有免费餐点，但这家咖啡馆的菜品都价格实惠。

搭：main menu 主菜单；主选单 menu option 菜单选择

12. employee [ɪmˈplɔɪi:] *n.* 雇员

例：In some companies, employees work in enclosed workstations or cubicles.
在一些公司，员工在封闭的工作站或小隔间里工作。

记：词根记忆 employ雇用 + ee指受动者→employee雇员

搭：employee turnover 员工流动；职工离职 senior employee 高级雇员

派：employer *n.* 雇主，老板 employ *v.* 雇佣

13. plant [plɑ:nt] *n.* 植物；工厂，发电厂 *v.* 栽种，种植

例：Tom planted different kinds of vegetables and herbs, and he decided to grow organically.
汤姆种植了不同种类的蔬菜和草药，他决定进行有机种植。

搭：in plant 在生长发育中 plant out 把……移植到地里

14. address [əˈdres] *n.* 地址，住址；网址；电子邮箱地址；演讲，演说 *v.* 演说，演讲；处理，设法解决

例：If you have any complaints, please address them to Mr. Cox, Director of Customer Service.
如果你有任何不满，请向客户服务部主任考克斯先生提出。

搭：permanent address 永久住址 inaugural address 就职演说

15. door [dɔ: (r)] *n.* 门；门口，门道；建筑，门户 *v.* 车门撞击（骑自行车经过的人）

例：John recommended just knocking on the doors of my neighbours and inviting them round for a cup of coffee and I really fancy trying that.
约翰建议我敲开邻居的门，请他们来喝杯咖啡，我真想试试。

搭：close/shut the door on sth. 使不可能；拒……于门外；把……的门堵死
out of doors 在户外；露天

16. air [eə(r)] *n.* 大气，空气；空中，天空　*v.* 使公开，宣扬；（使）通风；（使）晾干

例：Environmentalists agree that the continued use of private cars will worsen air pollution.

环保人士一致认为，继续使用私家车将加剧空气污染。

搭：in the air 在传播中；流行　a breath of fresh air 新鲜空气；透气

17. degree [dɪˈɡriː] *n.* 度，度数；学位课程，学位

例：On average，there are twice as many applicants for undergraduate degree programmes as there are places available.

平均而言，申请本科学位课程的人数是可提供名额的两倍。

搭：academic degree 学术型学位　high degree 高度；高地位

18. pilot [ˈpaɪlət] *n.* 飞行员；领航员　*adj.* 试点的　*v.* 驾驶（飞行器）；领航；试验，试行

例：He is a pilot, but he is not responsible for International flight.

他是一位飞行员，但他不负责国际航线。

搭：pilot test 小规模试验；初步试验　fighter pilot 战斗机飞行员

19. band [bænd] *n.* 乐队；一伙，一群；范围，段　*v.* 给……分级，把……分段

例：Joey plays the bass in a band with his friends.

乔伊和他的朋友们在乐队里弹贝斯。

搭：band together 联合；联手

20. exhibition [ˌeksɪˈbɪʃn] *n.* 展览，展出；表现，展示

例：We'd plan to go to an art exhibition in Central Gallery, but she called to say she was busy and could we go another day.

我们本来打算去中央美术馆看艺术展，但她打电话来说她很忙，问我们能不能改天再去。

记：词根记忆exhibit展出 + ion 行为，状态→exhibition展览，展出

搭：exhibition hall 展览厅　on exhibition 展出中

派：exhibit *v.* 展出

21. position [pəˈzɪʃn] *n.* 位置，地点；恰当位置，正确位置　*v.* 安置，使处于

例：Lily Geller and Arthur Green are the nominees for the position of manager.

莉莉·盖勒和亚瑟·格林被提名为经理一职。

记： **词根记忆** posit放 + ion行为，状态→position恰当位置

搭： financial position 财务状况　official position 官方立场

22. adult [ˈædʌlt] *n.* 成年人；成年动物　*adj.* 成年的，发育成熟的

例： The price of the ticket to Mountain Park is different, while it's $10 for children and $13 for adults.

山地公园的门票价格不同，儿童票价10美元，成人票价13美元。

搭： adult education 成人教育　mature adult 成熟的成年人

23. front [frʌnt] *n.* 前面；前线，前方　*adj.* 前面的，正面的

例： Buses leave from the front of the hotel.

大客车从酒店门口出发。

搭： front door 前门　front for sb./sth. 为……掩护（秘密、非法活动）

in front of 在……前面

24. treat [triːt] *v.* 对待，看待；治疗，医治；请客，招待　*n.* 乐事，享受；款待

例： He is mad at the way he is treated.

他对所受的待遇很生气。

搭： treat differently 区别对待　treat sb. to sth. 用……招待；以……款待

25. mistake [mɪˈsteɪk] *n.* 错误，过失　*v.* 误解，误会

例： I admit that when I first got there, I wondered if I had made a mistake by taking part in the program.

我承认，我第一次到那里的时候，我想知道我参加这个项目是否犯了一个错误。

记： **联想记忆** mis错误的 + take拿走，领取→引申为误会，错误→mistake错误

搭： by mistake 错误地；由疏忽所致　make a mistake 犯错误

26. process [ˈprəʊses] *n.* 步骤，程序　*v.* 处理，加工；审核，受理

例： I usually praise these movies, there are also some criticisms, but the whole filmmaking process fascinates me.

我通常会称赞这些电影，也会有一些批评，但整个电影制作过程让我着迷。

记： **词根记忆** pro前 + cess行走→process行进，过程

搭： in the process of 在……的过程中　production process 生产流程

27. colleague [ˈkɒliːg] n. 同事，同僚

例：His colleagues did not treat him friendly.

他的同事对他不友好。

记：**联想记忆** col共同，一起 + l- + leg 法律 + ue→共同担负法律赋予的劳动义务 →colleague引申为同事

28. journalist [ˈdʒɜːnəlɪst] n. 新闻工作者，新闻记者；报纸撰稿人

例：While at first glance they look like any other journalist, they develop special relationships with many of the celebrities they meet.

虽然乍一看，他们和其他记者没什么两样，但他们与遇到的许多名人都建立了特殊的关系。

记：**词根记忆** journal报纸，刊物 + ist表示从事某种职业的人→journalist新闻工作者

搭：accredited journalist 特派新闻记者

派：journal n. 报纸或期刊

29. river [ˈrɪvə (r)] n. 河，江

例：During their long trek, Joe and their team found that crossing the river had to be risky.

在他们的长途跋涉中，乔和他们的团队发现过河时必须冒着很大的风险。

搭：river basin 流域 by the river 在河边

30. applicant [ˈæplɪkənt] n. 申请人

例：We welcome applicants with work experience.

我们欢迎有工作经验的应聘者。

搭：job applicant 求职人 applicant for the credit 申请开证人

派：apply v. 申请

31. goal [gəʊl] n. 球门；进球得分；目标，目的 v. 射门，射门得分

例：My main goal was to reduce my dependence on store-bought food, but also to learn a basic skill.

我的主要目标是减少对从商店买的食物的依赖，但也要学习一项基本技能。

搭：ultimate goal 最终目标；终极目标 long-term goal 长期目标

32. lack [læk] n.&v. 缺乏，不足

例：Underwater artificial light lacks enough energy to achieve the desired effect.

水下的人造光缺乏足够的能量来达到所需的效果。

搭：for lack of 因缺乏　lack of confidence 缺乏自信

33. passenger ['pæsɪndʒə (r)] n. 乘客，旅客　adj. 乘客的，旅客的

例：Passengers are ready to disembark.

乘客们已准备好下船。

记：**联想记忆** pass- 通过 + eng + er 人→引申为通过的人是乘客→passenger乘客

搭：passenger transport 客运　passenger volume 客流量；承载量；乘客量

34. science ['saɪəns] n. 科学，科学知识

例：I know you don't like science fiction, and romantic comedies are all the same.

我知道你不喜欢科幻小说，浪漫喜剧也一样。

记：**词根记忆** sci知道，知晓 + ence性质→科学帮助人了解世界→science科学

搭：modern science 现代科学 social science 社会科学

35. collection [kə'lekʃn] n. 收藏品，收集物

例：There is one of the rarest things in his collection.

他的收藏中有一件最稀有的东西。

记：**词根记忆** collect收集 + ion 行为，状态→collection收藏品

搭：data collection 数据收集　collection agent 托收代理人

派：collect v. 收集

36. issue ['ɪʃuː] n. 议题，争论点；（报纸、杂志等的）期，号；发放，分配

例：Avoid taking photos when you are dealing with difficult environmental issues.

避免在处理棘手的环境问题时拍照。

记：**联想记忆** it（iss）强烈情感，愤怒 + ue名词后缀→对一个事情发怒→issue问题

搭：in the issue 结果，终于 at issue 争议中的；讨论中的

37. star [staː (r)] n. 星，恒星；明星　v. 主演，使主演；表现杰出　adj. 最好的，最出色的

例：Look up at the sky at night and watch the stars.

晚上抬头仰望天空看星星。

搭：reach for the stars 有九天揽月之志

38. case [keɪs] *n.* 具体情况，实例；病例；诉讼，官司；案件，案子；容器，箱子；事实，论据 *v.* 围绕，包盖；装入保护容器内

例：They get a magnificent view of the country if that was the case.

如果是这样的话，他们可以看到这个国家的壮丽景色。

搭：court case 诉讼案 make a case 说明理由 in that case 那样的话

39. image [ˈɪmɪdʒ] *n.* 形象，印象；影像，图像；比喻，意象；画像，塑像 *v.* 作……的像，描绘……的形象；幻想，想象

例：I spent five years touring, leading a rock band as vocalist and guitarist, changing my image.

我花了五年的时间巡回演出，以主唱和吉他手的身份带领一支摇滚乐队，改变了我的形象。

搭：self-image 自我形象 corporate image 企业形象

project an image 树立一种形象

派：imagination *n.* 想象力，幻想物 imaginative *adj.* 富有想象力的

imaginary *adj.* 假想的

40. nature [ˈneɪtʃə(r)] *n.* 大自然，自然界；性格，秉性；本质，特点；类型，种类

例：The man was moved by the positive nature of the interaction with an animal.

这名男子被与动物互动的积极天性所感动。

记：词根记忆 nat 出生，诞生 + ure 表名词→天生的→引申为大自然

搭：in nature 本质上，事实上 by nature 天生地；生性

派：natural *adj.* 自然的，天然的 naturalist *n.* 博物学家；自然主义者

巩固练习

扫码听音频

1. 扫码听写（根据所听音频写出本单元对应单词）

(1) _____　(2) _____　(3) _____　(4) _____

(5) _____　(6) _____　(7) _____　(8) _____

(9) _____　(10) _____　(11) _____　(12) _____

(13) _____　(14) _____　(15) _____　(16) _____

(17) _____　(18) _____　(19) _____　(20) _____

(21) _____	(22) _____	(23) _____	(24) _____
(25) _____	(26) _____	(27) _____	(28) _____
(29) _____	(30) _____	(31) _____	(32) _____
(33) _____	(34) _____	(35) _____	(36) _____
(37) _____	(38) _____	(39) _____	(40) _____

2. 实战演练（选出最符合句意的选项）

(1) Educational toys, videos, and a wide _____ of baby devices that claim to improve children's intelligence have flooded onto the market.

(A) range　　　　　　　　　(B) series

(C) chain　　　　　　　　　(D) extend

(2) It has a wider choice of shopping _____ than other supermarkets.

(A) options　　　　　　　　(B) choices

(C) alternatives　　　　　　(D) selections

(3) He _____ himself on his ability to match people's names with their faces.

(A) prides　　　　　　　　　(B) celebrates

(C) enjoys　　　　　　　　　(D) delights

(4) The flaw that needed to be _____ was a communicative one, not physical one.

(A) emphasized　　　　　　(B) addressed

(C) dealt　　　　　　　　　(D) given

(5) The result of the test tells HR a lot about _____ applicant's character.

(A) a　　　　　　　　　　　(B) the

(C) one　　　　　　　　　　(D) how

(6) It remains mystic to say with any _____ of truth which situation we will face next month.

(A) point　　　　　　　　　(B) degree

(C) scale　　　　　　　　　(D) grade

(7) Recently, more attention is being drawn to the _____ doctor plays in society.

(A) position　　　　　　　　(B) role

(C) function　　　　　　　　(D) part

(8) You have to book the ticket for a visit to this place at least a week in _____.

(A) front　　　　　　　　　(B) progress

(C) advance　　　　　　　　(D) future

(9) The shrill ringing of the doorbell suddenly interrupted my _____ of thought.

  (A) track   (B) path

  (C) train   (D) process

(10) The teacher describes this story as a myth that people who live here cling to despite _____ of evidence

  (A) lack   (B) shortage

  (C) absence   (D) loss

Day 13

扫码听音频

小试牛刀

浏览本单元所有单词，在你已掌握的单词前面打√。

☐ pound	☐ race	☐ stage	☐ term
☐ action	☐ award	☐ bag	☐ bank
☐ beginner	☐ century	☐ context	☐ council
☐ editor	☐ effort	☐ luxury	☐ match
☐ disadvantage	☐ practice	☐ round	☐ selection
☐ species	☐ tip	☐ tool	☐ access
☐ supermarket	☐ baby	☐ bar	☐ assistant
☐ decision	☐ matter	☐ care	☐ face
☐ temperature	☐ factory	☐ fashion	☐ knowledge
☐ pool	☐ direction	☐ image	☐ list

词汇精讲

1. pound [paʊnd] *n.* 磅；英镑 *v.* 连续重击，猛打；（心脏）剧烈地跳动

例：Clients can deduct 5 pounds from their supply bill.

客户可以在供货账单上减去5英镑。

搭：by the pound 按每磅（计价） pound on 重击；猛

2. race [reɪs] *n.* 赛跑，速度竞赛；竞争，角逐；人种，种族；民族 *v.* 比赛，参加比赛

例：About 50 people signed up for the bike race.

大约有50人报名参加了自行车比赛。

搭：race against time/the clock 和时间赛跑 a race of 一群……

派：racial *adj.* 种族的；种族间的；人种的 racist *n.* 种族主义者

3. stage [steɪdʒ] *n.* 阶段，时期；舞台；戏剧，戏剧表演 *v.* 上演，演出；主办，举行

例：Part of the left side of the stage is blurred.

舞台左侧的一部分模糊不清。

搭：critical stage 关键阶段 reach a stage 达到某一阶段

4. term [tɜːm] *n.* 时期，期限，任期 *v.* 把……称为，把……叫作

例：Ms. Black will teach the painting class this term.

布莱克女士这学期将教绘画课。

搭：in terms of 谈及；就……而言；在……方面

5. action ['ækʃn] *n.* 行动；行为；战斗；诉讼 *v.* 处理 *adj.* 动作（片）的，动作片中的

例：People have to take action quickly or we won't even be able to take them apart.

人们必须迅速采取行动，否则我们甚至无法把它拆开。

记：词根记忆 act 行动，做 + ion 行为，状态→action行动；行为

搭：take action 采取行动；提出诉讼 action on 对……的作用 in action 在活动；在运转

6. award [ə'wɔːd] *n.* 奖，奖品

例：They had about six times more nominations for a merit award than we were allowed to give out.

他们获得的优秀奖提名大约是我们被允许发放的六倍。

记：发音记忆 a（一个）+ ward（物）→一个额外的物品→award 奖，奖品

搭：award sth. to sb. 授予某人某物

7. bag [bæg] *n.* 袋，包；一袋的量；大量，很多 *v.* 把……装进袋子；抢占，占有

例：She has some candies in her bag.
她包里有一些糖。

8. bank [bæŋk] *n.* 银行；储蓄罐；库存，库；岸 *v.* 把（钱）存入银行，把……储存入库

例：Please tell me the location of the National bank.
请告诉我国家银行的位置。

搭：bank on 指望；依靠

9. beginner [bɪˈɡɪnə(r)] *n.* 初学者；新手

例：It is run by a craft teacher who has a flair for beginners.
它是由一位对初学者来说很有天分的工艺老师经营的。

记：词根记忆 begin开始 + n + er 某种人→刚开始的人→beginner 初学者，新人

10. century [ˈsentʃəri] *n.* 世纪；一百年

例：Penicillin was invented in the 20th century.
青霉素是在二十世纪发明的。

记：词根记忆 cent 百，百分之一 + ury 名词后缀→century 一百年

11. context [ˈkɒntekst] *n.* 背景，环境；上下文，语境

例：Her first year project was about a small building in an industrial context.
她第一年的项目是关于工业背景下的小型建筑。

记：词根记忆 con 共同，一起 + text 编织→共同编织构成上下文和背景→context 背景；上下文，语境

搭：in the context of 在……情况下；在……背景下　out of context 断章取义；脱离上下文

派：contextual *adj.* 文脉上的，前后关系的

12. council [ˈkaʊnsl] *n.* 委员会，理事会；政务委员会，地方议会；会议

例：The city council is likely to pass the proposal.
市议会很可能会通过这项提案。

搭：state council 国务院

派：councilor *n.* 政务会委员

---

13. editor [ˈedɪtə (r)] *n.* 编辑；记者；剪辑师；编辑程序

例：He was appointed as an **editor** of the main newspaper.

他被任命为主报社的编辑。

记：词根记忆 edit编辑 + or 人或物→editor编辑；记者

搭：chief editor 总编辑 senior editor 高级编辑，资深编辑

派：editorial *adj.* 编辑的，主笔的

---

14. effort [ˈefət] *n.* 努力，尽力

例：If you don't make **effort** to practice, no one will be interested in you.

如果你不努力练习，没有人会对你感兴趣。

记：**联想记忆** ef 出来，从……向外 + fort 力量；强壮→向外使自己力量更强→effort努力，尽力

搭：make an effort 努力，做出努力 spare no efforts 不遗余力，竭尽全力

派：effortful *adj.* 需要努力的，充满努力的

---

15. luxury [ˈlʌkʃəri] *n.* 奢华，华贵；奢侈品 *adj.* 奢侈的，豪华的

例：The average price of **luxury** goods in the store is 34，540 euros.

店内奢侈品均价是34，540欧元。

记：词根记忆 luxur 过度，奢华 + y 名词后缀→luxury奢侈品

搭：in the lap of luxury 生活优裕；养尊处优

派：luxurious *adj.* 奢侈的 luxe *n.* 奢侈

---

16. match [mætʃ] *n.* 比赛，竞赛；火柴；敌手，旗鼓相当的人；适合，匹配 *v.* 比得上，敌得过；使成对，使相配

例：There is an important football **match** tonight, so the traffic will definitely be much heavier than usual.

今晚有一场重要的足球比赛，所以交通肯定会比平时拥挤得多。

搭：match with 使和……相匹配 match up 使相配，使协调

派：matcher *n.* 匹配器

---

17. disadvantage [ˌdɪsədˈvɑːntɪdʒ] *n.* 不利条件，劣势；不利因素；损失，损害 *vt.* 使处于不利地位，损害

例：Candidates who can't learn the skill are at a **disadvantage**.

学不会该项技能的应聘者处于不利地位。

记：词根记忆 dis否定 + advantage 有利条件→disadvantage 不利条件

搭：at a disadvantage 处于不利地位 to the disadvantage of 对……不利

18. **practice** [ˈpræktɪs] *n.* 实践，实际操作；通常的做法，惯例；练习 *v.* 练习；经常做，养成……的习惯

例：You have many chances to practice your Spanish.

你有很多机会练习你的西班牙语。

记：词根记忆 pract做 + ice表示情况→practice做法，实践

搭：in practice 在实践中；实际上，事实上 into practice 实施；实行

派：practise *v.* 练习，实践 practised *adj.* 熟练的 practitioner *n.* 从业者

19. **round** [raʊnd] *adj.* 圆形的，球形的；圆弧的；丰满的；（声音）圆润的 *adv.* 旋转，环绕；周长，绕一整圈 *v.* 环绕，绕过 *prep.* 环绕，围绕 *n.* 轮次；（比赛的）轮，局，场

例：Mark usually travels round his city with bus.

马克通常乘公共汽车在他的城市里旅行。

搭：round off 使圆满结束 round on 严厉指责；抨击

round up 使聚拢；使聚集

20. selection [sɪˈlekʃn] *n.* 选择，挑选；可供选择的事物

例：You must attend the selection and cook some delicious food for judges.

你必须参加选拔，并为评委做一些美味的食物。

记：词根记忆 select选择，精选 + ion表示行为→selection挑选

搭：site selection 厂址选择 selection process 挑选过程

派：selected *adj.* 挑出来的 selecting *v.* 挑选

21. species [ˈspiːʃiːz] *n.* 种，物种；种类 *adj.* 原种的

例：In a world plagued by many environmental problems，zoos provide protection for the world's endangered species.

在一个受到许多环境问题困扰的世界里，动物园为世界濒危物种提供了保护。

记：词根记忆 speci 种类 + es 名词后缀→species 物种

搭：species diversity 物种多样性 species richness 物种丰富度

22. **tip** [tɪp] *n.* 指点，诀窍，建议；小费；末梢，尖端 *v.* （使）倾斜，（使）斜侧；给小费

例：Business visitors to the Britain can help communicate by reading these tips provided by companies.

来英国的商务访问者可以通过阅读公司提供的这些提示来帮助沟通。

搭：tip off 暗中告知 tip over 打翻；翻倒 tip up （使）倾斜；（使）倾翻

23. tool [tu:l] *n.* 工具，手段 *v.* 驱车兜风；（用工具）制作

例：There's plenty of room for tools in the trunk.

后备箱里有很多地方可以放工具。

搭：communication tool 通信手段 machine tool 机床

24. access ['ækses] *n.* 入口，通道；获得的机会，使用权 *v.* 接近，进入

例：How can customers request access to their shopping records?

客户如何查询他们的购物记录？

记：词根记忆 ac（＝ad，去）+ cess（＝cede，移动）→access接近

搭：access control 访问控制 have access to 使用；接近；可以利用

派：accessible *adj.* 可得到的 accessibility *n.* 易接近，可到达

25. supermarket ['su:pəma:kɪt] *n.* 超级市场，超市

例：A supermarket was opened in the suburbs last month.

上个月在郊区开了一家超级市场。

记：词根记忆 super 超级 + market集市→supermarket 超市

26. baby ['beɪbi] *n.* 婴儿，婴孩；动物幼崽 *v.* 把……当婴儿般对待，对……娇生惯养 *adj.*（蔬菜）幼嫩的；（幼）小的，小型的

例：She was holding the baby in one arm and a sheet in the other, and the baby was screaming and his face was red.

她一只胳膊夹着孩子，另一只胳膊夹着一张单子，婴儿在尖叫，脸都憋红了。

搭：baby boom 婴儿潮；生育高峰

派：babyish *adj.* 稚气的

27. bar [ba:（r）] *n.* 酒吧；块，棒；功能条 *v.* 阻止，禁止

例：I was in a coffee bar one day and I picked up a newspaper to read to wait for my friends.

有一天，我在咖啡厅里拿起一份报纸，边读边等我的朋友们。

搭：bar someone from 禁止某人……

28. assistant [əˈsɪstənt] *n.* 助理，助手；店员，售货员 *adj.* 助理的，副的

例：The reason why I can cope without an assistant is that I have a minimal office compared with others.

我之所以没有助理也能应付，是因为我的办公室比别人小得多。

记：词根记忆 assist帮助 + ant 某种人→assistant助理，助手

搭：shop assistant 店员

29. decision [dɪˈsɪʒn] *n.* 决定，抉择；判决，裁定；果断，决断力；做决定，决策

例：It might be better for her to travel as youngers do than to make a decision to go to university.

对她来说，像年轻人一样去旅行可能比决定上大学更好。

记：**联想记忆** de离开+ cis切 + ion名词词尾，行为→切开，过去，离开→decision决定，抉择

搭：make a decision 做出决定 difficult decision 艰难的决定

派：deciding *adj.* 无疑的

30. matter [ˈmætə (r)] *n.* 事情，问题；事态，情况

例：If people like it, it doesn't matter how easy it is, I promise I will sing it so loud that if you sing it wrong, no one will notice.

如果人们喜欢它，它有多容易并不重要，我保证我会唱得很大声，如果你唱错了，没有人会注意到。

搭：as a matter of fact 事实上；其实；说真的 be another/a different matter 另外一回事；又是一回事；另当别论

31. care [keə (r)] *n.* 照料，护理；小心，谨慎；忧虑，烦恼；收养，监护 *v.* 照顾，照料；在意，担忧；喜欢，想要

例：When we have a new exhibition opening, we will choose a new company to take care of food and beverage.

当我们有一个新的展览开幕时，我们会选择一家新公司负责食品和饮料。

搭：good care 很好的照顾 take care of 照顾；注意；抚养

派：careful *adj.* 认真的 carefully *adv.* 认真地 careless *adj.* 粗心大意的

32. face [feɪs] *n.* 脸，面部；面部表情，脸色 *v.* 面临，遭遇；正视，面对

例：Face-to-face teamwork is more effective in this situation.

在这种情况下，面对面的团队合作更有效。

搭：face down 挫败，反对　face up to （使）直面，正视

33. temperature [ˈtemprətʃə (r)] *n.* 温度，气温；体温；发烧

例：If stored at low temperatures, the shelf life of the product can be up to several years.

如果在低温下保存，该产品的保质期可达几年。

记：词根记忆 temper调节 + at + ure表示行为，结果→自然界的温度可进行自我调节→temperature温度

搭：reach a temperature 达到温度　raise/lower the temperature 升/降温；增加/减少热烈程度

34. factory [ˈfæktri; ˈfæktəri] *n.* 工厂，制造厂；（在外国的）代理店

例：He is the manager of a factory who gives up his job and becomes a singer.

他是一家工厂的经理，他放弃了工作，成为一名歌手。

记：词根记忆 fact做，造 + ory表示地点，场所→制造场所，即工厂→factory工厂

搭：clothing factory 服装厂；被服厂

35. fashion [ˈfæʃn] *n.* 时髦打扮，流行装扮 *v.* （尤指用手工）制作，使成形；塑造

例：It's sad that these lovely comfy T-shirts are old-fashioned.

很遗憾，这些可爱舒适的T恤已经过时了。

记：发音记忆 fashion "风尚"→引申为时尚

搭：fast fashion 快时尚　in fashion 合于时尚，流行

派：fashionable *adj.* 流行的，时髦的

36. knowledge [ˈnɒlɪdʒ] *n.* 知识，学问；知道，了解

例：All the courses are totally based on the newest knowledge and aims to extend the view of students.

所有课程均以最新知识为基础，旨在拓展学生的视野。

搭：knowledge management 知识管理　general knowledge 常识，各方面的知识

37. pool [puːl] *n.* 池塘，水坑；后备人员，备用物品；共用的资源

例：Josh loves swimming but even craves a challenge outside of the pool.

乔希喜欢游泳，但他也渴望泳池外的挑战。

搭：swimming pool 游泳池　car pool 汽车合伙；汽车合用组织

38. direction [daɪ'rekʃn] *n.* 方向，方位；趋势，动向

例：It's a good idea to learn the control method first，so this will make you used to grasping its **direction**.

首先学习控制方法是一个好主意，这样你就会习惯掌握它的方向。

记：词根记忆 direct朝着，指向 + ion表示行为，状态→direction方向

搭：in the direction　朝……方向，在……方向

派：directional *adj.* 方向的

39. image ['ɪmɪdʒ] *n.* 形象，印象 *v.* 作……的像，描绘……的形象

例：I spent five years doing sports and learning hard to change my **image**.

我花了五年时间做运动，努力学习以改变自己的形象。

搭：image processing 图像处理　public image 公众形象

40. list [lɪst] *n.* 列表，清单 *v.* 列清单，拟订清单；把……列入名单

例：Jason has already seen the **list** of sports class this year.

杰森已经看过今年的体育班名单了。

搭：a list of 一览表，清单；一列　on the list 在单子上，在名册中

巩固练习

1. 扫码听写（根据所听音频写出本单元对应单词）

(1) _____　(2) _____　(3) _____　(4) _____

(5) _____　(6) _____　(7) _____　(8) _____

(9) _____　(10) _____　(11) _____　(12) _____

(13) _____　(14) _____　(15) _____　(16) _____

(17) _____　(18) _____　(19) _____　(20) _____

(21) _____　(22) _____　(23) _____　(24) _____

(25) _____　(26) _____　(27) _____　(28) _____

(29) _____　(30) _____　(31) _____　(32) _____

(33) _____　(34) _____　(35) _____　(36) _____

(37) _____　(38) _____　(39) _____　(40) _____

扫码听音频

2. 实战演练（选出最符合句意的选项）

(1) He made great _____ to encourage people to read.

    (A) efforts   (B) courage

    (C) process   (D) move

(2) There are many casual _____ and restaurants.

    (A) slides   (B) bars

    (C) ban   (D) obstruction

(3) The product has lots of _____ that we need to improve.

    (A) disadvantages   (B) handicaps

    (C) errors   (D) drawbacks

(4) This practical course gives people chances to _____ their skills in real-life situations.

    (A) pursue   (B) practice

    (C) know   (D) train

(5) I was in two _____ about whether this was the right position for me, but I'm happy I picked it in the end.

    (A) minds   (B) choices

    (C) thoughts   (D) decisions

(6) The new methods used for shooting _____ are amazing and I've just come back from a course in this area.

    (A) behaviour   (B) manner

    (C) action   (D) fight

(7) Some expressions should be avoided in cross-cultural _____.

    (A) environment   (B) implication

    (C) relevance   (D) context

(8) The restaurant won several _____ for the good service for customers.

    (A) rewards   (B) awards

    (C) honours   (D) prizes

(9) Please hand _____ the papers to classmates.

    (A) up   (B) round

    (C) down   (D) about

（10）It is not easy to _____ the right teaching materials for courses.

　　（A）entry 　　　　　　　（B）access

　　（C）entrance 　　　　　　（D）accept

Day 14

小试牛刀

浏览本单元所有单词，在你已掌握的单词前面打√。

☐ background	☐ sense	☐ purpose	☐ thought
☐ object	☐ couple	☐ feature	☐ post
☐ performance	☐ complaint	☐ solution	☐ clinic
☐ pressure	☐ library	☐ impact	☐ wall
☐ relationship	☐ society	☐ technique	☐ doctor
☐ majority	☐ energy	☐ industry	☐ land
☐ atmosphere	☐ discount	☐ expectation	☐ dream
☐ education	☐ camp	☐ insect	☐ card
☐ attraction	☐ advance	☐ achievement	☐ drive
☐ title	☐ sound	☐ value	☐ topic

词汇精讲

1. background ['bækgraʊnd] *n.* 出身背景，学历，经历

例：It's good for me that the courses I can attend spreads over periods so that I can do some background reading.

我可以参加的课程分散在不同的时间段对我来说很好，这样我就可以做一些背景阅读。

记：联想记忆 back 后面的 + ground 土地→后面的土地即是背后的风景→引申为背景

搭：cultural/ethnic/family background 文化/民族/家庭背景 background music 背景音乐

2. sense [sens] *n.* 感觉官能；（对某物的）感觉；道理，合理性；理智，理性；意义，含义 *v.* 感觉到，觉察到

例：All you need is the love of the sky and a sense of adventure.

你所需要的只是对天空的热爱和冒险精神。

记：词根记忆 sens 感觉 + e→sense感觉

搭：common sense 常识 in a sense 在某种意义上

派：sensible *adj.* 理智的，合理的 sensitivity *n.* 感知，觉察

3. purpose ['pɜːpəs] *n.* 目的，意图；目标，计划 *v.* 有意，打算

例：The purpose of the lesson is to broaden the view of the world to people.

这节课的目的是拓宽人们对世界的看法。

记：词根记忆 pur(pro)前 + pos 放置+ e→放在前方的东西→purpose目的，意图

搭：on purpose 有意，成心地 for purpose of 为了；为了……的目的

4. thought [θɔːt] *n.* 想法，看法，主意

例：It is thought that the dog must have crossed the line and was waiting on the platform.

人们认为这只狗一定是过了线，在站台上等着。

搭：have second thoughts 转念一想

collect your thoughts 镇定下来，敛神专注；做好精神准备

5. object ['ɒbdʒɪkt] *n.* 物体，实物；目的，目标；宾语 *v.* 反对

例：He might start with the foundation first, or assemble the core of a piece depending on the type of object he wants to recreate with bricks.

他可能会先从基础开始，或者根据他想要用砖块重建的物体的类型来组装一个部件的核心。

记：词根记忆 ob在……前面 + ject扔，投掷→放置在前面的目标或物体→object物体，目标

搭：no object 不成问题 object to sb./sth. 反对

派：objection n. 反对的理由；反对，异议 objectify v. （使）具体化，（使）客观化

6. couple [ˈkʌpl] *n.* 两个，几个；一对夫妇/情侣 *v.* 加上，结合；（把设备等）连接；形成一双，配成一对

例：A couple are discussing the plan to the castle.
一对夫妇正在讨论去城堡的计划。

记：联想记忆 co与……一起 + up拿，伸向 + le→伸手与……连在一起→couple一对

搭：a couple of 三两个 couple sb./sth. with sb./sth. 把…与…连接起来

7. feature [ˈfiːtʃə(r)] *n.* 特点，特征 *v.* 以……为特色，以……为主要组成；起重要作用，占重要地位

例：One of the most interesting features of the city is the dialects people here use.
这个城市最有趣的特点之一是这里的人们所使用的方言。

记：联想记忆 feat做，制作 + ure表名词→上帝制造出来的即是特色→feature特点，特征

搭：basic feature 基本特性

8. post [pəʊst] *n.* 邮政，邮递；工作，职位 *v.* 张贴，公布

例：Based on the legislation, goods like fireworks are considered as unsafe things by post.
根据法规，邮寄像烟花这样的物品被认为是不安全的。

搭：post off 邮寄；投递 post up 张贴，贴出

9. performance [pəˈfɔːməns] *n.* 表演，演出；工作情况，表现 *adj.* 性能卓越的，高性能的

例：Nervousness can get in the way of a smooth performance.
紧张会妨碍演出顺利进行。

记：词根记忆 perform 执行 + ance 性质，状况→performance 表现

搭：performance appraisal 表现评估

10. complaint [kəmˈpleɪnt] *n.* 抱怨，投诉

例：I have no complaints about the sheer complexity of the book.

我对本书过于冗杂的内容毫无抱怨。

记：联想记忆 com表强调 + plaint捶胸顿足→强烈地捶胸顿足→complaint抱怨

搭：complaint against someone 对某人的投诉

11. solution [səˈluːʃn] *n.* 解决办法；解答，答案

例：Our supplier gives us a cost effective solution.

我们的供应商给了我们一个经济有效的解决方案。

搭：solution to a problem 解决问题的办法

12. clinic [ˈklɪnɪk] *n.* 诊所，门诊部

例：People who work at clinic must follow the instruction.

在诊所工作的人必须遵守说明。

搭：medical clinic 医疗诊所

派：clinical *adj.* 诊所的，医务室的 clinician *n.* 临床医生

13. pressure [ˈpreʃə (r)] *n.* 压力，挤压；催促，强迫

例：Chefs are under huge pressure in a busy restaurant.

厨师在繁忙的餐厅会承受巨大的压力。

记：词根记忆 press按，压 + -ure表名词→pressure压力

搭：put pressure on sb. to do sth. 强迫某人做某事 under pressure面临压力，在压力之下

14. library [ˈlaɪbrəri] *n.* 图书馆，藏书楼

例：Today's library will close early at 5 p.m. because of the disinfection.

因消毒，图书馆将提早在今天下午五点闭馆。

派：librarian *n.* 图书馆馆长

15. impact [ˈɪmpækt] *n.* 撞击，冲击力；巨大影响，强大作用 *v.* 冲击，撞击；挤入，压紧；（对……）产生影响

例：He did numerous tests to help understand the impacts of spaceflight on the human body.

他做了许多测试，以帮助了解太空飞行对人体的影响。

记：联想记忆 im 在内，进入，使 + pact 压紧，推进→使不断压紧→impact冲击，撞击

搭：have an impact on 对于……有影响

16. wall [wɔːl] *n.* 城墙，围墙 *v.* 用墙围住；砌墙封闭 *adj.* 墙壁的

例：When I did the test flight，I almost hit the wall.

当我进行试飞时，我几乎撞在墙上了。

17. relationship [rɪˈleɪʃnʃɪp] *n.* 关系，关联

例：If people establish some special relationship with specific people，then the life may be easier than they do not do that.

如果人们与特定的人建立了一些特殊的关系，那么生活可能会比他们不这样做更容易。

记：词根记忆 relation 关系 + ship 关系，状态→relationship 关系，关联

18. society [səˈsaɪəti] *n.* 社会；社群

例：You are invited to this special meeting of the horticultural society.

你被邀请参加园艺协会的这次特殊会议。

记：词根记忆 soc联合，结交 + ie + ty表示状态，性质→人与人之间的联合→society社会

搭：in society 在社会上

派：sociable *adj.* 善于交际的 sociability *n.* 社交能力

19. technique [tekˈniːk] *n.* 技巧，工艺

例：Our instructor paired us at random and then asked us to teach each other a favorite technique.

我们的导师把我们随机配对，然后让我们互相教彼此一个最喜欢的技巧。

记：词根记忆 techn技艺技术 + ique→technique技能，技术

派：technical *adj.* 技术的

20. doctor [ˈdɒktə(r)] *n.* 医生，大夫；博士 *v.* 篡改，伪造

例：If you want to see a doctor，please call the office after 10 a.m.

如果你想看医生，请在上午10点以后给办公室打电话。

记：词根记忆 doc教，授 + or与……相关的人→与教和学相关的人→doctor医生，博士

派：doctorate *n.* 博士学位

21. majority [məˈdʒɒrəti] *n.* 大多数 *adj.* 多数人的

例：This description actually includes majority of Susan's work.

这一描述实际上包括了苏珊的大部分工作。

记：词根记忆 major主要的 + ity表示状态→majority大部分，大多数

搭：majority opinion 多数派观点

22. energy ['enədʒi] *n.* 能力，力气；精力，活力

例：I have much more energy when I start to do sports.

当我开始做运动时，我有更多的精力。

记：词根记忆 en使……做某事，使进入 + erg工作 + y表示性质、状态→进入工作
状态，产生能量→energy能力，力气

搭：full of energy 精力充沛的

派：energetic *adj.* 精力充沛的

23. industry ['ɪndəstri] *n.* 工业，生产制造；行业，产业

例：By seeing his CV, you can know he has experience of this industry and he obviously wants to succeed.

通过他的简历，你可以知道他有这个行业的经验，而且很明显他想要成功。

记：词根记忆 in向内 + du + str（u）组成，建 + ry 表示行为→组织起来的行为
→industry 工业，勤劳

派：industrious *adj.* 勤劳的，勤奋的

24. land [lænd] *n.* 陆地，地面 *v.* 着陆，降落

例：This kind of car can travel on very uneven land.

这类车可以在极不平坦的地面上行驶。

搭：land up 最终抵达

25. atmosphere ['ætməsfɪə (r)] *n.* 大气，大气层；气氛，环境

例：The atmosphere between this two people is intimate.

这两个人之间的气氛很亲密。

记：联想记忆 atmo蒸汽 + sphere球体，球形→气体笼罩球体→atmosphere大气

搭：heavy atmosphere 令人尴尬（或不安）的气氛

26. discount ['dɪskaʊnt] *n.* 减价，折扣 *adj.* 打折的，减价出售的

例：Lots of shops offer discounts to students.

许多商铺给学生打折。

记：词根记忆 dis无，不 + count估计，计算，猜想→金额不计在内→discount打折

搭：at a discount 打折扣

27. expectation [ˌekspek'teɪʃn] *n.* 期待，预期；期望，指望

例：The large amount of the tuition fees raise expectations that people feel obliged
to get value for money.

高额的学费提高了人们的期望，人们觉得有义务让钱物有所值。

记：词根记忆 expect期待+ ation表示行为→expectation期待，期望

搭：sense of expectation 期待感

28. dream [dri:m] *n.* 梦；梦想 *v.* 做梦，梦见；梦想，想象 *adj.* 理想的，完美的

例：My dream job is to have both money and free time.

我理想的工作是有钱又有闲。

搭：dream of 梦想；梦见

29. education [ˌedʒuˈkeɪʃn] *n.* （尤指学校）教育；培养，训练；教育机构，教育界人士

例：Do you think education will be different in the future?

你认为未来的教育会有所不同吗？

记：词根记忆 educat（e）教育，教导+ ion表示行为，状态，结果→education 教育

搭：higher education 高等教育（指含大学以上的教育）

派：educational *adj.* 教育的；有教育意义的

30. camp [kæmp] *n.* 营地；兵营，军营；度假营 *v.* 野营，露营；据守，坚守

例：Tom had a rest with others in the camp where he was staying.

汤姆在他所住的营地和其他人一起休息。

搭：camp out 扎营；宿营；露宿；露营

31. insect [ˈɪnsekt] *n.* 昆虫；卑鄙的人

例：Her planted vegetables are suffered from insects.

她种的蔬菜遭了虫害。

搭：insect pest 害虫

32. card [kɑ:d] *n.* 银行卡，身份证；明信片，贺卡

例：The store cannot use credit card.

本店不能使用信用卡。

搭：play your cards right 办事精明

33. attraction [əˈtrækʃn] *n.* 有吸引力的事物；吸引力

例：Unknown things still are an attraction for many people.

未知的事物仍然吸引着许多人。

记：词根记忆 attract吸引 + ion表示行为，状态→attraction爱慕，引力

搭：tourist attraction 观光胜地 attraction for 对……的吸引力

34. advance [əd'vɑːns] v. （使）前进，（使）向前移动 n. 前进；进步，进展

例：She would like to see photos in advance.

她想要提前看照片。

记：词根记忆 ad去 + v. + ance（ante变形而来）先前，在……之前→先于他人从某地出发→advance 前进；提前

搭：in advance （of sth.）预先，提前

35. achievement [ə'tʃiːvmənt] n. 成绩，成就；完成，实现

例：One of my proudest achievements so far is a bicycle I made by my own.

到目前为止，我最自豪的成就之一是我自己做的一辆自行车。

记：词根记忆 achieve实现 + ment表示行为，行为的过程或结果→achievement 成就

36. drive [draɪv] v. 迫使，驱使；开车，驾驶 n. 驱车出行；强烈欲望，本能需求

例：He must have more important things to do than drive me everywhere.

他肯定有更重要的事要做，而不是开车带我到处跑。

搭：drive away 使不愿久留；使想离去 drive off 击退；赶走 drive out 驱逐；逐出；淘汰

派：driver n. 司机

37. title ['taɪtl] n. 名称，标题

例：Can you give me an appropriate title for your movie?

你能给你的电影取个合适的名字吗？

搭：job title 职称

派：entitle v. 给……命名

38. sound [saʊnd] n. 声音，声响 v. （使）发声，（使）作响 adj. 无损伤的，健康的，坚实的；合理的，明智的

例：In the material they sent out in advance, it sounded very relevant to what we want to do in next step.

在他们提前发出的材料中，听起来与我们下一步要做的事情非常相关。

记：联想记忆 son声音→sound声音，响声

搭：sound like 听起来像……

39. **value** ['vælju:] *n.* 价值；等值，等价 *v.* 尊重，重视；给……定价

例：The opera ticket is good value for money.

戏剧票物有所值。

搭：added value 附加价值

派：valuable *adj.* 值钱的

40. **topic** ['tɒpɪk] *n.* 题目，主题；一般规则，总论

例：Students can only choose one question from each topic area.

学生只能从每个主题区域中选择一个问题。

扫码听音频

巩固练习

1. 扫码听写（根据所听音频写出本单元对应单词）

(1) _____ (2) _____ (3) _____ (4) _____

(5) _____ (6) _____ (7) _____ (8) _____

(9) _____ (10) _____ (11) _____ (12) _____

(13) _____ (14) _____ (15) _____ (16) _____

(17) _____ (18) _____ (19) _____ (20) _____

(21) _____ (22) _____ (23) _____ (24) _____

(25) _____ (26) _____ (27) _____ (28) _____

(29) _____ (30) _____ (31) _____ (32) _____

(33) _____ (34) _____ (35) _____ (36) _____

(37) _____ (38) _____ (39) _____ (40) _____

2. 实战演练（选出最符合句意的选项）

(1) The top hotel in beach is a wonderful _____ for anyone who enjoys the sunshine!

　　(A) discount　　　　　　　　(B) luck

　　(C) prize　　　　　　　　　(D) sight

(2) We often get _____ from residents about all the rubbish that has piled up on the streets.

　　(A) complaints　　　　　　　(B) letters

(C) references   (D) notes

(3) One _____ doctor believes that even if a person only do sports once a week, it can make an extraordinary difference to their body.

    (A) main   (B) first

    (C) leading   (D) major

(4) This subject relies on highly sophisticated _____.

    (A) skills   (B) techniques

    (C) power   (D) methods

(5) They want to develop good _____ with people who live here.

    (A) relationships   (B) relatives

    (C) relates   (D) regularity

(6) Read the whole passage to get _____ general understanding of the topic and content.

    (A) a   (B) the

    (C) one   (D) whole

(7) These results _____ light on the way toddlers acquire features of verb meaning by catching the information that they were not involve in directly.

    (A) spread   (B) provide

    (C) offer   (D) shed

(8) There are lots of young people so the _____ is dynamic.

    (A) air   (B) condition

    (C) place   (D) atmosphere

(9) The _____ for Sam is that he can learn new skills in the lesson.

    (A) attraction   (B) attractive

    (C) charm   (D) action

(10) In the summer vacations we both went to summer _____.

    (A) camp   (B) buildings

    (C) campus   (D) visit

Day 15

扫码听音频

小试牛刀

浏览本单元所有单词，在你已掌握的单词前面打√。

☐ experiment	☐ resident	☐ vegetable	☐ bottle
☐ chocolate	☐ display	☐ spread	☐ risk
☐ occasion	☐ album	☐ standard	☐ budget
☐ engineer	☐ coach	☐ wave	☐ rock
☐ connection	☐ medicine	☐ population	☐ capital
☐ colour	☐ gallery	☐ survey	☐ lung
☐ proposal	☐ impression	☐ screen	☐ cartoon
☐ sauce	☐ hobby	☐ paper	☐ loss
☐ request	☐ resource	☐ ambition	☐ catalog
☐ decade	☐ lifestyle	☐ voyage	☐ taxi

词汇精讲

1. experiment [ɪkˈsperɪmənt] *n.* 实验，试验；尝试，实践　*v.* 做试验；试，尝试

例：For several years, he has been experimenting with lots of materials that we cannot image as his artistic medium.

几年来，他一直在尝试用许多我们无法想象的材料作为他的艺术媒介。

记：**联想记忆** exper→expert 专家→专家做实验→experiment 实验

搭：experiment on 对……进行实验；试用

派：experimentation *n.* 实验　experimental *adj.* 实验的，试验的

2. resident [ˈrezɪdənt] *n.* 居民，住户　*adj.*（在某地）居住的，居留的

例：The tour guide is happy to introduce this place to both visitors and local residents who want to learn more.

导游很乐意把这个地方介绍给想了解更多的游客和当地居民。

记：**词根记忆** resid居住 + ent表从事活动的人→resident居民

搭：permanent resident 永久性居民

派：residence *n.* 住处

3. vegetable [ˈvedʒtəbl] *n.* 蔬菜

例：The prices of fruits and vegetables vary widely.

水果和蔬菜的价格差别很大。

记：**联想记忆** veg鲜活的 + e + table桌子→新鲜的才能端上桌子→vegetable蔬菜

4. bottle [ˈbɒtl] *n.* 瓶子　*v.* 装瓶

例：Emily has a gas stove and a gas bottle as well.

艾米莉有一个煤气炉，还有一个煤气瓶。

搭：bottle up 压抑，抑制（强烈的感情）

5. chocolate [ˈtʃɒklət] *n.* 巧克力　*adj.* 巧克力味的

例：His friends want to know how to make chocolate.

他的朋友们想知道怎么做巧克力。

6. display [dɪˈspleɪ] *n.* 展览，陈列　*v.* 展示，陈列；显露，表现

例：We walked along the grassy slope, and then in front of us is the first display board.

我们沿着草坡走，在我们面前的是第一块展板。

记：**词根记忆** dis无，不 + play折叠（由ply而来）→不折叠，即展开展示→display陈列，展出

搭：on display 陈列，展出

7. spread ［spred］ n.&v. 扩散，蔓延；传播，传染

例：The crowds that soon gathered ensured the **spread** of his fame.

很快聚集起来的人群确保了他名声的传播。

搭：spread out 摊开，铺开

8. risk ［rɪsk］ n. 危险，风险 v. 使遭受（失去、毁坏或伤害的）危险

例：They will experience an unprecedented **risk** from the sun's rays.

他们将经历前所未有的太阳射线的危险。

搭：at risk （from/of sth.）有危险；冒风险 take a risk 冒险

9. occasion ［əˈkeɪʒn］ n. 时刻，时候；时机，适当的机会 v. <正式> 引起，惹起

例：Annie bought a dress for a special **occasion**.

安妮为特殊的场合买了一条裙子。

记：**词根记忆** ob + cas降临，发生 + ion名词词尾→occasion时刻，时候

搭：on occasion（s）偶尔，偶然；有时 sense of occasion 场合意识

派：occasional *adj.* 偶尔的

10. album ［ˈælbəm］ n. 唱片，专辑；相册，影集，集邮册

例：After he heard me play, he asked me to make an **album** with him.

他听了我的演奏后，邀请我和他一起做一张专辑。

11. standard ［ˈstændəd］ n. 标准，水平，规范 *adj.* 普通的，标准的

例：For more details on current safety **standards**, please email information@goods.com.

有关当前安全标准的更多详细信息，请发送电子邮件至information@goods.com。

记：**联想记忆** stand站立 + ard某种等级或标准→以某种标准存在→standard标准

派：standardize *v.* 使标准化，使符合标准

12. budget [ˈbʌdʒɪt] *n.* 预算；政府预算案 *v.* 制定预算，制定开支计划；计划，安排 *adj.* 廉价的，经济型的

例：Although the budget for our sector is reduced，we still have huge breakthrough.

虽然我们部门的预算减少了，但我们仍然有巨大的突破。

搭：budget for 在编制预算时考虑

派：budgetary *adj.* 预算的

13. engineer [ˌendʒɪˈnɪə(r)] *n.* 工程师，设计师 *v.* 设计，建造；策划，精心安排

例：My dream is to become an engineer.

我的梦想是成为一名工程师。

记：联想记忆 en里面 + gin产生 + eer表示人→知道内部原理的人→engineer工程师

派：engineering *n.* 工程学

14. coach [kəʊtʃ] *n.* 教练；私人教师 *v.* 训练，指导

例：In my 30 years as a coach，I have rarely felt so proud.

在我30年的教练生涯中，我很少感到如此自豪。

搭：head coach 主教练

15. wave [weɪv] *n.* 海浪；波 *v.* 挥手；挥手示意；挥舞，挥动

例：The wind will suddenly control your direction，and you need to control yourself and quickly pass the wave.

风会突然控制你的方向，你需要控制自己，快速通过海浪。

搭：wave sth. aside/away 对……置之不理；不理会 wave sb. off 挥手送别

16. rock [rɒk] *n.* 岩石；礁石 *v.* （使）轻轻摇晃，缓缓摆动

例：Everything was smooth until the boat struck some rocks in a strong wind.

一切都很顺利，直到船在大风中撞上了礁石。

搭：on the rocks 陷于困境

17. connection [kəˈnekʃn] *n.* 关系，联系；连接，接通

例：You can just go to a remote and alien place to find the connection with the world.

你可以去一个遥远而陌生的地方寻找与世界的联系。

记：词根记忆 connect连接，接通 + ion表示行为，状态→connection连接，关联

搭：in connection with sb./sth. 与……有关（或相关）

派：connective *adj.* 连接的

18. medicine [ˈmedsn] *n.* 药物，药剂　*v.* 用药物治疗，给……用药

例：I want some medicine for my cold.

我想要一些治感冒的药。

记：词根记忆 medic治疗，治愈 + ine 表名词→能治疗的物品→medicine 药物

搭：the best medicine （改进状况的）最佳方法

19. population [ˌpɒpjuˈleɪʃn] *n.* （地区、国家等的）人口，人口数量；某领域的生物，族群，人口

例：The population of rural areas has increased slightly.

农村地区人口小幅上涨。

记：词根记忆 popul人 + ation表示状态，结果→population全体人民，人口

派：populace *n.* 平民百姓

20. capital [ˈkæpɪtl] *n.* 资本，资金；资本家，资方；首都，首府，省会；大写字母　*adj.* 可处死刑的；大写的；首府的，省会的

例：If you travel to a country, you have to go to its capital.

如果你去一个国家旅行，你必须去它的首都。

记：词根记忆 capit头 + al与……相关的→与头有关的，首要的→capital首都；资本；大写字母

搭：make capital （out） of sth. 从……中捞取好处；利用……谋求私利

派：capitalism *n.* 资本主义　capitalize *v.* 使资本化

21. colour [ˈkʌlə（r）] *n.* 颜色；色彩，用色，配色　*v.* 给……染色，着色

例：People just want the same thing as they have, like the logo with the same colour.

人们只是想要和他们拥有的一样的东西，比如相同颜色的标志。

搭：colour in 为……上色

派：coloured *adj.* 有色的　colourful *adj.* 五颜六色的

22. gallery [ˈgæləri] *n.* 美术馆，画廊

例：The manager doesn't like artist's work in the gallery.

经理不喜欢画廊里艺术家的作品。

搭：play to the gallery 哗众取宠；行为惹人注目

23. survey ['sɜːveɪ] *n.* 民意调查，民意测验；考察，调查 *v.* 做民意测验，做民意调查；审视，检查

例：Students are going to do a **survey** about communication.

学生们将做一个关于交流的调查。

记：联想记忆 sur 跨越 + vey 很多人→横跨很多人的调查→survey 做民意调查

24. lung [lʌŋ] *n.* 肺；呼吸器

例：I checked my **lungs** and experiment its function to hope that can help people suffering from respiratory conditions down here.

我检查了我的肺，并试验了它的功能，希望能帮助这里患有呼吸系统疾病的人。

25. proposal [prə'pəʊzl] *n.* 提议，建议；提案

例：The **proposal** is rejected by the company executives.

该建议被公司高层拒绝了。

记：词根记忆 pro前，公开 + pos放置+al表示行为、状态→proposal 提议，建议

派：proposed *adj.* 被提议的 propose *v.* 建议

26. impression [ɪm'preʃn] n. 印象，感想；影响，作用

例：People's first **impression** to others may be mistaken.

人们对别人的第一印象可能是错误的。

记：词根记忆 impress使（人）赞赏尊敬，留下印象 + –ion 行为，状态→impression 印象，感想

搭：impression on 对……的印象 under the impression 记得

派：impressive adj. 给人印象深刻的

27. screen [skriːn] *n.* 屏幕，荧光屏 *v.* 检查，筛查；筛，筛选；检查排除

例：The **screen** kept crashing and everyone was saying "can you hear me now".

屏幕总是死机，每个人都在说"你现在能听到我说话吗"。

搭：screen out 筛取出；筛选排除；筛掉

28. cartoon [kɑː'tuːn] *n.* 漫画，讽刺画；动画片，卡通片；草图，底图 *v.* 给……画漫画；画漫画

例：Successful **cartoons** can provide people with rich emotional value.

成功的动画片可以给人提供丰富的情感价值。

记：词根记忆 cart纸，片 + o + on表示物→漫画起初都是一页一页纸→cartoon漫画；动画片

29. sauce [sɔːs] *n.* 酱，调味汁　*v.* 加酱汁于，用酱汁调味；使增加趣味

例：Dumplings are filled with either meat sauce or vegetables and served with tomato sauce.

饺子馅要么是肉酱，要么是蔬菜，再配上番茄酱。

30. hobby [ˈhɒbi] *n.* 业余爱好，嗜好

例：As a hobby, my girlfriend and I do quizzes on the Internet.

作为一种爱好，我和我的女朋友在网上做测验。

派：hobbyist *n.* 业余爱好者

31. paper [ˈpeɪpə (r)] *n.* 纸；报纸；论文　*adj.* 纸做的，纸质的

例：Kim sold some pictures to get money to pay for all his paint brushes and paper and art lessons.

金姆卖了一些画来赚钱支付他所有的画笔、纸张和美术课的费用。

搭：paper over 掩盖，掩饰　on paper 以书面形式

32. loss [lɒs] *n.* 失去，丧失；亏损；死亡，去世

例：I don't want to travel with a driver because I feel a loss of privacy.

我不想和司机一起旅行，因为我觉得失去了隐私。

搭：at a loss 不知所措；困惑　cut your losses 趁早罢手；及时止损

派：losing *n.* 失败　lose *v.* 失去　lost *adj.* 失去的

33. request [rɪˈkwest] *n.&v.* 要求，请求

例：Now we cannot process your request, please wait for four work days.

现在我们无法处理您的请求，请等待四个工作日。

搭：at the request of 应……的邀请，应……的要求

34. resource [rɪˈsɔːs] *n.* 自然资源；资源　*v.* 向……提供资金（或设备）

例：Social media is not a reliable resource of news.

社交媒体不是可靠的新闻来源。

记：词根记忆 re 向后，往回 + source 资源→resource资源

35. ambition [æm'bɪʃn] *n.* 追求的目标，抱负；雄心，野心；干劲
　　　 v. 追求，有……野心

例：I have my own long-term plans and ambitions in that area.
　　在这个领域，我有自己的长期计划和抱负。

记：联想记忆 amb周围 + it走 + ion表示行为，状态，结果→走向周围，不拘于一方天地→ambition雄心

36. catalog ['kætəlɒg] *n.* 目录；登记 *v.* 登记；为……编目录

例：The catalog also included reviews of the masters, which I had to write down and research.
　　目录中还包括对大师的评论，我必须写下来并进行研究。

记：联想记忆 cata 向下，相反，离开 + log 说话→向下记下说过的话→catalog 目录，登记

37. decade ['dekeɪd] *n.* 十年，十年期

例：About a decade ago, he was working as a little clerk and, in his own words：miserable.
　　大约十年前，他还是个小职员，用他自己的话来说：很痛苦。

记：词根记忆 dec十 + ade表示某种行动的个人或集体→decade十年，十年期

38. lifestyle ['laɪfstaɪl] *n.* 业余爱好，嗜好

例：My home does not match my lifestyle.
　　我的家乡和我的生活方式不匹配。

39. voyage ['vɔɪɪdʒ] 　 *n.* （尤指坐船或飞往太空的）航行，旅行

例：We sincerely hope that you can have a good voyage.
　　我们真诚地希望你一路顺风。

记：联想记忆 voy路 + age表示抽象名词→voyage航行

搭：maiden voyage 初航

40. taxi ['tæksi] *n.* 出租车，计程车，的士 *v.* （飞机）缓慢滑行

例：It's not in the city center, so you may need to get a taxi from the station.
　　它不在市中心，所以你可能需要从车站打一辆出租车。

巩固练习

1. 扫码听写（根据所听音频写出本单元对应单词）

（1）_____	（2）_____	（3）_____	（4）_____
（5）_____	（6）_____	（7）_____	（8）_____
（9）_____	（10）_____	（11）_____	（12）_____
（13）_____	（14）_____	（15）_____	（16）_____
（17）_____	（18）_____	（19）_____	（20）_____
（21）_____	（22）_____	（23）_____	（24）_____
（25）_____	（26）_____	（27）_____	（28）_____
（29）_____	（30）_____	（31）_____	（32）_____
（33）_____	（34）_____	（35）_____	（36）_____
（37）_____	（38）_____	（39）_____	（40）_____

2. 实战演练（选出最符合句意的选项）

（1）It's a good way to combine _____ school with periods in mainstream schools.

　　（A）residential　　　　　（B）domestic

　　（C）living　　　　　　　（D）inhabited

（2）Words _____ on screen from time to time to explain the story.

　　（A）developed　　　　　（B）happened

　　（C）appeared　　　　　　（D）displayed

（3）A certain homogeneity is _____ as the demand of customers is going to become the same.

　　（A）casting　　　　　　　（B）spreading

　　（C）providing　　　　　　（D）offering

（4）The _____ may interrupt the shooting.

　　（A）waves　　　　　　　（B）sea

　　（C）shutter　　　　　　　（D）gift

（5）We conducted a _____ about people's experiences and opinions in the village.

　　（A）learning　　　　　　　（B）paper

　　（C）goods　　　　　　　　（D）survey

(6) Their population is declining, caused by climate change, habitat _____, and so on.

(A) lost   (B) loss

(C) disappear   (D) losing

(7) All passengers are _____ to visit the ship's office in order to collect a landing card.

(A) requested   (B) imposed

(C) offered   (D) believed

(8) She has an/a _____ to explore new ideas.

(A) idea   (B) development

(C) understanding   (D) ambition

(9) Any further delays will be announced during the _____ when you on the sea.

(A) ship   (B) boat

(C) voyage   (D) trip

(10) With so little rainfall, plants grow slowly and only flower on rare _____.

(A) moment   (B) chance

(C) times   (D) occasions

Day 16

小试牛刀

浏览本单元所有单词，在你已掌握的单词前面打√。

☐ wedding	☐ character	☐ envelope	☐ pleasure
☐ refugee	☐ vehicle	☐ recipe	☐ tent
☐ tradition	☐ contrast	☐ forecast	☐ pollution
☐ surface	☐ theater	☐ habitat	☐ wood
☐ surroundings	☐ stimulate	☐ apartment	☐ priority
☐ waste	☐ satisfy	☐ reflect	☐ size
☐ adventure	☐ dinosaur	☐ ingredient	☐ progress
☐ support	☐ cruise	☐ secret	☐ store
☐ argument	☐ distance	☐ passport	☐ specialise
☐ quality	☐ crash	☐ branch	☐ prize

词汇精讲

1. wedding [ˈwedɪŋ] *n.* 婚礼，结婚庆典

例：What **wedding** gifts can I give for her?

我要送她什么结婚礼物？

搭：wedding ceremony 结婚典礼

2. character [ˈkærəktə (r)] *n.* 性格，品质；特色，特征；人物，角色

例：We want you to build a story with strong **characters** and create a sense of drama.

我们希望你能够构建一个具有强烈人物形象的故事，并创造一种戏剧感。

搭：in character/out of character 符合（或不符合）某人的性格

派：characteristic *adj.* 独特的，典型的

3. envelope [ˈenvələʊp] *n.* 信封，封皮

例：The company is also responsible for the **envelope** and post.

该公司还负责信封和邮寄。

记：词根记忆 en在……里面 + vel包裹 + ope→里面包裹着东西→envelope信封

4. pleasure [ˈpleʒə (r)] *n.* 快乐，满足，欣慰 *adj.* 游乐的，非公务的 *v.* 从……中获得乐趣；（使）高兴

例：When you share one thing with others, the **pleasure** of social connection will take things up a notch.

当你和别人分享一件事时，社会联系的乐趣会把事情提升一个档次。

记：词根记忆 pleas（e）使高兴 + ure表示行为，结果→pleasure乐事，愉快

搭：at one's pleasure 根据某人的意愿；随意

派：pleasurable *adj.* 快乐的

5. refugee [ˌrefjuˈdʒiː] *n.* 难民，避难者

例：A group of hardworking former **refugees** started a new company in our city.

一群努力工作的前难民在我们的城市开办了一家新公司。

记：词根记忆 re 再，又 + fug 逃走，离开 + ee 人或物→从家乡逃走的人们→refugee 难民，避难者

搭：refugee camp 难民营；难民收容所

6. vehicle [ˈviːəkl] *n.* 交通工具，车辆

例：It can be easily transported on land in most types of **vehicles**.

它可以很容易地用大多数类型的车辆在陆地上运输。

搭：motor vehicle 汽车；机动车辆

7. recipe ['resəpi] *n.* 烹饪法，食谱；诀窍，秘诀

例：This picture shows a **recipe** of making exclusive sauce.

图为制作独家酱料的菜谱。

记：词根记忆 re 向后，往回 + cip 拿，抓住，获取 + e→向前人去拿他们做出的东西→recipe 食谱

搭：secret recipe 秘方；秘密配方

8. tent [tent] *n.* 帐篷

例：She doesn't like to sleep in a **tent**.

她不喜欢睡帐篷。

9. tradition [trə'dɪʃn] *n.* 传统，惯例

例：As with any other aesthetic **tradition**, the art of handwriting has a noble history.

与其他任何美学传统一样，书法艺术有一段崇高的历史。

记：词根记忆 tra跨越 + dit给予，予以 + ion表示物→某物由一代人给予另一代人→tradition传统，传说

搭：by tradition 照传统；根据口传

派：traditional *adj.* 传统的

10. contrast ['kɒntrɑːst] *n.* 差异，对比 *v.* 对比，对照

例：There is a huge **contrast** between the houses in the village and those in the city.

村里的房子和城里的房子形成了巨大的对比。

记：词根记忆 contra 反对，相反 + st 站，立→contrast 对比，对照

搭：in contrast 与此相反；比较起来 by contrast 相比之下；与之相比

11. forecast ['fɔːkɑːst] *v.* &*n.* 预测，预报

例：They were predicting storms and heavy rain but the **forecast** has really improved so we can go out in the afternoon.

他们预报说会有暴风和大雨，但是预报确实有所改善，所以我们下午就可以出去了。

记：词根记忆 fore 前面，预先 + cast 投，发射→预先发布的→forecast预测，预报

搭：weather forecast 天气预测，天气预报

12. pollution [pə'luːʃn] *n.* 污染；污染物

例：In this game, players have to solve not only air **pollution** but also other environmental problems.

在这个游戏中，玩家不仅要解决空气污染问题，还要解决其他环境问题。

记：词根记忆 pollut（e）污染 + ion表示行为，状态，结果→pollution污染

派：polluted *adj.* 受污染的 pollutant *n.* 污染物

13. surface ['sɜːfɪs] *n.* 表面；水面，地面；桌面，台面 *v.* 浮出水面；（信息、情感或问题）显露，暴露 *adj.* 表面上的，外表上的；表面的

例：The surface of the wood was pitted with holes made by insects.

那块木头的表面被昆虫蛀了一个个的洞。

记：词根记忆 sur 上 + fac 脸，面+ e→surface 表面

搭：on the surface 在表面上，外表上

派：surfaced *adj.* 成平面的；刨平的

14. theater ['θɪətə(r)] *n.* 电影院，戏院，剧场

例：Pass the station and then you will find the café is opposite the theater.

你过了车站就会发现咖啡馆在剧院对面。

记：联想记忆 theat- 看，观察 + er 表示物→在该地能看到很多影片→theater 电影院

搭：movie theater 电影院

15. habitat ['hæbɪtæt] *n.* （动植物的）生活环境，栖息地

例：Ultimately，these conservation attempts may prove futile amid the challenges of climate change，habitat loss，and surging human numbers.

最终，在气候变化、栖息地丧失和人类数量激增的挑战下，这些保护尝试可能会被证明是徒劳的。

记：联想记忆 habit 居住 + at 地方→有动植物居住的地方→habitat 栖息地

搭：habitat destruction 生境破坏；毁坏栖息地 habitat condition 居住条件

16. wood [wʊd] *n.* 木材，木料，木头 *adj.* 木制的 *v.* 收集木材

例：Rachel's house is made by old wood.

瑞秋的房子是用旧木头建造的。

搭：solid wood 实木 wood furniture 木制家具

17. surroundings [sə'raʊndɪŋz] *n.* 周围环境，周围事物

例：We were told that because this kind of animal had less contact with people there，we'd be able to watch them in natural surroundings.

我们被告知，因为这种动物与那里的人接触较少，所以我们可以在自然环境中观察它们。

18. stimulate ['stɪmjuleɪt] v. 促进，激发（某事物）；激发，鼓励

例：Manual work stimulates and uses parts of your brain that are dormant.
手工工作刺激和使用你大脑中处于休眠状态的部分。

记：词根记忆 stimul刺，刺激 + ate做，造成→stimulate促进，激发

派：stimulation n. 刺激，鼓励

19. apartment [əˈpɑːtmənt] n. 公寓套房；（总统等要人的）房间，套间

例：The apartment will be available for rent next Wednesday at 8 a.m.
这套公寓将在下星期三上午8点开始出租。

记：词根记忆 a远离，偏离 + part部分，分开 + ment具体的物→从楼房中分出来的房间→apartment公寓套房

20. priority [praɪˈɒrəti] n. 优先事项，最重要的事；优先，优先权，重点；<英>优先通行权 adj. 优先的

例：The priority is keeping to an exact safety when you go under water with your team.
当你和你的团队在水下时，最重要的是确保安全。

记：词根记忆 prior优先的 + ity……状态，性质→priority优先事项

搭：give priority to 优先考虑；认为优先

21. waste [weɪst] n. 浪费，滥用 v. 浪费，滥用；未能充分利用

例：This table shows the amount of waste that produced by five countries and districts.
这张表显示了五个国家和地区产生的废物量。

搭：waste disposal 废物处理　waste away 变消瘦；变衰弱

派：wastrel n. 废品；浪费者

22. satisfy [ˈsætɪsfaɪ] v. 使满意，使满足；满足（要求、需要等）；符合（规定、条件或标准）

例：Can you think what things mostly satisfy you when you speak another language?
当你说另一种语言时，你能想到什么最让你满意吗？

记：词根记忆 satis足够，饱足 + fy 动词后缀→satisfy使满意，使满足

搭：satisfy a need 满足需要；符合需求

派：satisfactory *adj.* 令人满意的，合适的

23. reflect [rɪ'flekt] *v.* 反射；反映

例：Maybe the animal can **reflect** the human behavior.

也许动物可以反映人类的行为。

搭：reflect upon 反思，考虑　reflect well, badly, etc. on sb./sth. 使给人以好的（坏的或其他）印象

派：reflection *n.* 映像，倒影

24. size [saɪz] *n.* 大小，尺寸　*v.* 依大小分类（或排列）；按一定大小制作

例：This magazine has same **size** as newspaper.

这本杂志和报纸一样大。

搭：size up 打量；估计；判断；评估

派：sizable *adj.* 相当大的，颇大的

25. adventure [əd'ventʃə (r)] *n.* 冒险（经历），奇遇　*v.* 冒险；大胆说出

例：My hard work makes these posts about exciting **adventures**.

我的辛勤劳作促成了这些记录令人兴奋的冒险的帖子。

记：词根记忆 ad朝向 + vent到，来 + ure表示行为，结果→到某地去→adventure 冒险

派：adventurous *adj.*爱冒险的

26. dinosaur ['daɪnəsɔː (r)] *n.* 恐龙；守旧落伍的人

例：Some **dinosaurs** have four legs，but in the earliest time they have two legs.

有些恐龙有四条腿，但在最早的时候它们有两条腿。

记：词根记忆 dino 害怕 + saur 蜥蜴→令人害怕的大蜥蜴→dinosaur 恐龙

27. ingredient [ɪn'griːdiənt] *n.* （食品的）成分，原料；要素，因素　*adj.* 构成组成部分的

例：Nothing is more complicated than preparing the **ingredients** for cooking.

没有比准备烹饪材料更复杂的了。

搭：food ingredient 食品配料成分

28. progress ['prəʊɡres] *n.&v.* 进步，进展；前进，行进

例：In recent years，scientists studying serious health problems have made significant **progress**.

近年来，研究严重健康问题的科学家取得了重大进展。

记：词根记忆 pro向前，在前 + gress走，步伐→一直向前走→progress进步，进展

搭：progress to do sth. 接着做（另一件事） in progress 在进行中

派：progression *n.* 前进

29. support [səˈpɔːt] *v.* 支持，拥护，鼓励；帮助，援助 *n.* 支持，拥护；帮助，援助；赞助

例：Students with health issues will be given support.

有健康问题的学生将得到支持。

记：词根记忆 sup自下而上 + port承担，承受→从下方托住承担重量→support支持

30. cruise [kruːz] *n.* 巡游，乘船游览 *v.* 乘船游览；以平稳的速度行驶

例：Lee is looking forward to travelling on a cruise ship.

李期待着乘坐游轮旅行。

搭：cruise ship 游轮，游艇

31. secret [ˈsiːkrət] *adj.* 秘密的，保密的 *n.* 秘密，内情

例：He is worried about that someone may discover his secret.

他担心有人会发现他的秘密。

记：词根记忆 se分开 + cret分离→区分开，并隐藏→secret秘密的，机密的

搭：in secret 秘密地；暗中

派：secrecy *n.* 保密 secretive *adj.* 保密的

32. store [stɔː(r)] *n.* 商店；仓库，储存处 *v.* 贮存，储藏

例：If all the food is stored properly, the cooks can leave.

如果所有食物都存储妥当，那厨师们就可以离开了。

搭：store away 贮存；储备；存放 store up 储备；囤积

派：storable *adj.* 可储存的；耐贮藏的 storer *n.* 存储器；仓库保管员

33. argument [ˈɑːɡjumənt] *n.* 争论，争吵；论据，理由

例：Communication is important when friends resolve argument with each other.

当朋友们解决彼此的争论时，沟通是很重要的。

记：词根记忆 argu(e) 争论 + ment 行为或结果→argument 争论，争吵

搭：argument against/for 反对/支持……的论证

派：arguably *adv.* 可论证地，按理 argue *v.* 争论，辩论

34. distance ['dɪstəns] *n.* 远处；疏远，隔阂；进展；距离 *v.* 疏远，远离 *adj.* 远距离的

例：The town has a short distance from the city.

这个小镇离城市很近。

记：词根记忆 di分离 + st站，立 + ance性质，状况→离得很远→distance距离

搭：at/from a distance 离一段距离　keep sb. at a distance 对……冷淡；同……疏远

派：distant *adj.* 遥远的

35. passport ['pɑːspɔːt] *n.* 护照；途径，手段

例：Staff will record the information of passport.

工作人员会记录护照信息。

记：联想记忆 pass 通过 + port 港口→通过港口去另一方的事物→passport 护照

36. specialize ['speʃəlaɪz] *vi.* 专门研究（或从事），专攻

例：The zoo vet specializes in giant pandas.

这位动物园兽医专治大熊猫。

记：词根记忆 special 特别的 + ize 动词后缀→specialize 专门研究

搭：specialize in 专门研究……

派：specialized *adj.* 专门的　specialty *n.* 专业　specialization *n.* 专业化

37. quality ['kwɒləti] *n.* 质量，品质 *adj.* 优质的，高质量的

例：They were dissatisfied with the quality of new system.

他们对新系统的质量不满意。

记：发音记忆 quality 夸了梯→指梯子的质量好→质量，品质

38. crash [kræʃ] *v.* 撞车，坠毁；猛撞 *n.* 撞车事故，失事；巨响，碰撞声 *adj.* 应急的，速成的

例：His friend was injured in an air crash.

他的朋友在一次飞机失事中受了伤。

搭：air crash 飞机失事；空难　car crash 车祸

39. branch [brɑːntʃ] *n.* 树枝，分枝；分支机构，分店 *v.* 分岔，岔开；出枝，发出新枝

例：I knew all those intricate branches were tangled up because the tree was so old.

我知道那些复杂的树枝都缠绕在一起了，因为这棵树太古老了。

搭：branch off 分叉；分岔；（在某处）改变方向　branch out 扩大范围；拓展领域

40. prize [praɪz] *n.* 奖品，奖项　*adj.* 可获奖的，优等的　*v.* 珍视，高度重视

例：If you win **prizes**，people will get to know your work.

如果你赢了奖，人们就会知道你的工作。

记：词根记忆 priz 价值，估价＋e→一件有价值的东西→prize 奖品，奖项

巩固练习

扫码听音频

1. 扫码听写（根据所听音频写出本单元对应单词）

(1) _____　(2) _____　(3) _____　(4) _____

(5) _____　(6) _____　(7) _____　(8) _____

(9) _____　(10) _____　(11) _____　(12) _____

(13) _____　(14) _____　(15) _____　(16) _____

(17) _____　(18) _____　(19) _____　(20) _____

(21) _____　(22) _____　(23) _____　(24) _____

(25) _____　(26) _____　(27) _____　(28) _____

(29) _____　(30) _____　(31) _____　(32) _____

(33) _____　(34) _____　(35) _____　(36) _____

(37) _____　(38) _____　(39) _____　(40) _____

2. 实战演练（选出最符合句意的选项）

(1) —So kind of you! Thank you for receiving our invitation.

　　—It's my _____.

　　(A) pleasure　　　　　　(B) pleasant

　　(C) pleased　　　　　　(D) please

(2) Drivers were not allowed to stay in their _____.

　　(A) lorries　　　　　　(B) vehicles

　　(C) trucks　　　　　　(D) cars

(3) She doesn't want discuss others out of _____.

　　(A) character　　　　　(B) appearance

　　(C) regard　　　　　　(D) respect

(4) To see wild animals in their natural _____ is always a wonderful experience.

　　(A) habitat　　　　　　(B) habitant

（C）extinction   （D）living

（5）They hope toys can ＿＿＿＿ children's intelligence and improve their emotion.

（A）stimulate   （B）reproduce

（C）duplicate   （D）simulate

（6）She think the environment can ＿＿＿＿ people's personality.

（A）relief   （B）remote

（C）inflect   （D）reflect

（7）You need an/a ＿＿＿＿ to new places.

（A）adventure   （B）experience

（C）sense   （D）feeling

（8）The school issues a ＿＿＿＿ report each term.

（A）progress   （B）pursuit

（C）move   （D）development

（9）The lion managed to run a ＿＿＿＿ of 150 kilometers while still carrying a camera.

（A）distance   （B）distant

（C）distinction   （D）distinct

（10）A ＿＿＿＿ is a group of shops or hotels all owned by the same company.

（A）branch   （B）chain

（C）row   （D）line

Section 3
拓展词汇

Day 17

小试牛刀

浏览本单元所有单词，在你已掌握的单词前面打√。

☐ guarantee	☐ decorate	☐ fashionable	☐ separate
☐ assume	☐ cancel	☐ bake	☐ divide
☐ considerable	☐ domestic	☐ relevant	☐ sufficient
☐ attach	☐ ancient	☐ anxious	☐ false
☐ highlight	☐ familiar	☐ distinctive	☐ economic
☐ disabled	☐ doubtful	☐ flexible	☐ handle
☐ aggressive	☐ nervous	☐ romantic	☐ bright
☐ exotic	☐ casual	☐ rough	☐ legal
☐ administrative	☐ original	☐ demonstrate	☐ potential
☐ annual	☐ climb	☐ reliable	☐ direct

1. guarantee [ˌɡærən'tiː] *v.&n.* 确保，保证；担保

例：If people want to guarantee a ticket to the conference，they should send the email to us.

如果有人想要参加会议的票，他们应该发电子邮件给我们。

记：词根记忆 guar保护 + an用于加强语气 + tee名词→guarantee保证，担保

搭：be guaranteed to do sth. 肯定会；必定会

2. decorate ['dekəreɪt] *v.* 装饰，装点

例：The restaurant has been decorated with that totally in her mind.

餐厅完全是按照她的想法装饰的。

记：词根记忆 dec合适 + or + ate做某事→采取适合的装饰→decorate装饰

搭：decorate with 以……来装饰

派：decoration *n.* 装饰 decorative *adj.* 装饰性的

3. fashionable ['fæʃnəbl] *adj.* 流行的，时髦的；有钱人光顾的

例：The mall has stylish and fashionable places to eat.

商场里有时尚的就餐场所。

记：词根记忆 fashion（时尚）+ able （形容词后缀）→ fashionable 流行的，时髦的

派：fashionably *adv.* 赶时髦的

4. separate ['sepəreɪt] *adj.* 单独的，分开的；不同的，不相关的 *v.* （使）分离；（把……）分成不同部分

例：You will be asked to fill out a separate form，which may result in a long delay.

您将被要求填写一份单独的表格，这可能会导致长时间的延迟。

记：词根记忆 se 分开 + par 平等，相等 + ate 做，造成→平等地把这些东西分开→separate单独的，分开的

搭：separate out 分辨；区分；区别

5. assume [ə'sjuːm] *v.* 假定，假设，认为；装出，做出

例：I'd assumed eating out costs quite a bit more but actually I think it is worthy.

我原以为在外面吃饭要花很多钱，但实际上我认为这是值得的。

记：词根记忆 as朝向 + sum拿，取 + e→拿自己认可的论点做假设→assume假设

派：assumed *adj.* 假定的；假设的 assumption *n.* 假定；设想

6. cancel ['kænsl] *v.* 取消（计划好的事情）；终止，废除　*n.* 取消，撤销

例：The sports event has been **cancelled** for the bad weather.

由于天气不好，运动会取消了。

搭：cancel out 抵消

派：cancelled *adj.* 被取消的　cancelling *v.* 取消

7. bake [beɪk] *v.* 炎热，灼热；烤，烘，焙　*n.* 烤制食品

例：Margaret likes to **bake** cakes for her children.

玛格丽特喜欢为她的孩子们烤蛋糕。

8. divide [dɪ'vaɪd] *v.* （使）分开，分散　*n.* 差异，分歧

例：They **divided** this task into several stages.

他们把这项任务分成几个阶段。

记：词根记忆 divid 分，分离 + e→divide 分开

搭：divide up 划分；分割　divide into 分成

9. considerable [kən'sɪdərəbl] *adj.* 相当大的，相当重要的

例：**Considerable** evidence exists to support global warming, but people do not have plan to deal with this problem.

有相当多的证据证实全球变暖，但是人们没有计划来解决这个问题。

派：considerably *adv.* 非常，相当多地　inconsiderable *adj.* 微小的，价值低的

10. domestic [də'mestɪk] *adj.* 国内的，本国的；家用的，家庭的　*n.* 家庭纠纷，家庭矛盾

例：I have qualification to treat **domestic** animals but I cannot treat zoo animals.

我有治疗家畜的资格，但我不能治疗动物园的动物。

记：联想记忆 dome（圆屋顶）+ st（缩写:街道）+ic（名词后缀）→街道上圆屋顶的房子里住着家里人→domestic 家庭的

搭：domestic market 国内市场

派：domestically *adv.* 家庭式地

11. relevant ['reləvənt] *adj.* 有关的，切题的

例：They sent **relevant** materials for joining this meeting.

他们送来了参加这次会议的有关材料。

记：词根记忆 re 再 + lev + ant→再举起→relevant 有关的

派：relevance *n.* 相关性　irrelevant *adj.* 不相干的

12. sufficient [səˈfɪʃnt] *adj.* 足够的，充足的

例：The machine does not have sufficient power to turn on.

这台机器没有足够的电力启动。

记：词根记忆 suffice使足够，足以 + ent ……的→sufficient足够的

派：insufficient *adj.* 不足的

13. attach [əˈtætʃ] *v.* 系上，贴上；连接；赋予；把……固定住

例：Oddly enough，it turns out that rooting for a less successful team actually makes supporters more attached to the team.

奇怪的是，事实证明，支持一支不太成功的球队实际上会让支持者更依恋球队。

记：词根记忆 at朝，向，去 + tach 钉子→用钉子固定住→attach把……固定住

派：attachment *n.* 附件 attaching *adj.* 附属的

14. ancient [ˈeɪnʃənt] *adj.* 古代的，远古的 *n.* （尤指埃及、希腊和罗马的）古代人

例：The newly unearthed relics provide us with more traces of the life of ancient people.

新出土的文物为我们提供了更多古代人生活的痕迹。

记：词根记忆 anci古老 + ent……的→ancient古老的

派：anciently *adv.* 在古代

15. anxious [ˈæŋkʃəs] *adj.* 焦虑的，担心的；渴望的，急切的；（时间或局势）紧张的，令人焦虑的

例：She felt anxious when she faced the newspaper editor.

她面对报纸编辑时感到焦虑。

记：发音记忆 anxious 俺可想死→焦虑导致的→焦虑的

搭：anxious for something 渴望某事

派：anxiously *adv.* 焦虑地

16. false [fɔːls] *adj.* 错误的，不真实的

例：Most people's false idea of him probably stems from their own prejudices.

大多数人对他的错误看法可能源于他们自己的偏见。

记：发音记忆 false否事→否定的事物→错误的

搭：by/under/on false pretences 靠欺诈手段；以虚假的借口 ring false 给人以虚假的印象

派：falsely *adv.* 错误地

17. highlight [ˈhaɪlaɪt] *v.* 突出，强调；挑染 *n.* 最好（或最精彩、最激动人心）的部分；挑染的头发；强光部分

例：Her mother helped him **highlight** the problem in his school assignment.
她的母亲帮助他强调了他在学校作业中出现的问题。

记：词根记忆 high高处；主要的 + light 光亮；点亮→highlight高光；突出

18. familiar [fəˈmɪliə (r)] *adj.* 熟悉的；常见的，普通的；非正式的，随和的

例：This novel includes some **familiar** scenes.
这部小说中有一些熟悉的场景。

记：词根记忆 family家庭 + ar（形容词词缀）→家人是熟悉的→familiar熟悉的

搭：get familiar with 熟悉；变得熟悉

派：familiarly *adv.* 不拘礼节地；亲密地

19. distinctive [dɪˈstɪŋktɪv] *adj.* 独特的，与众不同的

例：Everyone comments on my **distinctive** style.
每个人对我独特风格有所评论。

记：词根记忆 dis分开 + stinct刺 + ive形容词后缀→把刺分开→distinctive独特的

派：distinctively *adv.* 特殊地

20. economic [ˌiːkəˈnɒmɪk] *adj.* 经济的，经济学的

例：You have to solve social problems like mass migration and **economic** problems like the third world debt in the game.
你必须在游戏中解决像大规模移民这样的社会问题和像第三世界债务这样的经济问题。

记：词根记忆 econom(y)经济 + -ic ……的→economic经济的

派：economical *adj.* 经济实惠的

21. disabled [dɪsˈeɪbld] *adj.* 丧失能力的，有残疾的 *v.* 使丧失能力，使伤残

例：This place is for **disabled** driver parking.
这里是残疾人停车的地方。

记：词根记忆 disabl(e)使失去能力 + ed被……的，已……的→disabled使丧失能力

搭：disabled people 残疾人

派：disablement *n.* 残废；无资格

22. doubtful [ˈdaʊtfl] *adj.* 怀疑的，不确定的

例：She is **doubtful** that satellites will improve the internet coverage.

她对卫星能否提高互联网覆盖率表示怀疑。

记：词根记忆 doubt怀疑，疑惑 + -ful形容词后缀→doubtful怀疑的，不确定的

搭：be doubtful of/about 对……表示怀疑

派：doubtfully *adv.* 怀疑地

23. flexible [ˈfleksəbl] *adj.* 灵活的；柔韧的，易弯曲的

例：Tour guide must be **flexible** to deal with everything that may happen.

导游必须灵活应对可能发生的一切事情。

记：词根记忆 flex弯曲 + ible能……的→flexible能弯曲的，易弯曲的

搭：flexible working hours/patterns 弹性工作时间/模式

派：flexibility *n.* 灵活性

24. handle [ˈhændl] *v.* 拿；处理，应付 *n.* 把手，拉手

例：This airport has long history and **handles** more international flights than any other airport in the world.

这个机场历史悠久，应付的国际航班比世界上任何其他机场都多。

记：联想记忆 hand手 + le了→用手拿的东西是把手→handle处理，应付

搭：handle with 处理

派：handleability *n.* 可操作性　handleable *adj.* 可操作的　handled *adj.* 已处理的

25. aggressive [əˈgresɪv] *adj.* 好斗的，挑衅的；积极进取的

例：**Aggressive** behaviour in kitchen cannot make people work effectively.

厨房里的攻击性行为不能使人们有效地工作。

记：词根记忆 aggress攻击，侵略 + ive有……倾向的→aggressive侵略性的；好斗的

派：aggressively *adv.* 挑衅地　aggressiveness *n.* 攻击性

26. nervous [ˈnɜːvəs] *adj.* 神经紧张的，担忧的

例：The lack of communication with team members makes him **nervous**.

缺乏与团队成员的沟通使他感到紧张。

记：词根记忆 nerv(e)神经 + ous ……的→神经紧绷的→nervous神经紧张的，担忧的

派：nervously *adv.* 不安地　nervousness *n.* 紧张，不安

27. romantic [rəʊˈmæntɪk] *adj.* 浪漫的，有情调的；富有浪漫色彩的

例：The couple decided to see a romantic comedy movie.

这对夫妇决定去看爱情喜剧片。

记：词根记忆 roman(ce)浪漫 + tic ……的→romantic浪漫的

派：romantically *adv.* 浪漫地

28. bright [braɪt] *adj.* 明亮的；鲜艳的

例：When you try to sleep，there shouldn't be bright light in the room.

当你想睡觉的时候，房间里不应该有明亮的光线。

派：brightly *adv.* 明亮地　brightness *n.* 明亮

29. exotic [ɪgˈzɒtɪk] *adj.* 奇异的，异国风情的　*n.* 外来植物，外来动物

例：Traveling to those exotic places is part of my work.

去那些充满异国情调的地方旅行是我工作的一部分。

记：词根记忆 exo外部，外面 + tic ……的→外面的→exotic充满异国风情的

派：exotically *adv.* 外来地，奇异地

30. casual [ˈkæʒuəl] *adj.* 休闲的，便装的　*n.* 便服，便装

例：This kind of dress is casuals in 1920s' America.

这种衣服是20世纪20年代美国的休闲装。

派：casually *adv.* 随便地　casualty *n.* 意外事故；伤亡人员　casualness *n.* 偶然，漫不经心

31. rough [rʌf] *adj.* 粗糙的，不平的　*n.* 草稿，草图　*v.* 粗制，对……粗加工

例：The bowl isn't exactly beautiful，not straight and it has rough edges.

这个碗并不漂亮，不直，边缘粗糙。

搭：in the rough 未完成的；未加工的

派：roughness *n.* 粗糙

32. legal [ˈliːgl] *adj.* 法律允许的，合法的

例：He once worked in a legal firm，which closed down three years ago.

他曾在一家三年前倒闭的律师事务所工作。

记：词根记忆 leg 法律 + al ……的→legal 合法的

派：legally *adv.* 合法地

33. administrative [əd'mɪnɪstrətɪv] *adj.* 管理的，行政的

例：Linda would like to have an assistant to help her do the administrative work.
琳达想要一个助手帮她做行政工作。

派：administratively *adv.* 行政地，管理地

34. original [ə'rɪdʒənl] *adj.* 起初的，原先的　*n.* 原件，原稿

例：They called last night to change the appointment back to the original time.
他们昨晚打电话把预约时间改回原来的时间了。

记：词根记忆 origin起源 + al与……相关的→original原始的，最初的

搭：in the original 用原著的语言；未经翻译

35. demonstrate ['demənstreɪt] *v.* 证明；示范，演示

例：The architecture she designed demonstrates her own style.
她设计的建筑体现了她自己的风格。

记：词根记忆 de完全地 + monstr神的预兆，引申为指出，显示 + ate表示做→demonstrate表现，说明

36. potential [pə'tenʃ(ə)l] *adj.* 潜在的，可能的　*n.* （事物的）潜力，可能性

例：The potential of dance to bring people together is well known.
舞蹈将人们团结在一起的潜力是众所周知的。

记：词根记忆 potent强有力的 + ial表示有……性质的→potential可能的，潜在的

派：potentially *adv.* 可能地

37. annual ['ænjuəl] *adj.* 一年一度的；年度的　*n.* 一年生植物；年刊

例：We must dress up for the annual dinner.
我们必须盛装出席年度晚宴。

记：词根记忆 ann年，每年 + ual与……相关的→annual每年的，一年的

38. climb [klaɪm] *v.&n.* 攀登，攀爬

例：The view from the mountains is amazing if you don't mind climbing them.
如果你不介意爬上去的话，从山上看出去的景色真是太棒了。

记：联想记忆 c + limb →抓住 + 肢体/枝干/树枝→抓住树干树枝→攀登

搭：climb down （在辩论、争论中）认错；服输；改变意图

39. reliable [rɪˈlaɪəbl] *adj.* 可靠的，可信赖的　*n.* 可靠的人

例：Many modern electronic devices are more **reliable** than the mechanical devices of the past.

许多现代电子设备比过去的机械设备更可靠。

记：词根记忆 rel(y)依赖 + i + able可……的→reliable可信赖的

派：reliability *n.* 可靠性　reliably *adv.* 可靠地

40. direct [daɪˈrekt] *adj.* 径直的，笔直的　*v.* 指引，引导　*adv.* 径直地，直达地

例：Questions relating to course requirements should be **directed** to Dr. Geller by email.

有关课程要求的问题应通过电子邮件直接向盖勒博士进行询问。

巩固练习

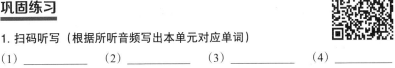

扫码听音频

1. 扫码听写（根据所听音频写出本单元对应单词）

(1) _____　(2) _____　(3) _____　(4) _____

(5) _____　(6) _____　(7) _____　(8) _____

(9) _____　(10) _____　(11) _____　(12) _____

(13) _____　(14) _____　(15) _____　(16) _____

(17) _____　(18) _____　(19) _____　(20) _____

(21) _____　(22) _____　(23) _____　(24) _____

(25) _____　(26) _____　(27) _____　(28) _____

(29) _____　(30) _____　(31) _____　(32) _____

(33) _____　(34) _____　(35) _____　(36) _____

(37) _____　(38) _____　(39) _____　(40) _____

2. 实战演练（选出最符合句意的选项）

(1) Many people _____ that all my work is sitting in front of the computer trying out new games.

　　(A) assume　　　　　　　(B) presume

　　(C) assure　　　　　　　(D) exclude

(2) The week was _____ up into weekdays and weekends.

　　(A) departed　　　　　　(B) divided

(C) taken (D) given

(3) This show will be successful because the presenter has _____ TV experience.

    (A) considerate (B) collective

    (C) considerable (D) sensible

(4) An outline of the event is _____.

    (A) associated (B) appealed

    (C) tied (D) attached

(5) He was _____ that the progress of the project is so quickly.

    (A) doubtful (B) good

    (C) wanted (D) uneasy

(6) You cannot do these _____ behavior in the classroom.

    (A) invasive (B) aggressive

    (C) predominant (D) stubborn

(7) Many students plan their _____ journey when they graduate.

    (A) foreign (B) exotic

    (C) royal (D) opposite

(8) By day, he wrote _____ contrasts, while by night he spent up to 8 hours painting.

    (A) legal (B) authority

    (C) equitable (D) legislative

(9) Secretary is not her _____ career choice.

    (A) actual (B) genuine

    (C) real (D) original

(10) Your job is to be persuasive, sound _____, and emphasize the value of the product.

    (A) reliable (B) rely

    (C) reliance (D) reliability

Day 18

扫码听音频

小试牛刀

浏览本单元所有单词，在你已掌握的单词前面打√。

☐ aesthetic	☐ assemble	☐ promote	☐ terrible
☐ wealthy	☐ private	☐ modify	☐ dirty
☐ investigate	☐ privileged	☐ affordable	☐ justify
☐ upload	☐ specific	☐ occupy	☐ sweet
☐ interrupt	☐ mention	☐ anticipate	☐ switch
☐ warn	☐ straight	☐ claim	☐ edible
☐ unpredictable	☐ combine	☐ apologize	☐ violent
☐ consist	☐ abandon	☐ damage	☐ shut
☐ anonymous	☐ calculate	☐ vulnerable	☐ ordinary
☐ estimate	☐ polite	☐ eminent	☐ cruel

词汇精讲

1. aesthetic [iːsˈθetɪk] *adj.* 审美的，美学的；美的，艺术的

  n. 美感，审美观；

例：More and more people around the world share their aesthetic aspirations on the same large social media platform.

世界各地越来越多的人在同一个大型社交媒体平台上分享他们的审美倾向。

记：词根记忆 aesthet感觉 + ic……的→感觉到的→aesthetic审美的

派：aestheticism *n.* 唯美主义

2. assemble [əˈsembl] *v.* （使）集合，（使）聚集；装配，组装

例：They can assemble in a short time when they stay in a small building.

当他们待在一个小建筑里时，他们可以在很短的时间内集合起来。

记：联想记忆 as(加强) + sembl(相似) + e→不断集合类似的东西→assemble 集合

搭：assemble line 装配线

3. promote [prəˈməʊt] *v.* 促进，提倡；升职，晋升

例：TV and social media may help me promote my restaurant.

电视和社交媒体可以帮助我推广我的餐厅。

记：词根记忆 pro向前，在前 + mot运动，移动 + e→promote提升

派：promotion *n.* 推广

4. terrible [ˈterəbl] *adj.* 糟糕的，令人感到可怕的

例：We are upset about the terrible oil spill on our beach.

我们对海滩上可怕的石油泄漏感到不安。

记：词根记忆 terr害怕(由词根ter演变而来) + ible形容词，可……的→能让人感到害怕的→terrible糟糕的，恐惧的

派：terribly *adv.* 非常地

5. wealthy [ˈwelθi] *adj.* 富有的，丰富的

例：He began to feel entitled to hang out with the wealthy.

他开始觉得自己有资格和富人混在一起。

记：词根记忆 wealth钱财 + y……的→wealthy富有的

6. private [ˈpraɪvət] *adj.* 私有的，自用的

例：You don't need to cook because you have private chef.

你不需要做饭，因为你有私人厨师。

记：词根记忆 priv个人，私人 + ate具有……的→private私有的

搭：in private 私下地；没外人在场

派：privately *adv.* 私下地

7. modify ['mɒdɪfaɪ] *v.* 修改，改进；修饰，限定

例：We took the bike into pieces and modified it.

我们把自行车拆开改装了一下。

记：联想记忆 mod(模型) + ify(改变)→modify 修改

派：modification *n.* 修改

8. dirty ['dɜːti] *adj.* 肮脏的；下流的 *v.* 弄脏，使变脏；变脏 *adv.* 很，非常；卑鄙地，不诚实地

例：The bus has a dirty condition inside.

公共汽车里面很脏。

记：词根记忆 dirt烂泥 + y(形容词后缀)→dirty肮脏的

搭：give sb. a dirty look 厌恶地瞪某人一眼 dirty word 脏话

9. investigate [ɪn'vestɪgeɪt] *v.* 侦察（某事）；调查（某人）；研究

例：The developers have already investigated the problem of the software.

开发人员已经调查了这个软件的问题。

记：联想记忆 invest(投资) + i(连接字母) + gate(大门)→投资应该从调查、研究入门

搭：investigate into 对……进行调查

派：investigation *n.* 调查

10. privileged ['prɪvəlɪdʒd] *adj.* 享有特权的；荣幸的 *v.* 特免，免除

例：I felt privileged to stand there.

我很荣幸站在这里。

搭：privileged position 特权地位

11. affordable [ə'fɔːdəbl] *adj.* 便宜的，付得起的

例：This new machine is easily affordable.

这种新机器很容易买得起。

记：词根记忆 afford支付 + able能→affordable支付得起

搭：affordable housing 经济适用房

12. justify ['dʒʌstɪfaɪ] *v.* 是……的正当理由；对……做出解释，为……辩解

例：He justified himself with the suffering he had experienced at the hands of others.

他以自己在别人手里所遭受的痛苦为自己辩护。

记：词根记忆 just法律，公正 + ify动词后缀→正义的行为→justify 辩解

派：justification *n.* 正当理由　justificatory *adj.* 辩护的

13. upload [ˌʌp'ləʊd] *v.* 上传，上载　*n.* 上载（或上传）的数据

例：I will try to upload some pictures soon so that we can continue the work.

我会尽快上传一些图片，以便我们继续工作。

记：词根记忆 up上 + load 装载→upload上传

14. specific [spə'sɪfɪk] *adj.* 明确的，具体的；特定的；特有的

例：His work is to design tour to specific people.

他的工作是为特定的人群设计旅游路线。

记：词根记忆 speci(es)种类 + fic使具有某种性质的→成为某一特定种类→specific特定的，特有的

派：specificity *n.* 独特性

15. occupy ['ɒkjupaɪ] *v.* 使用（房屋、建筑），居住；占据

例：Problems in life continue to occupy his mind for a long time.

生活中的问题长期占据着他的思想。

记：联想记忆 oc再次 + cupy抓→抓住地盘→占领

派：occupied *adj.* 被占领的

16. sweet [swiːt] *adj.* 含糖的，甜的

例：Jack likes sweet food more than savoury food.

比起咸味的食物，杰克更喜欢甜食。

搭：in your own sweet time/way 任凭自己的意愿

派：sweetly *adv.* 甜美的

17. interrupt [ˌɪntə'rʌpt] *v.* 打断，打扰；使暂停，使中断；阻断，遮挡

例：Isabel is used to be interrupted by clients and supplier.

伊莎贝尔习惯了被客户和供应商打断。

记：词根记忆 inter在……之间，相互 + rupt打破，破裂→打破之间的联系→interrupt打断

派：interruption *n.* 中断

18. mention ['menʃn] *v.* 提到，谈到；提名，推荐 *n.* 提及，说起

例：The writer mentions the old people gave advice for him to write this book.

作者提到老人给了他写这本书的建议。

记：词根记忆 ment头脑，智力 + ion行为，状态→在头脑智力都存在的情况下提出→mention提到

搭：not to mention 更不用说；且不说 make no mention of someone/something 只字未提……

19. anticipate [æn'tɪsɪpeɪt] *v.* 预期，预料；期望，盼望

例：The problem the young man anticipates in school show is that a big volume of music makes people hard to listen to each other.

这个年轻人在学校演出中预料到的问题是，大音量的音乐使人们难以倾听彼此的声音。

记：词根记忆 anti先前，在……之前 + cip拿，取 + ate做，造成→提前拿到消息→anticipate预料，期望

派：anticipatory *adj.* 预期的

20. switch [swɪtʃ] n. 开关，电闸 *v.* 打开，关闭；交换，调换

例：I wanted to ring you but your mobile phone was switched off.

我想给你打电话，但你的手机关机了。

搭：switch off/on 关闭/打开 switch over 转换；改变

21. warn [wɔːn] *v.* 提醒，使警惕；警告，告诫

例：I'd like to warn you he won't be able to join the party.

我要提醒你，他不能参加聚会了。

搭：warn off 警告……离开；告诫……停止做……

22. straight [streɪt] *adj.* 直的，笔直的 *adv.* 直线地，径直地

例：One of the advantages to shop here is that you can get your purchases straight away.

在这里购物的好处之一是你可以马上拿到买到的东西。

记：发音记忆 straight "似垂的" →垂直的，笔直的

搭：straight away 立即；马上

派：straightness *n.* 直度

23. claim [kleɪm] *v.&n.* 声称，断言；索取，索要

例：The supporters of this football team claim they make a lot of efforts for the match.

这支足球队的支持者声称他们为这场比赛付出了很多努力。

搭：claim sth. back 索回；要回

24. edible [ˈedəbl] *adj.* 可食用的 *n.* 食物

例：An edible insect vaccine was developed from a kind of moth.

从一种飞蛾中研制出了一种可食用的昆虫疫苗。

记：词根记忆 ed吃 + ible能……的→edible可食用的

25. unpredictable [ˌʌnprɪˈdɪktəbl] *adj.* 无法预测的，不定的 *n.* 不可预言的事

例：These people behave in an unpredictable way.

这些人的行为难以捉摸。

26. combine [kəmˈbaɪn] *v.* (使)结合，组合 *n.* 联盟，联合体；联合收割机

例：It's hard to combine being a painter and a lawyer.

画家和律师的身份很难兼得。

记：词根记忆 com同，一起 + bin个 + e→两个在一起的→combine组合，结合

搭：join/combine forces (with sb.) (同……)联合；(与………)合作

派：combination *n.* 结合(体)；联合(体)；混合

27. apologize [əˈpɒlədʒaɪz] *v.* 道歉，谢罪

例：I want to apologize to you for my mistake.

我想为我的错误向你道歉。

记：词根记忆 apology道歉 + ise动词后缀→apologize道歉，谢罪

28. violent [ˈvaɪələnt] *adj.* 暴力的；(人)有暴力倾向的；含暴力行为的；剧烈的

例：No research can show that violent crimes are linked to computer game.

没有研究表明暴力犯罪与电脑游戏有关。

记：词根记忆 viol暴力，力量 + ent……的→violent暴力的

派：violently *adv.* 猛烈地

29. consist [kən'sɪst] *v.* 由……组成，由……构成

例：Will much home-made food **consist** of even more fast food in the future?

将来会有更多的家庭自制食品由快餐组成吗？

搭：consist of 由……构成　consist in 在于；存在于　consist with 符合；与……一致

30. abandon [ə'bændən] *v.* 抛弃，遗弃　*n.* 放任，放纵

例：Professor **abandoned** what he was planning to say, and let the student take over for a while.

教授放弃了他本来打算讲的话，让那个学生替他讲一会儿。

记：词根记忆 a没有，不能 + ban宣布 + don给→不再宣布的事情→abandon抛弃；中止

搭：with abandon 恣意地，放纵地

31. damage ['dæmɪdʒ] *n.* （有形的）损坏，损失；损害，伤害；损害赔偿金；费用，代价　*v.* 损坏，损害；对……造成坏影响

例：One point is that travelling **damages** the environment.

一个观点是旅游破坏环境。

记：联想记忆 dam大门 + age年纪 →上年岁的大门容易被破坏→damage破坏

搭：damage caused by/to sth. 由……引起的/对……的损害

派：damaging *adj.* 有破坏性的，损害的

32. shut [ʃʌt] *v.* 关闭，合上　*adj.* 关闭的，关上的　*n.* 关闭

例：She usually **shuts** the door away and thinks for a few minutes in the morning.

她通常在早上关上门，思考几分钟。

搭：shut down 倒闭，停业　shut off 关闭　shut up （使）住口；（使）闭嘴

33. anonymous [ə'nɒnɪməs] *adj.* 匿名的，不知名的；不记名的，不具名的

例：I can write something about this **anonymous** reader.

我可以写点关于这位匿名读者的事。

记：词根记忆 an否定 + onym名字 + ous ……的→anonymous匿名的

派：anonymously *adv.* 化名地　anonymity *n.* 匿名

34. calculate ['kælkjuleɪt] *v.* 计算，核算；预测，推测

例：A scientist has **calculated** that this car was as heavy as an African elephant.

一位科学家计算出这辆车和一头非洲象一样重。

记：词根记忆 calc石头 + ul + ate表示做→以石头计数→calculate计算

35. vulnerable ['vʌlnərəbl] *adj.* 脆弱的，易受伤的；易受攻击的，易受伤害的

例：Sensitive people are often more **vulnerable**.

敏感的人往往更容易受到伤害。

记：词根记忆 vulner伤害 + able充满……的，招致……→容易伤痕累累→vulnerable脆弱的

派：invulnerable *adj.* 无懈可击的

36. ordinary ['ɔːdnri] *adj.* 普通的，平常的　*n.* 常见的人（或事物）

例：**Ordinary** women in Africa and south-east Asia do not buy expensive creams for their skin.

非洲和东南亚的普通女性不会为了皮肤购买昂贵的护肤霜。

搭：out of the ordinary 不寻常

派：ordinariness *n.* 平凡性

37. estimate ['estɪmət] *v.* 估计；判断，评价　*n.* 估计，估价；估价单；看法，判断

例：It was **estimated** that their patrons may lose over 100,000 balls per year to the surrounding environment when they play Golf.

据估计，他们的顾客在打高尔夫球时，每年可能会向周围环境损失超过10万个球。

记：词根记忆 estim评判价值 + ate表示做→estimate估计，估算；评价

搭：estimate for 为……估价

派：estimated *adj.* 估计的

38. polite [pə'laɪt] *adj.* 有礼貌的，客气的

例：It's important to be **polite** to other people.

对别人礼貌是很重要的。

派：politely *adv.* 礼貌地　politeness *n.* 礼貌

39. eminent ['emɪnənt] *adj.* 卓越的，出众的；突出的，明显的

例：**Eminent** scientists came to the conclusion that this monkey could understand human speech and do arithmetic.

知名科学家得出结论，这只猴子能听懂人类的语言，还能做算术。

记：词根记忆 e向外，离开 + min伸出，突出 + ent……的→向外突出的→eminent

出众的

40. cruel [ˈkruːəl] *adj.* 残酷的，残忍的；引起痛苦的

例：Zoos may show people's cruel attitude to wild animals.

动物园可能展示了人们对野生动物的残酷态度。

派：cruelly *adv.* 残忍的

扫码听音频

巩固练习

1. 扫码听写（根据所听音频写出本单元对应单词）

(1) _____ (2) _____ (3) _____ (4) _____

(5) _____ (6) _____ (7) _____ (8) _____

(9) _____ (10) _____ (11) _____ (12) _____

(13) _____ (14) _____ (15) _____ (16) _____

(17) _____ (18) _____ (19) _____ (20) _____

(21) _____ (22) _____ (23) _____ (24) _____

(25) _____ (26) _____ (27) _____ (28) _____

(29) _____ (30) _____ (31) _____ (32) _____

(33) _____ (34) _____ (35) _____ (36) _____

(37) _____ (38) _____ (39) _____ (40) _____

2. 实战演练（选出最符合句意的选项）

(1) Many people actively support or _____ the charity.

    (A) compile   (B) promote

    (C) complicate   (D) rise

(2) He began to _____ this material by changing their colour.

    (A) modify   (B) change

    (C) alter   (D) adjust

(3) Food in this menu for me is _____.

    (A) affordable   (B) affirmative

    (C) reachable   (D) approachable

(4) Please _____ my passage on this website.

    (A) load   (B) participate

    (C) upload   (D) uplight

(5) Finding the owner of the lost keys was more time-consuming than he _____.

    (A) anticipated   (B) eradicated

    (C) predicted   (D) corroborated

(6) Health specialists _____ that around the world people's eating habits are changing.

    (A) pose   (B) clam

    (C) claim   (D) shout

(7) Each year, thousands of people _____ together for the beautiful moon in that time.

    (A) cooperate   (B) undertake

    (C) participate   (D) combine

(8) The principle can be slightly _____ for her words.

    (A) abandoned   (B) avoided

    (C) explained   (D) intended

(9) The safeguard in the game is _____ today.

    (A) harmful   (B) vulnerable

    (C) numerous   (D) difficult

(10) You will increase your appreciation of pieces of art and their creators, and soon be able to _____ the difference among these artists.

    (A) expect   (B) anticipate

    (C) foresee   (D) measure

Day 19

小试牛刀

浏览本单元所有单词，在你已掌握的单词前面打√。

☐ government	☐ competitor	☐ military	☐ sensible
☐ oblige	☐ obsess	☐ district	☐ solid
☐ conclusion	☐ awareness	☐ feedback	☐ smooth
☐ frozen	☐ concept	☐ drama	☐ ban
☐ entertainment	☐ identical	☐ extinction	☐ dumpling
☐ mixed	☐ gentle	☐ neutral	☐ field
☐ congratulation	☐ inflatable	☐ remarkable	☐ addition
☐ bargain	☐ guilty	☐ element	☐ severe
☐ appreciation	☐ certificate	☐ generation	☐ possess
☐ agency	☐ decline	☐ launch	☐ reject

词汇精讲

1. government [ˈɡʌvənmənt] *n.* 政府，内阁；政体，国家体制

例：You can see the announcement on your local **government** website.

你可以在当地政府网站上看到这个公告。

记：词根记忆 govern统治 + ment名词词缀→government政府

2. competitor [kəmˈpetɪtə(r)] *n.* 竞争者，对手；选手，参赛者

例：The number of **competitors** will decrease this year.

今年竞争对手的数量将会减少。

记：词根记忆 compet(e)竞争 + itor人→competitor竞争者

3. military [ˈmɪlətri] *adj.* 军事的，军队的　*n.* 军人，军方

例：**Military** and rescue organizations are using the new equipment to quickly access hard to reach locations.

军方和救援组织正在使用新设备快速进入难以到达的地点。

记：词根记忆 milit兵 + ary……的→military军事的

4. sensible [ˈsensəbl] *adj.* 理智的，合理的；能感觉到的

例：Buying something you need is a more **sensible** choice.

买你需要的东西是一个更明智的选择。

记：词根记忆 sens(e)感觉 + ible能……的→sensible感觉到的

派：sensibly *adv.* 明显地

5. oblige [əˈblaɪdʒ] *v.* 迫使，责成；施恩惠于，帮……的忙

例：He was **obliged** to do as other people in society.

他必须像社会上的其他人那样做。

记：词根记忆 ob加强 + lig捆绑 + e→加强捆绑束缚→oblige迫使

6. obsess [əbˈses] *v.* 使着迷；使心神不宁；挂牵，念念不忘

例：They were **obsessed** by the superficial sense of history so they used this old-fashioned style of interior design.

他们痴迷于肤浅的历史感，所以他们采用了这种老式的室内设计风格。

派：obsessively *adv.* 使人着迷地　obsession *n.* 困扰

7. district [ˈdɪstrɪkt] *n.* 地区，区域；行政区，辖区

例：There are many young people working in the central business **district**.

有许多年轻人在中央商务区工作。

记：联想记忆 di(分开) + strict(严格)→分开严格管理，各管各的→district行政区

8. solid [ˈsɒlɪd] *adj.* 坚硬的；固体的，固态；结实的，牢固的

例：The company provided the solid core for the flexibility and durability of the machine.

该公司为机器的灵活性和耐用性提供了坚实的核心。

派：solidate *v.* 加固

9. conclusion [kənˈkluːʒn] *n.* 结论，推论；结局，结尾；缔结，商定

例：Her conclusion about separate education for the deaf was proved to be wrong.

她关于聋人分开接受教育的结论被证明是错误的。

记：联想记忆 con(共同) + clude(关闭) + ion→大家关闭讨论→conclusion结论

搭：in conclusion 总而言之

派：conclusive *adj.* 结论性的

10. awareness [əˈweənəs] *n.* 认识，意识；感悟能力

例：This game aims to raise the political and social awareness of gamers in developing countries.

这款游戏旨在提高发展中国家玩家的政治和社会意识。

11. feedback [ˈfiːdbæk] *n.* 反馈意见

例：After the interview，he got really positive feedback.

面试结束后，他得到了非常积极的反馈。

记：联想记忆 feed喂 + back回原处；后的→将后面的结果喂给收到的人→feedback 反馈意见

12. smooth [smuːð] *adj.* 光滑的，平坦的，平整的；顺利的，无困难的

例：The top priority is smooth operation of automatic equipment.

自动设备的顺利运行是重中之重。

记：发音记忆 smooth似慕斯→像慕斯一样光滑→smooth光滑的，平整的

搭：smooth sth. away/out 消除　smooth sth. over 缓和；调解；斡旋

派：smoothness *n.* 平滑，平稳　smoothly *adv.* 流畅地

13. frozen [ˈfrəʊzn] *adj.* 结冰的，冻硬的

例：They could hunt on the frozen ice.

它们可以在结冰的冰面上捕猎。

14. concept [ˈkɒnsept] *n.* 概念，观念　*adj.* （围绕）某一主题的；为表达一种想法而创造的

例：The **concept** of "blues" is hard to describe.
"忧郁"的概念很难描述。

记：词根记忆 con表强调 + cep拿，取 + t→最初指接住，握住，后指萌生的想法
→concept概念

派：conception *n.* 概念，观念

15. drama [ˈdrɑːmə] *n.* 剧本，戏剧；戏剧研究

例：I was playing a famous doctor in that TV **drama** at the moment.
那时我正在那部电视剧中扮演一位著名的医生。

搭：make a drama out of sth. 小题大做；大惊小怪

派：dramatic *adj.* 戏剧性的

16. ban [bæn] *n.* 禁止，禁令；逐出令

例：Some people are happy with the traffic **ban** in the city centre.
有些人对市中心的交通禁令很满意。

派：banned *adj.* 被禁的，被取缔的

17. entertainment [ˌentəˈteɪnmənt] *n.* 娱乐，娱乐表演；招待，款待

例：The home **entertainment** is improved nowadays.
现在家庭娱乐得到了改善。

记：词根记忆 entertain 给……娱乐 + ment 行为或结果→entertainment 娱乐

18. identical [aɪˈdentɪkl] *adj.* 完全相同的；同一的

例：The tool he used is **identical** to the ones used by medieval scribes.
他使用的工具和中世纪抄写员使用的工具一模一样。

记：词根记忆 ident相同 + ical与……有关的→identical同一的，完全相同的

搭：be identical with 与……相同

派：identically *adv.* 相同地

19. extinction [ɪkˈstɪŋkʃn] *n.* 灭绝，消亡；（债务的）偿清；消光

例：It's important to provide breeding programmes for animals that are on the verge of **extinction**.
为濒临灭绝的动物提供繁殖计划很重要。

记：词根记忆 extinct灭绝的 + ion表示行为→extinction消失，灭绝

20. dumpling [ˈdʌmplɪŋ] *n.* 汤团，饺子；水果布丁，水果馅点心

例：The most popular class is making dumplings.

最受欢迎的课程是包饺子。

21. mixed [mɪkst] *adj.* （感情）矛盾的，复杂的　*v.* （使）混合，掺和

例：The weather looks mixed tomorrow，with sunshine in at least some parts of the country.

明天的天气看起来好坏参半，至少这个国家的部分地区会有阳光。

搭：mixed up 混淆不清的

22. gentle [ˈdʒentl] *adj.* 文静的，温柔的　*v.* 使（或变）温柔，（使）平静；使驯服

例：After a year，she told me the whole story in a gentle way，and I realised it was my fault.

一年后，她温和地告诉了我整个故事，我意识到这是我的错。

记：词根记忆 gen出身 + tle→出身好的→gentle和蔼的；温和的

派：gently *adv.* 温和地

23. neutral [ˈnjuːtrəl] *adj.* 中立的，不偏不倚的　*n.* 中立者，中立国

例：I'm more inclined to stand in a neutral place to avoid any kind of distraction.

我更倾向于站在中间的地方，以避免任何分心。

记：词根记忆 neutr 中间 + al ……的→neutral 中立的

搭：on neutral ground/territory 在中立地区；在第三方地区

派：neutrality *n.* 中立

24. field [fiːld] *n.* 田地，田野；战场；现场，实地　*v.* 处理，回应

例：I'm going to play basketball with Tony on the field behind the school，and will you join us?

我打算和托尼在学校后面的操场上打篮球，你和我们一起去吗？

搭：leave the field clear for sb. 为……的胜利铺平道路

派：fielding *n.* 守备

25. congratulation [kənˌɡrætʃuˈleɪʃn] *n.* 恭喜，祝贺；恭贺，贺辞

例：Congratulation on your promotion!

祝贺你升职！

记：词根记忆 congratulat（e）祝贺 + ion 行为，状态→congratulation 祝贺

26. inflatable [ɪnˈfleɪtəbl] *adj.* 膨胀的，可充气的；得意的

例：This inflatable boat is the first commercial amphibious vessel.

这艘充气船是第一艘商用两栖船。

27. remarkable [rɪˈmɑːkəbl] *adj.* 引人注目的，非凡的

例：This system they invented is remarkable for a few reasons.

他们发明的这个系统之所以引人注目是有几个原因的。

记：联想记忆 remark说 + able可……的→可说的有很多→remarkable引人注目的，非凡的

派：remarkably *adv.* 非常，极为

28. addition [əˈdɪʃn] *n.* 增加物，新增人员；增加；加法

例：In addition，the experiments may help to advance medicine.

此外，这些实验可能有助于医学的进步。

记：词根记忆 add添加 + it + ion表示行为，行为的结果→addition添加；增加物

搭：in addition （to sb./sth.）除……以外（还）

派：additional *adj.* 附加的

29. bargain [ˈbɑːgən] *n.* 便宜货，减价品；协议，交易 *v.* 讨价还价，谈判

例：She kept telling me what a bargain it was.

她一直在告诉我这是多么划算。

记：联想记忆 bar酒吧 + gain得到→在酒吧里讨价还价得到了便宜货→bargain便宜货

搭：bargain for 讨价还价 strike a bargain/deal 达成（对双方都有利的）协议

30. guilty [ˈgɪlti] *adj.* 内疚的，羞愧的；有罪的，有过失的

例：He felt guilty about wasting time.

他对浪费时间感到内疚。

派：guiltily *adv.* 内疚地

31. element [ˈelɪmənt] *n.* 基本部分，要素；元素；有点，少量

例：We should focus on what elements students may focus on more.

我们应该关注学生可能更关注的要素。

搭：in your element 如鱼得水；得心应手

派：elementary *adj.* 基本的；初级的

32. severe [sɪ'vɪə(r)] *adj.* 十分严重的，极为恶劣的；艰巨的，严峻的

例：Dr. Joseph has a severe penalty for plagiarism.

约瑟夫博士因剽窃受到严厉处罚。

派：severely *adv.* 严重地　severity *n.* 严重

33. appreciation [əˌpriːʃi'eɪʃn] *n.* 欣赏，鉴赏；感激，感谢；理解，领会

例：The course may deepen your appreciation of art.

这门课可以加深你对艺术的欣赏。

记：词根记忆 appreciat（e）欣赏 + ion表示行为，结果→appreciation欣赏

34. certificate [sə'tɪfɪkət] *n.* 证明，证书　*v.* 发证书给……，用证书证明

例：International applicants need English translations of certificates from their home country.

国际申请者需要其本国证书的英文翻译件。

记：词根记忆 certif(y)证明，证实 + ic + ate名词词缀→certificate证明；合格证书

35. generation [ˌdʒenə'reɪʃn] *n.* 一代

例：They are three generations living in one village.

他们三代人住在一个村子里。

记：词根记忆 gener出生，产生；种族 + ation行为，过程，状态，结果→generation产生；一代

36. possess [pə'zes] *v.* 拥有，持有

例：You ought to possess self-knowledge.

你应该有自知之明。

记：联想记忆 poss力量 + sess停留→有力量（把东西）留下来→possess拥有，持有

派：possession *n.* 拥有

37. agency ['eɪdʒənsi] *n.* 代理行，经销处；政府专门机构，政府内的局，部，处

例：I register with an accommodation agency by the Internet.

我通过互联网在一家住宿中介登记。

搭：through the agency of 由于……的作用

38. decline [dɪˈklaɪn] *v.* 下降，衰退；拒绝，谢绝　*n.* 减少，衰退

例：There is a decline in people's interest of DIY.

人们对DIY的兴趣下降了。

记：词根记忆 de 从，分离，向下 + clin 倾斜，弯曲 + e→向下倾斜即下降→decline 下降；减少

搭：on the decline 在走下坡路

39. launch [lɔːntʃ] *v.* 发动，发起；上市，发行　*n.* （航天器的）发射；（产品的）上市；（事件的）发起

例：This kind of product was launched under a complicate situation.

这种产品是在复杂的形势下推出的。

搭：launch into 积极投入；猛烈展开

40. reject [rɪˈdʒekt] *v.* 拒绝，否决　*n.* 次品，废品

例：He rejected to use simple material to create his art work.

他拒绝使用简单的材料来创作他的艺术作品。

记：联想记忆 re 相对，相反 + ject 投掷，扔→向相反方扔去→reject 拒绝

派：rejection *n.* 拒绝

扫码听音频

巩固练习

1. 扫码听写（根据所听音频写出本单元对应单词）

(1) _____　(2) _____　(3) _____　(4) _____

(5) _____　(6) _____　(7) _____　(8) _____

(9) _____　(10) _____　(11) _____　(12) _____

(13) _____　(14) _____　(15) _____　(16) _____

(17) _____　(18) _____　(19) _____　(20) _____

(21) _____　(22) _____　(23) _____　(24) _____

(25) _____　(26) _____　(27) _____　(28) _____

(29) _____　(30) _____　(31) _____　(32) _____

(33) _____　(34) _____　(35) _____　(36) _____

(37) _____　(38) _____　(39) _____　(40) _____

2. 实战演练（选出最符合句意的选项）

(1) It's not _____ to do it yourself.

    (A) sensible   (B) aware

    (C) conscious   (D) reasonable

(2) You feel _____ to get value for money, however, that's measured.

    (A) compelled   (B) obliged

    (C) thanked   (D) extended

(3) Advertisements are required not to give a misleading _____.

    (A) effect   (B) impression

    (C) awareness   (D) interpretation

(4) This antique can also provide new _____ into how people in ancient cultures lived.

    (A) concepts   (B) insights

    (C) perceptions   (D) judgements

(5) What I earn is _____ to about 500 dollars a month.

    (A) equivalent   (B) identical

    (C) matching   (D) corresponding

(6) He wants to convey the necessary information in a _____ manner.

    (A) positive   (B) negative

    (C) neutral   (D) disinterested

(7) They use the _____ boat to travel in the sea.

    (A) inflammable   (B) inflammatory

    (C) inflated   (D) inflatable

(8) With this kind of _____, this language became cool for young people.

    (A) element   (B) ornament

    (C) essence   (D) point

(9) Insects do not _____ antibodies.

    (A) possession   (B) own

    (C) possess   (D) tangle

(10) This company has _____ just last year.

    (A) launched   (B) appeared

    (C) happened   (D) pushed

Day 20

小试牛刀

浏览本单元所有单词，在你已掌握的单词前面打√。

☐ playground	☐ classmate	☐ overview	☐ grammar
☐ scratch	☐ spring	☐ analysis	☐ key
☐ vocabulary	☐ captain	☐ package	☐ reception
☐ channel	☐ judge	☐ picnic	☐ seal
☐ hometown	☐ measure	☐ participant	☐ reference
☐ patient	☐ refund	☐ balcony	☐ reply
☐ merchandise	☐ interior	☐ sentence	☐ chemical
☐ signal	☐ ground	☐ barrier	☐ video
☐ invitation	☐ workshop	☐ aspiration	☐ charity
☐ silence	☐ mission	☐ belief	☐ taste

词汇精讲

1. playground [ˈpleɪɡraʊnd] *n.* 操场，游乐场；（某一群体的）游憩胜地，度假场所

例：There is a children's playground, which is just opened.

这里有一个刚刚开业的儿童游乐场。

记：联想记忆 play玩 + ground大地→能够游乐的场所→playground操场，游乐场

2. classmate [ˈklɑːsmeɪt] *n.* 同班同学

例：It's important to discuss with your classmates when you do your school assignment.

当你做作业的时候和你的同学讨论是很重要的。

3. overview [ˈəʊvəvjuː] *n.* 概述，综述

例：Now zoo keepers need to get an overview before they are responsible for a particular section.

现在，动物园管理员在负责某一特定区域之前需要对其进行全面了解。

4. grammar [ˈɡræmə (r)] *n.* 语法，文法

例：He created a language with simple grammar.

他创造了一种语法简单的语言。

记：词根记忆 gram写，画 + m + ar与……有关的→与写有关的，即与文字有关的→grammar语法

5. scratch [skrætʃ] *v.*（用指甲）挠，轻抓；抓破，划破；划出，刮出 *n.* 划痕，划伤 *adj.* 仓促拼凑的，匆匆组成的；碰巧的；打草稿用的

例：He would build complete bicycles from scratch.

他会从零开始组装完整的自行车。

搭：scratch about/around (for sth.)（尤指艰难地）搜寻，查寻，查找 scratch sth. out 画掉，勾掉，删除

6. spring [sprɪŋ] *n.* 春天，春季；泉，泉水 *v.* 跳，跃；突然弹开，突然移动

例：This castle is just open in spring, summer and autumn.

这座城堡只在春、夏、秋开放。

搭：spring up 突然出现

7. analysis [əˈnæləsɪs] *n.* 分析；化验分析；心理分析

例：While she was studying, she also worked part time for a market analysis company.

在学习期间，她还在一家市场分析公司兼职。

记：**联想记忆** ana向上，遍及 + lysis分解，切开→将整篇文章分开解析→analysis 分析

搭：in the final/last analysis 归根结底；总之

8. key [kiː] *n.* 钥匙；关键，要诀　*v.* 键入；成为（获胜）的关键 *adj.* 关键的，主要的

例：I've been looking for my keys everywhere.

我到处找我的钥匙。

搭：key in 用键盘输入　keep sth./put sth./be under lock and key 把……安全地锁起来；在押；被囚禁

9. vocabulary [vəˈkæbjələri] *n.* 词汇；（某个学科的）专业词汇，术语

例：Josh has easy books on grammar and vocabulary.

乔希有一些简单的语法和词汇方面的书。

记：**联想记忆** voc说 + abul + ary构成抽象名词→组织成语句的单元→vocabulary 词汇

搭：technical vocabulary 术语词汇

10. captain [ˈkæptɪn] *n.* 队长，首领；上尉，上校；船长，机长 *v.* 率队，指挥

例：Actually I wanted to throw whales a ball, but the captain said that only dolphins play with balls.

其实我想扔给鲸鱼一个球，但是船长说只有海豚才玩球。

记：**联想记忆** capt拿，抓，握住 + ain 表人→掌握一群人→captain首领

11. package [ˈpækɪdʒ] *n.* 包裹　*v.* 把……打包，把……装箱

例：We'll ship your package today and it'll be with you next Monday.

我们今天会把您的包裹寄出去，下周一就会送到您那里。

记：**词根记忆** pack包裹 + age表行为→package把……打包

12. reception [rɪ'sepʃn] *n.* 接待处，服务台

例：All visitors must report to reception on arrival.

所有访客到达时必须到接待处报到。

13. channel ['tʃænl] *n.* 频道，电视频道；管道，通道，航道 *v.* 引导，把……用于；输送，传送

例：They want comments from audience of particular TV channels or radio stations.

他们希望得到特定电视频道或广播电台观众的评论。

14. judge [dʒʌdʒ] *n.* 法官，审判官 *v.* 判断，认为；裁判，评判

例：She believes these judges are fair.

她相信这些法官是公正的。

记：词根记忆 judg判断 + e→judge审判，判官

派：judgement *n.* 判定

15. picnic ['pɪknɪk] *n.* 野餐，野餐活动

例：No picnics allowed in the park.

公园里不准野餐。

派：picnicker *n.* 野餐者

16. seal [si:l] *n.* 印章，图章；海豹 *v.* 封上（信封）；密封（容器）

例：When you get off the car, it is just like getting out of a sealed box.

当你下车的时候，就像从一个密封的盒子里出来一样。

搭：seal in 保留；保存 seal up 封闭；密封 seal off 封闭，隔离

17. hometown ['həʊmtaʊn] *n.* 家乡，故乡

例：What aspect do you like about your hometown?

你喜欢你家乡的哪一方面？

记：联想记忆 home 家 + town 镇→家乡是座小镇→hometown家乡

18. measure ['meʒə(r)] *n.* 措施，办法；适量，适度；判断，衡量 *v.* 测量；估量，判定

例：We measure how much stress fans experience when they watching matches.

我们衡量球迷在观看比赛时所承受的压力。

记：词根记忆 meas 计量，测量 + ure 表名词→measure 衡量

搭：measure out（按需）量出，量取 measure up 符合，达到（标准或期望）

in full measure 最大限度地

19. participant [pɑː'tɪsɪpənt] *n.* 参加者，参与者

例：The organizers appreciate the support of the **participants**.

主办方很感谢参与者的支持。

记：词根记忆 particip（ate）参与，参加 + ant表示人→participant参与者

20. reference ['refrəns] *n.* 提及，谈到；参考，查阅 *adj.* 参考的，用于查阅的 *v.* 列出……的参考书目；提及，提到

例：The customer's booking **reference** is wrong.

客户的预订参考是错的。

记：词根记忆 refer参考 + ence表示行为，状态，性质→reference提及，参考

搭：in/with reference to（所述内容）关于

21. patient ['peɪʃnt] *adj.* 能忍耐的，有耐心的 *n.* 病人，患者

例：This hospital can no longer accept new **patients** at this time.

这家医院现在不能再接受新病人了。

记：词根记忆 pati忍受 + ent某种人→能够忍受的某种人→patient病人，患者

派：patiently *adv.* 耐心地

22. refund ['riːfʌnd] *n.* 退款，偿还金额 *v.* 退还（钱款）

例：We cannot give you **refund** without receipt.

没有收据我们不能给您退款。

记：词根记忆 re重新 + fund基金→重新将基金退回→refund退款

23. balcony ['bælkəni] *n.* 露台，阳台；楼座，楼厅

例：Sometimes we see the sunset on the apartment **balcony**.

有时我们在公寓的阳台上看日落。

24. reply [rɪ'plaɪ] *v.* 回答，答复；（以行动）做出回应，回击 *n.*（口头或书面）回答，答复

例：When you send back your **reply**, be sure to clip the payment in the envelope.

当你寄回回信时，一定要把付款夹在信封里。

记：联想记忆 re回 + ply重叠，折叠→(把问题)叠回去→reply回答

搭：make a reply 做出回复

派：replier *n.* 回答者

25. merchandise [ˈmɜːtʃəndaɪs] *n.* 商品，货品　*v.*（用广告等方式）推销（商品或服务）

例：The amount of band merchandise on sale cannot satisfy fans.

销售的乐队商品数量不能让歌迷满意。

记：联想记忆 merch交易 + and + ise……化→商品化的东西→merchandise商品

26. interior [ɪnˈtɪəriə（r）] *adj.* 内部的，里面的；国内的，内政的　*n.* 内部，里面

例：The design of the interior of her restaurant is special.

她餐厅的室内设计很特别。

27. sentence [ˈsentəns] *n.* 句子，句；判决，判刑；命题　*v.* 判决，宣判，判刑

例：The team presented sentences as ambient noise, independent of a particular speaker or situation.

该团队将句子作为环境噪音呈现，与特定的说话者或情境无关。

记：词根记忆 sent 感觉 + ence 名词词尾→sentence句子

28. chemical [ˈkemɪkl] *adj.* 化学的，与化学有关的　*n.* 化学品，化学制品

例：I don't want to use chemical things to plant my vegetables.

我不想用化学的东西来种植我的蔬菜。

记：词根记忆 chemic化学相关的 + al……的→chemical与化学相关的

29. signal [ˈsɪɡnəl] *n.* 信号，暗号；标志，预示　*v.* 发信号，示意；标志，预示　*adj.* 重大的，显要的

例：Sometimes eyes may not send right signals to the brain.

有时眼睛可能不会向大脑发送正确的信号。

记：词根记忆 sign标记 + al……的→signal标记，信号

派：signally *adv.* 显著地，非凡地

30. ground [ɡraʊnd] *n.* 地，地面；观点，立场　*v.* 以……为根据　*adj.* 切碎的，磨碎的

例：The job suited me down to the ground because I have related knowledge.

这份工作非常适合我，因为我有相关知识。

搭：hold/stand your ground 坚持立场

31. barrier [ˈbæriə (r)] *n.* 障碍，壁垒；障碍物，关卡

例：The first step of these startups is to cross international barriers.

这些初创公司的第一步是跨越国际壁垒。

记：词根记忆 bar词根有"阻碍""妨碍"之意 + er表示一类人或者一类事物→barrier障碍

32. video [ˈvɪdiəʊ] *n.* 录像 *adj.* 电视的，视频的 *v.* 录下

例：We supply the information you need like constant news updates，videos and data themes.

我们提供您需要的信息，如不断更新的新闻，视频和数据主题。

33. invitation [ˌɪnvɪˈteɪʃn] *n.* 邀请；引起，招致；征求，请求；请帖，请柬

例：I think you'd better accept the invitation because it's a chance for you to get a new job.

我认为你最好接受邀请，因为这是你获得新工作的机会。

记：词根记忆 invit(e)邀请，招致 + ation名词后缀→invitation邀请

34. workshop [ˈwɜːkʃɒp] *n.* 车间，工作室，作坊；研讨会，讲习班

例：He felt impressed with the painting workshop for the new teaching approach.

他对绘画工作室的新教学方法印象深刻。

记：词根记忆 work工作 + shop车间→workshop工坊

35. aspiration [ˌæspəˈreɪʃn] *n.* 渴望，抱负，志向

例：The sameness of these products is due to the aspirations of the producer.

这些产品的相同之处是由于生产者的愿望造成的。

36. charity [ˈtʃærəti] *n.* 慈善组织，慈善机构

例：She is going to do some charity work in Africa.

她要去非洲做一些慈善工作。

记：词根记忆 charit词根，意为"爱意"，"慈善" + y名词词尾→charity慈善，慈善组织

37. silence [ˈsaɪləns] *n.* 寂静，无声；沉默，默不作声 *v.* 使安静，使不说话

例：The sudden silence appeared but she would emerge and bring the topic.

突然的沉默出现了，但她会现身并带来话题。

记：词根记忆 sil安静 + ence性质；状态→silence安静

派：silent *adj.* 安静的

38. mission [ˈmɪʃn] *n.* 使命，重要任务；职责，天职

例：David received a lot of encouragement from people throughout his mission.

在整个任务过程中，大卫从人们那里得到了很多鼓励。

记：词根记忆 miss发送 + ion表示行为→发送，引申为使命→mission使命

搭：mission accomplished 任务已完成；大功告成

39. belief [bɪˈliːf] *n.* 相信，信心；看法，信念，观点；信仰，信条

例：The belief of keeping busy is becoming normal today.

如今，保持忙碌的观点正变得司空见惯。

记：发音记忆 belief必立夫→必须做一个顶天立地的大丈夫，这是我的信念→belief信念

搭：beyond belief 令人难以置信

派：believer *n.* 信徒

40. taste [teɪst] *n.* 味道，滋味；味觉；爱好 *v.* 尝起来

例：I cook all kinds of dishes now, some of which are difficult, however, they taste good.

我现在做各种各样的菜，有些菜虽然很难做，但是味道很好。

搭：be in bad taste 趣味低级

派：tasty *adj.* 美味的

扫码听音频

巩固练习

1. 扫码听写（根据所听音频写出本单元对应单词）

(1) _____	(2) _____	(3) _____	(4) _____
(5) _____	(6) _____	(7) _____	(8) _____
(9) _____	(10) _____	(11) _____	(12) _____
(13) _____	(14) _____	(15) _____	(16) _____
(17) _____	(18) _____	(19) _____	(20) _____
(21) _____	(22) _____	(23) _____	(24) _____
(25) _____	(26) _____	(27) _____	(28) _____
(29) _____	(30) _____	(31) _____	(32) _____

(33) _____ (34) _____ (35) _____ (36) _____

(37) _____ (38) _____ (39) _____ (40) _____

2. 实战演练（选出最符合句意的选项）

(1) I don't know what I did wrong, so I have to start from _____ and do it all over again.

   (A) outset   (B) scratching

   (C) source   (D) beginning

(2) This picture of flower was taken last _____.

   (A) spring   (B) water

   (C) season   (D) jump

(3) You can check your _____ at any help desk, freeing up more arm room for more shopping bags.

   (A) treasure   (B) objects

   (C) package   (D) wrap

(4) Are you thinking about the _____ to take to ban the use of mobile phone in the public?

   (A) telling   (B) measure

   (C) way   (D) price

(5) She is going to _____ the washing machine which didn't work.

   (A) buy   (B) purchase

   (C) demand   (D) refund

(6) Please _____ to me quickly.

   (A) except   (B) answer

   (C) reply   (D) maintain

(7) The horse responded to almost invisible _____ to start and stop.

   (A) performs   (B) signals

   (C) leadings   (D) information

(8) You've already smelled and _____ the new food.

   (A) tasted   (B) cooked

   (C) made   (D) drew

(9) We are going abroad to finish our own _____.

   (A) task   (B) target

（C）work　　　　　　　　　　（D）mission

（10）The referee gave a fair _____.

　　（A）revolution　　　　　（B）result

　　（C）judge　　　　　　　（D）solution

Day 21

小试牛刀

浏览本单元所有单词，在你已掌握的单词前面打√。

☐ volunteer	☐ dollar	☐ furniture	☐ knife
☐ memory	☐ juice	☐ climate	☐ snack
☐ structure	☐ dozen	☐ principle	☐ label
☐ comedy	☐ garage	☐ rule	☐ diet
☐ manufacturer	☐ episode	☐ infection	☐ manual
☐ muscle	☐ file	☐ sample	☐ craft
☐ qualification	☐ proportion	☐ invention	☐ sympathy
☐ ocean	☐ deposit	☐ satellite	☐ trick
☐ motivation	☐ fruit	☐ politician	☐ medium
☐ passion	☐ release	☐ seminar	☐ root

词汇精讲

1. volunteer [ˌvɒlənˈtɪə (r)] *n.* 志愿者，义务工作者 *v.* 自愿做，义务做，无偿做

例：They'll need plenty of **volunteers** to do charity work.

他们需要大量的志愿者来做慈善工作。

记：词根记忆 volunt意愿，志愿 + eer人员→volunteer志愿者

搭：volunteer service 义工服务；志工服务台

派：voluntary *adj.* 自愿的

2. dollar [ˈdɒlə (r)] *n.* 美元；元

例：You can pay me a few **dollars** to find out all kinds of animals in our zoo.

你可以付我几美元，让我去了解我们动物园里的各种动物。

3. furniture [ˈfɜːnɪtʃə (r)] *n.* 家具；装置

例：This website sells various kinds of electronic things and some **furniture**.

这个网站出售各种电子产品和一些家具。

4. knife [naɪf] *n.* 餐刀；刀子，刀具 *v.* 用刀伤害

例：If I plan to go into the wildness, I will take a **knife** and other equipment which can give me a shelter and make fires.

如果我打算去野外，我会带一把刀和其他可以给我遮风挡雨和生火的装备。

搭：the knives are out （for sb.）（对某人）磨刀霍霍，兴师问罪

5. memory [ˈmeməri] *n.* 记忆力，记性；记忆，回忆；（计算机存储器的）存储量

例：This new computer is not cheap but it has an amazing amount of **memory** so I think you'll like it.

这台新电脑不便宜，但内存大得惊人，所以我想你会喜欢的。

记：词根记忆 mem记忆 + ory名词词尾→memory回忆，记忆

搭：to the memory of sb. 作为对某人的纪念

派：memorable *adj.* 难忘的，值得纪念的 memorize *v.* 记住，熟记

6. juice [dʒuːs] *n.* （水果和蔬菜的）汁，水果（蔬菜）汁饮料

例：Could we take some **juice** or soda to drink?

我们可以带一些果汁或苏打水喝吗？

7. climate [ˈklaɪmət] *n.* 气候；气候区

例：Humans are facing lots of environmental challenges now like climate change.

人类现在面临着许多环境挑战，比如气候变化。

记：联想记忆 clim倾斜 + ate……的状态，性质，特性→一个地区的气候与太阳光线的倾斜角度有关→climate气候

8. snack [snæk] *n.* 零食，点心，小吃；快餐

例：During the voyage the main cafeteria serves hot and cold meals, drinks and snacks.

在航行中，主餐厅供应冷热餐、饮料和小吃。

9. structure [ˈstrʌktʃə (r)] *n.* 结构，构造；结构体

例：The structure of the building was carefully designed to withstand earthquakes.

这座建筑的结构经过精心设计，可以抵御地震。

记：词根记忆 struct建造，建立 + ure表名词→structure结构，构造

派：structural *adj.* 结构的

10. dozen [ˈdʌzn] *n.* 一打，十二个

例：A dozen passengers didn't notice the cat went on the train.

十几个乘客没有注意到那只猫上了火车。

11. principle [ˈprɪnsəpl] *n.*（行为）准则，（道德）原则；道义，正直

例：Her principle of writing novels is to abandon some unnecessary characters.

她写小说的原则是抛弃一些不必要的人物。

记：联想记忆 prin第一 + cip拿，取 + le表示做某种动作时所使用的东西→首要可取之物→principle原则

搭：in principle 原则上；理论上

12. label [ˈleɪbl] *n.* 标签，标牌；称号，绰号 *v.* 贴标签；把……不公正地称为

例：All the trendy labels want to open an outlet in this town.

所有的时尚品牌都想在这个城市开一家分店。

记：词根记忆 lab实验室 + el名词后缀→实验室里的试剂瓶上贴有标签→label标签

13. comedy [ˈkɒmədi] *n.* 喜剧，喜剧片

例：The couple's common hobby is watching romantic comedies.

这对情侣的共同爱好是看爱情喜剧片。

记：联想记忆 come来 + dy电影→来电影院看喜剧→comedy喜剧

14. garage [ˈɡærɑːʒ] *n.* 车库；加油站，汽车修理厂；车库音乐　*v.* 把……送入车库（或修车厂）

例：There are some tools stored in the garage.

车库里存放着一些工具。

记：联想记忆 gar保护 + age→保护，防御→保护（汽车的地方）→garage车库

15. rule [ruːl] *n.* 规章，条例　*v.* 统治，管辖；支配，控制；占首要地位

例：He followed the safety rules to build this house.

他按照安全规定建造了这栋房子。

搭：rule in 决定，确定　rule out 排除

派：ruler *n.* 统治者

16. diet [ˈdaɪət] *n.* 规定饮食；大量单调的活动；日常饮食

例：Special diet is available，including vegan food.

提供特别的饮食，包括素食。

搭：on a diet 在节食

派：dietary *adj.* 饮食的

17. manufacturer [ˌmænjuˈfæktʃərə (r)] *n.* 生产商，制造商

例：By the 1960s the surfing manufacturer produced a kind of skateboard in a new size.

到了20世纪60年代，冲浪板制造商生产了一种新尺寸的滑板。

记：词根记忆 manufactur(e)产品；制造 + er某种人→manufacturer生产商，制造商

18. episode [ˈepɪsəud] *n.* 一段经历，一段时期；集，一集

例：The first episode of this book starts with a girl leaving from her hometown.

这本书的第一节是从一个女孩离开家乡开始的。

记：联想记忆 epi另外，其他+ s + od路 + e→其他插入的路→episode插曲

19. infection [ɪnˈfekʃn] *n.* 传染病；感染；玷污，污染

例：They don't have antibodies, which mean they lack a "memory" for fighting infections.

它们没有抗体，这意味着它们缺乏对抗感染的"记忆"。

记：词根记忆 infect传染 + ion表示状态，结果→infection传染，感染

派：infected *adj.* 被感染的

20. manual [ˈmænjuəl] *adj.* 手工的，体力的；手动的，用手操作的
n. 使用手册，说明书

例：When you have two or three manuals, you can quickly change the machine.

当你有两个或三个手册时，你可以快速更换机器。

记：词根记忆 man手 + ual与……相关的→manual手工的

搭：on manual 处于非自动状态；处于手动状态

派：manually *adv.* 手动；手动地

21. muscle [ˈmʌsl] *n.* 肌肉；体力，力气　*v.* 用力搬动；挤

例：I pulled a muscle reaching for jar on the top shelf.

我拿最上面架子上的罐子时拉伤了肌肉。

搭：muscle in 强行介入，强行插手

派：muscled *adj.* 肌肉发达的

22. file [faɪl] *n.* 文件夹（或箱、柜等）；（计算机的）文档；档案；
纵列　*v.* （把文件等）归档，存档；提起（诉讼），提出（申请）

例：You can see lots of files in my computer.

你可以在我的电脑里看到很多文件。

搭：single file 单行

23. sample [ˈsɑːmpl] *n.* 样本，样品；试用产品　*v.* 品尝，尝试
adj. 样品的，实例的

例：We cannot believe this result because of the small sample number.

我们不能相信这个结果，因为样本数太少了。

记：联想记忆 s向外 + ample掌→从整体中取出来的一小份→sample样品

24. craft [krɑːft] *n.* 工艺，手艺；船，艇，飞行器；诡计，骗术；行
业，职业；手工艺品　*v.* 精心制作

例：On land, this huge craft can get around on 400 inch all terrain tires.

在陆地上，这艘小艇也可以使用400英寸的全地形轮胎在地面上行驶。

25. qualification [ˌkwɒlɪfɪˈkeɪʃn] *n.* 资格，学历；资历，技能条件

例：Working experience is more important than having the **qualifications**.

工作经验比资格证书更重要。

记：词根记忆 quali(fy)使……符合；合格 + fication表示使，致使→qualification 合格

搭：without qualification无条件地

26. proportion [prəˈpɔːʃn] *n.* 部分，份额；比例；正确的比例 *v.* 使（某物）成比例，使相称

例：It's not a bad thing to have smaller **proportion** students in university.

大学生比例小并不是一件坏事。

记：词根记忆 pro 在前 + port部分；分开 + ion表名词→按之前的量分开→proportion比例

搭：keep sth. in proportion 恰当地处事

27. invention [ɪnˈvenʃn] *n.* 发明物；发明，创造

例：When the telephone was an amazing new **invention**, government used much money to build phone boxes.

当电话是一项惊人的新发明时，政府花了很多钱建造电话亭。

记：词根记忆 invent 发明 + ion 行为，状态→invention 发明

28. sympathy [ˈsɪmpəθi] *n.* 同情（心），理解；赞同，支持

例：The interviewee has **sympathy** for those actors who don't have acting skills.

受访者对那些没有演技的演员表示同情。

记：词根记忆 sym共同，相同 + pathy感受，受苦的→sympathy同情

搭：in sympathy with 同情；支持

派：sympathetic *adj.* 同情的

29. ocean [ˈəʊʃn] *n.* 海洋，大海

例：I've been scuba diving for years in **ocean**.

我在海里潜水好几年了。

派：Oceania *n.* 大洋洲

30. deposit [dɪˈpɒzɪt] *v.* 放下，放置；储蓄；存放，寄存 *n.* 沉积物，沉积层

例：For the ATM is broken, you have to make the **deposit** in bank.

自动取款机坏了，你得去银行存钱。

记：联想记忆 de向下 + posit放→放下→deposit储蓄

搭：on deposit 存放着

31. satellite [ˈsætəlaɪt] *n.* 卫星，人造卫星

例：Reporters are talking about satellites around the earth.

　　记者们正在谈论围绕地球运行的卫星。

32. trick [trɪk] *n.* 花招，诡计，骗局；窍门 *v.* 欺骗，哄骗

例：The proper use of colour is a trick in advertising.

　　色彩的恰当运用是广告中的一个技巧。

搭：trick sb. into sth./into doing sth. 诱使某人做某事　trick sb. out of sth. 从某人处

　　骗走某物

派：发音记忆 trick吹客→吹嘘的客人心怀诡计→trick花招，诡计

33. motivation [ˌməʊtɪˈveɪʃn] *n.* 动力，诱因；积极性，干劲

例：Her motivation of becoming a chef is that many chefs don't take potential train-

　　ees seriously.

　　她成为一名厨师的动机是许多厨师不把潜在的学员当回事。

记：词根记忆 motivat(e)推动 + ion行为，状态→motivation动力，诱因

34. fruit [fruːt] *n.* 水果；（植物的）果实；成果，结果，后果

例：Fruit growers may have a big harvest in this autumn.

　　今年秋天果农可能会有大丰收。

搭：bear fruit 成功；取得成果

派：fruitless *adj.* 不成功的，不结果实的　fruitful *adj.* 成果丰硕的

35. politician [ˌpɒləˈtɪʃn] *n.* 从政者，政治家

例：Politicians may use their way to control the vote.

　　政客们可能会用他们的方式来控制投票。

记：词根记忆 polit与政治相关的 + ician人→爱国家之人→politician政客

36. medium [ˈmiːdiəm] *n.* 媒介，媒体；方法，手段　*adj.* 中等的，

　　　　中间的，适中的

例：He is restricting his medium to create his own art.

　　他正在限制他的媒介来创造他自己的艺术。

记：词根记忆 medi中间 + um→medium中间的

搭：in the medium term 中期内

37. passion ['pæʃn] *n.* 爱恋，情欲；激情，热情；酷爱，热衷的爱好（或活动等）

例：Monica's greatest **passion** is to teach her neighbor cooking skills.

莫妮卡最大的爱好就是教她的邻居烹饪技巧。

记：联想记忆 pass痛苦，忍耐 + ion表示行为，状态→感情，激情通常也会带来痛苦→passion激情

38. release [rɪ'liːs] *v.* 释放，放走；公布，发布；发行，上映 *n.* 释放，放出；排放，泄漏；公开，发布

例：Fans are waiting for the new **release**.

粉丝们正在等待新发行的版本。

记：联想记忆 re重新 + lease松开→将人松开→release释放

39. seminar ['semɪnɑː(r)] *n.* 研讨会，培训会

例：Our doctor's **seminar** will begin at 11 a. m.

我们的医生研讨会将在上午11点开始。

记：发音记忆 seminar散没那→研讨会散没呐？→研讨会

40. root [ruːt] *n.* （植物的）根，根茎；根用作物 *v.* 生根；扎根于

例：That spirit **roots** firmly in the country's traditions and its past.

这种精神牢牢扎根于这个国家的传统和过去。

搭：root around 翻找；搜寻 root for 支持；为……鼓劲 root out 铲除；清除

巩固练习

1. 扫码听写（根据所听音频写出本单元对应单词）

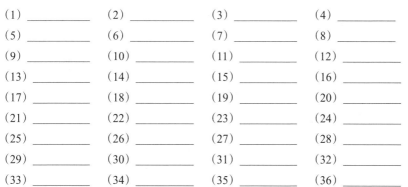

(1) ＿＿＿＿＿＿ (2) ＿＿＿＿＿＿ (3) ＿＿＿＿＿＿ (4) ＿＿＿＿＿＿

(5) ＿＿＿＿＿＿ (6) ＿＿＿＿＿＿ (7) ＿＿＿＿＿＿ (8) ＿＿＿＿＿＿

(9) ＿＿＿＿＿＿ (10) ＿＿＿＿＿＿ (11) ＿＿＿＿＿＿ (12) ＿＿＿＿＿＿

(13) ＿＿＿＿＿＿ (14) ＿＿＿＿＿＿ (15) ＿＿＿＿＿＿ (16) ＿＿＿＿＿＿

(17) ＿＿＿＿＿＿ (18) ＿＿＿＿＿＿ (19) ＿＿＿＿＿＿ (20) ＿＿＿＿＿＿

(21) ＿＿＿＿＿＿ (22) ＿＿＿＿＿＿ (23) ＿＿＿＿＿＿ (24) ＿＿＿＿＿＿

(25) ＿＿＿＿＿＿ (26) ＿＿＿＿＿＿ (27) ＿＿＿＿＿＿ (28) ＿＿＿＿＿＿

(29) ＿＿＿＿＿＿ (30) ＿＿＿＿＿＿ (31) ＿＿＿＿＿＿ (32) ＿＿＿＿＿＿

(33) ＿＿＿＿＿＿ (34) ＿＿＿＿＿＿ (35) ＿＿＿＿＿＿ (36) ＿＿＿＿＿＿

(37) _____   (38) _____   (39) _____   (40) _____

2. 实战演练（选出最符合句意的选项）

(1) Mr Hadison wants students to _____ to get things ready for the activity day.

　(A) volunteer　　　　　　　(B) voluntary

　(C) oblige　　　　　　　　(D) prepare

(2) The style of a painting has its _____ in the particular period.

　(A) root　　　　　　　　　(B) principle

　(C) cause　　　　　　　　　(D) footing

(3) The man prefer _____ to tragedy.

　(A) film　　　　　　　　　(B) series

　(C) comedy　　　　　　　　(D) opera

(4) In spring, the lung _____ attacked me.

　(A) infective　　　　　　　(B) infection

　(C) infectious　　　　　　　(D) infected

(5) I'll keep your report on _____ in my computer.

　(A) paper　　　　　　　　　(B) core

　(C) file　　　　　　　　　　(D) table

(6) We hope you _____ at least $250 over the period.

　(A) deposit　　　　　　　　(B) refund

　(C) money　　　　　　　　　(D) cash

(7) As a beginner, I will not play the _____.

　(A) trick　　　　　　　　　(B) treat

　(C) fraud　　　　　　　　　(D) game

(8) The applicant do not have _____ so he seems lack passion when he works.

　(A) adaptation　　　　　　　(B) motivation

　(C) application　　　　　　　(D) competition

(9) Her movie became successful because of her _____ for innovative style.

　(A) optimism　　　　　　　(B) caution

　(C) deliberation　　　　　　(D) passion

(10) The topic of this _____ is to discuss the pollution of the river.

　(A) seminar　　　　　　　　(B) school

　(C) fair　　　　　　　　　　(D) company

练习答案

Day 1

1. 扫码听写（根据所听音频写出本单元对应单词）

(1) even	(2) great	(3) know	(4) find	(5) look
(6) next	(7) quite	(8) school	(9) student	(10) job
(11) question	(12) film	(13) same	(14) start	(15) special
(16) explain	(17) young	(18) actually	(19) still	(20) learn
(21) ask	(22) old	(23) small	(24) however	(25) article
(26) course	(27) animal	(28) sport	(29) important	(30) local
(31) people	(32) time	(33) friend	(34) new	(35) always
(36) think	(37) different	(38) last	(39) say	(40) way

2. 实战演练（选出最符合句意的选项）

(1)【答案】B

【解析】本题考查名词词汇。（A）bonus 奖金；（B）task 任务；（C）job 工作；（D）sign 标志。根据句意，应为"部门给她布置的任务"，故选（B）。

【翻译】她觉得要在周末之前完成部门给她布置的任务是很困难的。

【词汇积累】department 部门 set 布置

(2)【答案】D

【解析】本题考查形容词词汇。（A）only 唯一的；（B）any 任何的；（C）same 同样的；（D）various 各种各样的。根据句意，应为"各种各样的形状和颜色"，故选（D）。

【翻译】掌上电脑有各种各样的形状和颜色。

【词汇积累】shape 形状

(3)【答案】A

【解析】本题考查动词词汇。（A）understood 明白；（B）thought 思考；（C）knew 知道；（D）taught 教授。根据句意，应为"明白了这道数学难题"，故选（A）。

【翻译】经过老师的讲解，我终于明白了这道数学难题。

【词汇积累】math 数学

(4)【答案】C

【解析】本题考查形容词词汇。（A）unique 独特的；（B）particular 特定的；（C）special 特别的；（D）especial 特殊的。special sale 为固定搭配，意为"特价销售"，故选（C）。

【翻译】这家百货公司决定在本月底对库存商品进行特价销售。

【词汇积累】stock 库存，存货

(5)【答案】C

【解析】本题考查副词词汇。（A）normally 通常；（B）loudly 大声地；（C）actually 实际上；（D）significantly 显著地。根据句意，应为"实际上比我们最初预计的要高得多"，故选（C）。

【翻译】成本实际上比我们最初预计的要高得多。

【词汇积累】initially 最初地

(6)【答案】A

【解析】本题考查名词词汇。（A）mate 伴侣；（B）parents 父母；（C）relative 亲戚；（D）friend 朋友。根据句意，应为"理想伴侣"，故选（A）。

【翻译】单身多年后，约翰终于找到了他的理想伴侣。

【词汇积累】single 单身的

(7)【答案】C

【解析】本题考查名词词汇。（A）issue 议题；（B）list 清单；（C）question 问题；（D）schedule 日程安排。根据句意，应为"对问题的回答"，故选（C）。

【翻译】球员对问题的回答使主教练满意。

【词汇积累】coach 教练

(8)【答案】D

【解析】本题考查动词词汇。（A）explore 探索；（B）describe 描述；（C）subscribe 订阅；（D）explain 解释。根据句意，应为"无法解释来源"，故选（D）。

【翻译】校长无法解释学校教学资格的来源。

【词汇积累】principal 校长

(9)【答案】B

【解析】本题考查形容词词汇。（A）utter 彻底的；（B）great 棒的；（C）ugly 丑陋的；（D）simple 普通的。根据句意，应为"夕阳下的森林多么棒啊"，故选（B）。

【翻译】夕阳下的森林多么棒啊！那一幕给我留下了深刻的印象。

【词汇积累】sunset 夕阳

（10）【答案】D

【解析】本题考查副词词汇。（A）thoroughly 彻底地；（B）always 总是；（C）seldom 几乎不；（D）regularly 定期地。根据句意，应为"定期服药"，故选（D）。

【翻译】医生建议他定期服药以抑制病情。

【词汇积累】suppress 抑制

Day 2

1. 扫码听写（根据所听音频写出本单元对应单词）

（1）enjoy	（2）review	（3）useful	（4）website	（5）famous
（6）read	（7）music	（8）social	（9）play	（10）life
（11）popular	（12）family	（13）meet	（14）appropriate	（15）possible
（16）try	（17）talk	（18）magazine	（19）language	（20）exactly
（21）available	（22）opinion	（23）several	（24）travel	（25）city
（26）leave	（27）home	（28）live	（29）difficult	（30）idea
（31）long	（32）visit	（33）recently	（34）restaurant	（35）child
（36）sure	（37）interesting	（38）buy	（39）food	（40）free

2. 实战演练（选出最符合句意的选项）

（1）【答案】D

【解析】本题考查动词词汇。（A）settle 定居；（B）search 搜索；（C）count 数；（D）live 居住。根据句意，应为"住在农村"，而且settle应与介词down搭配，故选（D）。

【翻译】他们辞去城市的工作后，选择住在宜人的农村。

【词汇积累】pleasant 宜人的

（2）【答案】B

【解析】本题考查副词词汇。（A）meanwhile 与此同时；（B）recently 最近；（C）lately 最近；（D）past 过去。根据句意，应为"最近有了新的证据"，而且recently多用于肯定句，故选（B）。

【翻译】关于这个案件最近有了新的证据。

【词汇积累】evidence 证据

（3）【答案】C

【解析】本题考查名词词汇。（A）food 食物；（B）meal 饭；（C）provisions 补给；（D）dishes 菜肴。根据句意，应为"准备了充足的补给"，而且与voyage搭配的词，比起food还是provisions更为精准，故选（C）。

【翻译】船员们为这次航行准备了充足的补给。

【词汇积累】voyage 航行

（4）【答案】C

【解析】本题考查形容词词汇。（A）respectable 受人尊敬的；（B）famous 著名的；（C）notorious 臭名昭著的；（D）reasonable 有道理的。根据句意，应为"粗鲁在社区里早已臭名昭著"，故选（C）。

【翻译】他的粗鲁在社区里早已臭名昭著。

【词汇积累】community 社区

（5）【答案】A

【解析】本题考查形容词词汇。（A）appropriate 适合的；（B）grateful 感激的；（C）proper 适合的；（D）responsible 负责的。根据句意，应为"适合这个庄严的场合"，而且appropriate常后接介词for/to。故选（A）。

【翻译】简单朴素的衣服适合这个庄严的场合。

【词汇积累】solemn 庄严的

（6）【答案】A

【解析】本题考查名词词汇。（A）couple 夫妇；（B）parents 父母；（C）family 家庭；（D）home 家。根据句意和动词前面的has，应为family（集合名词表单数），故选（A）。

【翻译】这个家庭已经在这栋大楼的八楼预订了一套公寓。

【词汇积累】apartment 公寓

（7）【答案】B

【解析】本题考查名词词汇。（A）flight 飞行；（B）trip 旅行；（C）travel 旅行；（D）service 服务。根据句意，应为"为期两周的澳大利亚之旅"，travel泛指旅行的行为而非某次具体的旅行，不强调目的地。而trip强调目的地或出行原因，故选（B）。

【翻译】为期两周的澳大利亚之旅使大学生们兴奋不已。

【词汇积累】Australia 澳大利亚

（8）【答案】A

【解析】本题考查副词词汇。（A）exactly 精确地；（B）normally 通常；（C）precisely 精确地；（D）accordingly 相应地。根据句意，应为"对形势的判断和事实完全一致"，而exact强调抽象的事物与事实吻合。故选（A）。

【翻译】他对当前形势的判断和事实完全一致。

【词汇积累】judgement 判断

（9）【答案】D

【解析】本题考查形容词词汇。（A）available 可用的；（B）delightful 高兴的；（C）visible 可看见的；（D）accessible 可进入的。根据句意，应为"仅供获得授权的人员进入访问"，故选（D）。

【翻译】本网站仅供获得授权的人员进入访问。

【词汇积累】authorize 授权

（10）【答案】B

【解析】本题考查动词词汇。（A）saved 拯救；（B）released 释放；（C）sent 发送；（D）liberated 解放。根据句意，应为"释放了孩子"，故选（B）。

【翻译】绑匪在收到赎金后释放了孩子。

【词汇积累】kidnapper 绑匪

Day 3

1. 扫码听写（根据所听音频写出本单元对应单词）

(1) name	(2) kind	(3) busy	(4) love	(5) international
(6) right	(7) world	(8) wild	(9) change	(10) future
(11) experience	(12) suggest	(13) beautiful	(14) style	(15) exciting
(16) pay	(17) watch	(18) hotel	(19) move	(20) public
(21) happen	(22) ready	(23) improve	(24) main	(25) receive
(26) company	(27) easy	(28) decide	(29) quickly	(30) country
(31) eat	(32) shop	(33) choose	(34) expensive	(35) problem
(36) keep	(37) information	(38) advice	(39) happy	(40) listen

2. 实战演练（选出最符合句意的选项）

（1）【答案】A

【解析】本题考查动词词汇。（A）named 任命；（B）designed 设计；（C）arranged 安排；（D）ensured 确保。根据句意，应为"任命乔纳森为新的首席执行官”，故选（A）。

【翻译】董事会任命乔纳森为新的首席执行官。

【词汇积累】board 董事会

（2）【答案】C

【解析】本题考查动词词汇。（A）seeing 看到；（B）accepting 接受；（C）receiving 收到；（D）watching 观看。根据句意，应为“收到这封信后尽快采取行动”，故选（C）。

【翻译】请在收到这封信后尽快采取行动以减少损失。

【词汇积累】loss 损失

（3）【答案】B

【解析】本题考查动词词汇。（A）laid 躺；（B）selected 选择；（C）ensured 确保；（D）chose 选择。根据句意，应为“选择了这枚钻戒作为信物”，而且比起choose，还是select强调精心挑选，故选（B）。

【翻译】他最终选择了这枚钻戒作为对女友的爱的信物。

【词汇积累】token 信物

（4）【答案】C

【解析】本题考查形容词词汇。（A）timid 胆怯的；（B）beautiful 美丽的；（C）handsome 英俊的；（D）faithful 忠实的。根据句意，应为“英俊的绅士”，故选（C）。

【翻译】别看他现在这个样子，他年轻的时候是一个英俊的绅士。

【词汇积累】gentleman 绅士

（5）【答案】D

【解析】本题考查动词词汇。（A）indulged 沉溺于；（B）favoured 支持；（C）prided 使……自豪；（D）engaged 从事。根据句意，应为“忙于从政府申请土地来建立他们自己的工厂”，故选（D）。

【翻译】保罗兄弟正忙于从政府申请土地来建立他们自己的工厂。

【词汇积累】factory 工厂

（6）【答案】C

【解析】本题考查动词词汇。（A）remind 提醒；（B）forget 忘记；（C）experience 经历；（D）realize 意识到。根据句意，应为“经历很多痛苦和挑战”，故选（C）。

【翻译】要成为一名宇航员，候选人必须经历很多痛苦和挑战。

【词汇积累】astronaut 宇航员

（7）【答案】A

【解析】本题考查名词词汇。（A）data 数据；（B）progress 进步；（C）information 信息；（D）sample 样本。根据句意，应为"掌握战斗机相关数据有重要意义"，data表示详细具体的数据， information表示信息概况，故选（A）。

【翻译】掌握该型战斗机的相关数据对我国的军事技术发展具有十分重要的意义。

【词汇积累】military 军事的

（8）【答案】D

【解析】本题考查动词词汇。（A）search 搜索；（B）seek 寻求；（C）listen 听；（D）overhear 偶然听到。根据句意，应为"碰巧听到总统和他秘书的谈话"，故选（D）。

【翻译】他碰巧听到总统和他秘书的谈话。

【词汇积累】secretary 秘书

（9）【答案】D

【解析】本题考查名词词汇。（A）reflection 反映；（B）style 风格；（C）fashion 时尚；（D）reason 原因。根据句意，应为"舞蹈风格狂野"，故选（D）。

【翻译】评委认为他的舞蹈风格对节目来说太狂野了。

【词汇积累】judge 评委，裁判

（10）【答案】C

【解析】本题考查形容词词汇。（A）crafty 狡猾的；（B）grand 伟大的；（C）kind 善良的；（D）simple 普通的。根据句意，应为"善良的行为"，故选（C）。

【翻译】捡起别人的钱包并把它交给警察是一种善良的行为。

【词汇积累】wallet 钱包

Day 4

1. 扫码听写（根据所听音频写出本单元对应单词）

（1）build	（2）answer	（3）include	（4）month	（5）night
（6）plan	（7）water	（8）remember	（9）grow	（10）reason
（11）collect	（12）agree	（13）competition	（14）believe	（15）computer
（16）photo	（17）win	（18）club	（19）allow	（20）minute
（21）weekend	（22）book	（23）number	（24）park	（25）provide
（26）point	（27）successful	（28）skill	（29）recommend	（30）team
（31）send	（32）bring	（33）hour	（34）follow	（35）wait
（36）writer	（37）money	（38）mean	（39）teach	（40）stop

2. 实战演练（选出最符合句意的选项）

(1)【答案】D

【解析】本题考查动词词汇。（A）fight 战斗；（B）persuade 说服；（C）prevail 战胜；（D）conquer 征服。根据句意，应为"征服欧洲的失败"，故选（D）。

【翻译】征服欧洲的失败是拿破仑一生的遗憾。

【词汇积累】lifelong 一生的

(2)【答案】B

【解析】本题考查动词词汇。（A）answer 回答；（B）provide 提供；（C）supply 提供；（D）respect 尊重。根据句意，应为"提供新的发展机会"，而且 provide sth. for sb. 为固定搭配，意为"为某人提供某物"，故选（B）。

【翻译】政策变化可能会给公司提供新的发展机会。

【词汇积累】policy 政策

(3)【答案】B

【解析】本题考查名词词汇。（A）paper 纸张；（B）currency 货币；（C）label 标签；（D）money 钱。根据句意，应为"兑换货币"，故选（B）。

【翻译】如果你想去西班牙，你会兑换哪种货币？

【词汇积累】change 兑换

(4)【答案】A

【解析】本题考查动词词汇。（A）permitted 允许；（B）allowed 允许；（C）followed 跟随；（D）brought 带来。根据句意，应为"允许建工厂"，而且 permit 指准许某人做某事，含权威正式的意味，故选（A）。

【翻译】政府允许他在工业园区建工厂。

【词汇积累】park 园区

(5)【答案】C

【解析】本题考查动词词汇。（A）understand 理解；（B）agree 同意；（C）approve 赞成；（D）accept 接受。approve of 为固定搭配，意为"赞成"，故选（C）。

【翻译】这位官员不赞成政府的经济政策。

【词汇积累】official 官员

(6)【答案】C

【解析】本题考查动词词汇。（A）worried 担心；（B）believed 相信；（C）trusted 信任；（D）disliked 不喜欢。根据句意，应为"信任这位有经验的雇员"，而且trust表达的感情程度高于believe，故选（C）。

【翻译】公司信任这位有经验的雇员，让他负责保险箱。

【词汇积累】safe 保险箱

（7）【答案】A

【解析】本题考查动词词汇。（A）replied 回复；（B）answered 回答；（C）sent 发送；（D）made 制作。根据句意，应为"迅速回复了电报"，故选（A）。

【翻译】她迅速回复了客户发来的电报。

【词汇积累】telegram 电报

（8）【答案】D

【解析】本题考查名词词汇。（A）computer 电脑；（B）projector 投影仪；（C）camera 照相机；（D）radio 收音机。根据句意，应为"听收音机"，故选（D）。

【翻译】许多老年人保留了听收音机的习惯。

【词汇积累】retain 保留

（9）【答案】B

【解析】本题考查名词词汇。（A）concept 概念；（B）contest 比赛；（C）faith 信仰；（D）match 比赛。根据句意，应为"演讲比赛"，而且contest尤指某种技能活动的比赛，match多指体育比赛，故选（B）。

【翻译】文学院赢得了演讲比赛。

【词汇积累】faculty 全体教职员工

（10）【答案】D

【解析】本题考查名词词汇。（A）chances 机会；（B）talents 天赋；（C）reasons 原因；（D）excuses 借口。根据句意，应为"找新的借口"，故选（D）。

【翻译】她总能为自己的低效率找新的借口。

【词汇积累】inefficiency 低效率

Day 5

1. 扫码听写（根据所听音频写出本单元对应单词）

(1) space	(2) publish	(3) sleep	(4) ticket	(5) customer
(6) centre	(7) share	(8) worry	(9) office	(10) technology
(11) activity	(12) example	(13) equipment	(14) system	(15) camera

(16) concert	(17) party	(18) message	(19) notice	(20) announcement
(21) business	(22) view	(23) summer	(24) bear	(25) sell
(26) discuss	(27) finish	(28) staff	(29) achieve	(30) art
(31) fly	(32) create	(33) event	(34) interview	(35) spell
(36) expect	(37) project	(38) relax	(39) increase	(40) letter

2. 实战演练（选出最符合句意的选项）

（1）【答案】D

【解析】本题考查动词词汇。（A）close 结束；（B）oversee 监督；（C）finish 结束；（D）terminate 终止。根据句意，应为"合同将在今年年底终止"，而且 terminate 指合同、协议等终止或使之终止，故选（D）。

【翻译】他与俱乐部的合同将在今年年底终止。

【词汇积累】contract 合同

（2）【答案】B

【解析】本题考查动词词汇。（A）object 反对；（B）reach 达成；（C）achieve 完成；（D）sign 签字。根据句意，应为"达成协议"，而且 reach an agreement 为固定搭配，意为"达成协议"，故选（B）。

【翻译】大会花了五个小时才达成协议。

【词汇积累】congress 大会

（3）【答案】C

【解析】本题考查动词词汇。（A）invent 发明；（B）advise 建议；（C）create 创造；（D）lend 借出。根据句意，应为"创造一种激励机制"，故选（C）。

【翻译】社会改革的实际目的是为经济发展创造一种激励机制。

【词汇积累】reform 改革

（4）【答案】A

【解析】本题考查名词词汇。（A）accident 意外；（B）example 范例；（C）expectation 期待；（D）incident 事故。根据句意，应为"撞到你是个意外"，而且 accident 强调偶然或意外发生的不幸事情，故选（A）。

【翻译】我今天训练时撞到你是个意外。

【词汇积累】practice 练习

（5）【答案】B

【解析】本题考查动词词汇。（A）expand 扩大；（B）increase 增加；（C）loosen 放松；（D）enlarge 放大。根据句意，应为"增加你通过考试的概率"，故选（B）。

【翻译】课后认真学习一定会增加你通过考试的概率。

【词汇积累】rate 比率，率

(6)【答案】B

【解析】本题考查名词词汇。（A）line 线；（B）space 空间；（C）seat 座位；（D）time 时间。根据句意，应为"腾出空间放家具"，故选（B）。

【翻译】我们怎么腾出空间放这么多家具？

【词汇积累】furniture 家具

(7)【答案】C

【解析】本题考查动词词汇。（A）heard 听见；（B）smelled 闻到；（C）noticed 注意到；（D）recorded 记录。根据句意，应为"注意到诺拉正坐出租车去购物中心"，故选（C）。

【翻译】我无意中注意到诺拉正坐出租车去购物中心。

【词汇积累】cab 出租车

(8)【答案】D

【解析】本题考查动词词汇。（A）read 读；（B）choose 选择；（C）change 改变；（D）remember 记住。根据句意，应为"不可能记住每个人的名字"，故选（D）。

【翻译】教授不可能在选修课上记住每个人的名字。

【词汇积累】elective 随意选择的

(9)【答案】A

【解析】本题考查名词词汇。（A）scenery 风景；（B）emptiness 空虚；（C）fantasy 幻想；（D）scene 风景。根据句意，应为"风景激发了创作灵感"，而且scenery指一个国家或某一地区的整体自然风景，故选（A）。

【翻译】英国的风景激发了莎士比亚创作他最伟大诗歌的灵感。

【词汇积累】poetry 诗歌

(10)【答案】B

【解析】本题考查名词词汇。（A）event 事件；（B）banquet 宴会；（C）activity 活动；（D）party 派对。根据句意，应为"邀请参加国宴"，而且state banquet为固定搭配，意为"国宴"，故选（B）。

【翻译】能被邀请参加国宴，我感到非常荣幸。

【词汇积累】honoured 荣幸的

Day 6

1. 扫码听写（根据所听音频写出本单元对应单词）

（1） media	（2） museum	（3） flight	（4） ship	（5） condition
（6） story	（7） light	（8） beach	（9） guest	（10）advertisement
（11） conference	（12） culture	（13） diagram	（14） level	（15） report
（16） sign	（17） result	（18）environment	（19） challenge	（20） attitude
（21） mountain	（22） career	（23） wind	（24） text	（25） bed
（26） advantage	（27） birthday	（28） member	（29） order	（30） service
（31） guide	（32） table	（33） task	（34） programme	（35） research
（36） clothes	（37） sea	（38） weather	（39） garden	（40） history

2. 实战演练（选出最符合句意的选项）

（1）【答案】D

【解析】本题考查名词词汇。（A）sky 天空；（B）sea 大海；（C）land 陆地；（D）ocean 海洋。根据句意和常识，应为"海洋约占地球总面积的70%"，而且ocean特指地球表面最广阔的水体的总称，故选（D）。

【翻译】海洋约占地球总面积的70%。

【词汇积累】percent 百分之……

（2）【答案】B

【解析】本题考查名词词汇。（A）circumstance 情况；（B）condition 情况；（C）situation 形势；（D）environment 环境。根据句意，应为"健康状况已大为改善"，而且health condition为固定搭配，意为"健康状况"，故选（B）。

【翻译】经过医生的努力，病人的健康状况已大为改善。

【词汇积累】patient 病人

（3）【答案】A

【解析】本题考查名词词汇。（A）attitude 态度；（B）altitude 海拔；（C）position 立场；（D）market 市场。根据句意，应为"漠不关心的态度"，而且attitude指对某人或某事物的一般看法。故选（A）。

【翻译】这种对政治漠不关心的态度在美国选民中很常见。

【词汇积累】indifferent 漠不关心的

（4）【答案】C

【解析】本题考查名词词汇。（A）reason 原因；（B）result 结果；（C）consequence 后果；（D）start 开端。根据句意和常识，应为"鲁莽行动的后果"，而且consequence强调产生的不良结果，故选（C）。

【翻译】鲁莽行动的后果是犯令你后悔一生的错误。

【词汇积累】reckless 鲁莽的

（5）【答案】B

【解析】本题考查名词词汇。（A）shoes 鞋；（B）uniform 校服；（C）clothes 衣服；（D）socks 袜子。根据句意和常识，应为"在升旗仪式上穿校服"，故选（B）。

【翻译】学校要求学生在升旗仪式上穿校服。

【词汇积累】ceremony 仪式

（6）【答案】B

【解析】本题考查名词词汇。（A）definition 定义；（B）level 程度；（C）rank 等级；（D）class 阶级。根据句意，应为"恐怖程度让我很难接受"，而level一般指水平等级，rank是指工作级别上的高低，故选（B）。

【翻译】这部电影的恐怖程度让我很难接受。

【词汇积累】horror 恐怖性

（7）【答案】D

【解析】本题考查名词词汇。（A）sign 签名；（B）name 名字；（C）gender 性别；（D）autograph 签名。根据句意，应为"打算向那位著名演员要签名"，而 autograph指名人在书籍、照片等上面签名。故选（D）。

【翻译】演出结束后，他打算向那位著名演员要签名。

【词汇积累】performance 表演，演出

（8）【答案】C

【解析】本题考查名词词汇。（A）culture 文化；（B）peace 和平；（C）civilization 文明；（D）happiness 幸福。根据句意，应为"把文明带到了土地上"，而且civilization指广义的文明，标志人类发展的进程，故选（C）。

【翻译】罗马人把文明带到了他们征服的许多土地上。

【词汇积累】conquer 征服

（9）【答案】A

【解析】本题考查名词词汇。（A）climate 气候；（B）temperature 温度；（C）weather 天气；（D）wind 风。根据句意，应为"湿热的气候不适合长期居住"，而且climate指某一地区常年的气候情况，故选（A）。

【翻译】巴西湿热的气候不适合东亚人长期居住。

【词汇积累】residence 居住

（10）【答案】A

【解析】本题考查名词词汇。（A）investigation 调查；（B）survey 调查；（C）report 报告；（D）research 调查。根据句意，应为"对犯罪现场进行了彻底的调查"，而且investigation指有系统的、彻底细致的调查以得到希望发现或需要知道的事，故选（A）。

【翻译】警方对犯罪现场进行了彻底的调查。

【词汇积累】thorough 彻底的

Day 7

1. 扫码听写（根据所听音频写出本单元对应单词）

（1）fast	（2）obviously	（3）currently	（4）suddenly	（5）academic
（6）extra	（7）late	（8）polar	（9）hot	（10）immediately
（11）comfortable	（12）properly	（13）welcome	（14）common	（15）present
（16）mobile	（17）proud	（18）professional	（19）suitable	（20）modern
（21）similar	（22）friendly	（23）top	（24）wide	（25）perfect
（26）especially	（27）certainly	（28）short	（29）strong	（30）practical
（31）high	（32）keen	（33）quiet	（34）eventually	（35）definitely
（36）generally	（37）unusual	（38）lucky	（39）cold	（40）natural

2. 实战演练（选出最符合句意的选项）

（1）【答案】C

【解析】本题考查名词词汇。（A）vigorous 强壮的；（B）large 大的；（C）strong 强烈的；（D）severe 严重的。根据句意，应为"强烈的责任感"，而且strong sense of duty为固定搭配，意为"强烈的责任感"，故选（C）。

【翻译】强烈的责任感使他坚持要继续调查下去。

【词汇积累】duty 责任

（2）【答案】D

【解析】本题考查副词词汇。（A）suddenly 突然地；（B）specially 专门地；

（C）certainly 当然；（D）especially 尤其。根据句意，应为"尤其是沉迷于游戏的年轻人"，故选（D）。

【翻译】这款游戏吸引了广泛的人群，尤其是沉迷于游戏的年轻人。

【词汇积累】obsess 使着迷

（3）【答案】A

【解析】本题考查形容词词汇。（A）sharp 敏锐的；（B）stupid 愚蠢的；（C）keen 敏锐的；（D）clever 聪明的。根据句意，应为"头脑仍像年轻人一样敏锐"，而且sharp指头脑反应敏锐灵活。故选（A）。

【翻译】他虽然八十岁了，但头脑仍像年轻人一样敏锐。

【词汇积累】eighty 八十

（4）【答案】B

【解析】本题考查形容词词汇。（A）flourishing 繁荣的；（B）peak 高峰时期的；（C）prospective 有希望的；（D）top 顶端的。根据句意，应为"旅游旺季"，而且peak season为固定搭配，意为"旺季"，故选（B）。

【翻译】旅游局预计8月份将是今年的旅游旺季。

【词汇积累】tourism 旅游业

（5）【答案】C

【解析】本题考查形容词词汇。（A）comfortable 舒适的；（B）useful 有用的；（C）practical 实际的；（D）personal 个人的。根据句意，应为"走得远只为赏樱花不实际"，故选（C）。

【翻译】我们走那么远只是为了赏樱花是不实际的。

【词汇积累】blossom 花

（6）【答案】A

【解析】本题考查形容词词汇。（A）professional 专业的；（B）successful 成功的；（C）reasonable 合理的；（D）desirable 令人向往的。根据句意，应为"专业顾问"，故选（A）。

【翻译】我们必须请专业顾问来帮助我们削减预算。

【词汇积累】budget 预算

（7）【答案】D

【解析】本题考查形容词词汇。（A）calm 冷静的；（B）irritable 急躁的；（C）brave 勇敢的；（D）quiet 安静的。根据句意，应为"是个文静的人"，故选（D）。

【翻译】他是个文静的人，很少主动和陌生人说话。

【词汇积累】initiative 主动性

(8)【答案】B

　　【解析】本题考查形容词词汇。(A) confident 自信的；(B) arrogant 自大的；(C) proud 骄傲的；(D) humble 谦虚的。根据句意，应为"自大到认为能够改变地球"，故选(B)。

　　【翻译】人类是如此自大，以为他们可以改变地球。

　　【词汇积累】earth 地球

(9)【答案】D

　　【解析】本题考查形容词词汇。(A) affordable 负得起的；(B) valuable 珍贵的；(C) fit 符合的；(D) suitable 适合的。根据句意，应为"适合过敏的人使用"，而且"be suitable for"为固定搭配，意为"适合"，故选(D)。

　　【翻译】这种药膏适合过敏的人使用。

　　【词汇积累】ointment 药膏

(10)【答案】C

　　【解析】本题考查动词词汇。(A) greeted 欢迎；(B) accepted 接受；(C) welcomed 欢迎；(D) guided 指导。根据句意，应为"欢迎邻国首脑"，而且welcome多指热情、官方或正式的迎接或欢迎，故选(C)。

　　【翻译】总统在机场欢迎了邻国的首脑。

　　【词汇积累】neighbouring 邻近的

Day 8

1. 扫码听写（根据所听音频写出本单元对应单词）

(1) gym	(2) commercial	(3) extended	(4) physical	(5) brilliant
(6) warm	(7) afraid	(8) digital	(9) typical	(10) enormous
(11) positive	(12) single	(13) electronic	(14) fair	(15) boring
(16) dry	(17) grateful	(18) independent	(19) delicious	(20) modern
(21) impossible	(22) global	(23) initial	(24) low	(25) personal
(26) underwater	(27) previous	(28) unique	(29) effective	(30) cheap
(31) fresh	(32) daily	(33) funny	(34) incredible	(35) simple
(36) deep	(37) regular	(38) major	(39) serious	(40) basic

2. 实战演练（选出最符合句意的选项）

(1)【答案】B

【解析】本题考查形容词词汇。（A）useful 有用的；（B）private 私人的；（C）commercial 商业的；（D）personal 个人的。根据句意，应为"私人媒体"，而且private指只供某个人或某群体使用的，强调非公用性，故选（B）。

【翻译】他们故意压制私人媒体以掩盖丑闻。

【词汇积累】scandal 丑闻

(2)【答案】C

【解析】本题考查形容词词汇。（A）later 以后的；（B）recent 最近的；（C）former 之前的；（D）previous 之前的。根据句意，应为"前首相"，而且former指曾有过某种职务或地位的，故选（C）。

【翻译】这位前首相在论坛上表达了他对恐怖袭击问题的看法。

【词汇积累】terrorist 恐怖分子

(3)【答案】A

【解析】本题考查形容词词汇。（A）fair 公平的；（B）sincere 真诚的；（C）possible 可能的；（D）comparable 可比的。根据句意，应为"在比赛中使用规定以外的器具对其他选手是不公平的"，故选（A）。

【翻译】在比赛中使用规定以外的器具对其他选手是不公平的。

【词汇积累】prescribe 规定

(4)【答案】B

【解析】本题考查形容词词汇。（A）effective 有效的；（B）efficient 高效的；（C）diligent 勤奋的；（D）stubborn 顽固的。根据句意，应为"高效率地以低成本完成复杂的任务"，而且efficient 强调效率高，不浪费时间、金钱、能源等，故选（B）。

【翻译】他以如此低的成本完成了这项复杂的任务，真有效率。

【词汇积累】complicated 复杂的

(5)【答案】D

【解析】本题考查形容词词汇。（A）practical 实际的；（B）optimistic 乐观的；（C）negative 消极的；（D）positive 积极的。根据句意和空格前的a，应为"积极的眼光"，故选（D）。

【翻译】用积极的眼光看待世界会让你少很多压力。

【词汇积累】light 眼光

(6)【答案】C

【解析】本题考查形容词词汇。（A）strange 奇怪的；（B）alien 异域的；（C）foreign 外国的；（D）radical 激进的。根据句意，应为"外籍教师"，而且foreign teacher为固定搭配，意为"外教"，故选（C）。

【翻译】罗杰教授在校园里是一位很受尊敬的外籍教师。

【词汇积累】respected 受尊敬的

（7）【答案】A

【解析】本题考查形容词词汇。（A）impossible 不可能的；（B）difficult 困难的；（C）incredible 不可思议的；（D）boring 无聊。根据句意，应为"长生不老是不可能的"，故选（A）。

【翻译】对于21世纪的人类来说，长生不老是不可能的。

【词汇积累】immortality 长生不老

（8）【答案】A

【解析】本题考查形容词词汇。（A）humorous 幽默的；（B）tedious 乏味的；（C）simple 简单的；（D）irritating 使人恼火的。根据句意，应为"幽默的演讲赢得了学生们的掌声和笑声"，故选（A）。

【翻译】校长幽默的演讲赢得了学生们的掌声和笑声。

【词汇积累】applause 掌声

（9）【答案】C

【解析】本题考查形容词词汇。（A）Coppery 铜的；（B）Electronic 电子的；（C）Electrical 电的；（D）Wooden 木制的。根据句意，应为"电气设备"，而且electrical指与电有关的或设备等用电、发电的，故选（C）。

【翻译】电气设备将点燃新的火花为汽车提供动力。

【词汇积累】ignite 点燃

（10）【答案】B

【解析】本题考查形容词词汇。（A）promising 前途光明的；（B）enormous 巨大的；（C）regular 恒定的；（D）typical 典型的。根据句意，应为"巨大的市场潜力"，故选（B）。

【翻译】据预测，这种新产品具有巨大的市场潜力。

【词汇积累】predict 预测

Day 9

1. 扫码听写（根据所听音频写出本单元对应单词）

（1）organize	（2）realize	（3）design	（4）express	（5）identify
（6）repair	（7）admire	（8）delay	（9）admit	（10）perform
（11）prevent	（12）prove	（13）borrow	（14）raise	（15）explore
（16）inform	（17）necessary	（18）dangerous	（19）average	（20）constant
（21）valuable	（22）noisy	（23）financial	（24）dark	（25）manage
（26）prepare	（27）suppose	（28）apply	（29）encourage	（30）cook
（31）compare	（32）affect	（33）avoid	（34）celebrate	（35）surprise
（36）wear	（37）arrange	（38）break	（39）imagine	（40）return

2. 实战演练（选出最符合句意的选项）

（1）【答案】D

【解析】本题考查动词词汇。（A）distribute 分配；（B）govern 管理；（C）dominate 统治；（D）manage 管理。根据句意，应为"管理公司"，而且manage指管理公司、组织等，故选（D）。

【翻译】这个年轻人管理他父亲的企业还为时过早。

【词汇积累】corporation 企业

（2）【答案】B

【解析】本题考查动词词汇。（A）designed 设计；（B）applied 应用；（C）used 使用；（D）invented 发明。根据句意，应为"应用纳米技术"，而且apply指将技术、方法等用于某一流程中以发挥其作用，故选（B）。

【翻译】科学家们在实验中应用纳米技术培育出能够发光的植物。

【词汇积累】nanotechnology 纳米技术

（3）【答案】C

【解析】本题考查动词词汇。（A）admitted 承认；（B）seen 见过；（C）acknowledged 承认；（D）supposed 假定。根据句意，应为"被公认为是最好的教授"，而且acknowledge指承认某一情况属实或接纳某种权威性。故选（C）。

【翻译】他被公认为是学术界最好的化学教授。

【词汇积累】circle 圈子

(4)【答案】A

【解析】本题考查动词词汇。（A）impressed 使留下深刻印象；（B）annoyed 使生气；（C）affected 影响；（D）disturbed 打扰。根据句意，应为"出色表现给我留下了深刻的印象"，故选（A）。

【翻译】他在比赛中的出色表现给我留下了深刻的印象。

【词汇积累】excellent 出色的

(5)【答案】B

【解析】本题考查动词词汇。（A）remember 记住；（B）avoid 避免；（C）evade 避免；（D）practice 练习。根据句意，应为"避免单独会面"，而且 avoid 指回避某人、某物或不使用某物，故选（B）。

【翻译】在昨天的尴尬之后，杰克逊试图避免与迈克尔单独会面。

【词汇积累】embarrassment 尴尬

(6)【答案】C

【解析】本题考查动词词汇。（A）take 接受；（B）fantasize 幻想；（C）imagine 想象；（D）think 思考。根据句意，应为"无法想象经历了多少痛苦"，故选（C）。

【翻译】我无法想象他为完成这项任务经历了多少痛苦。

【词汇积累】mission 任务

(7)【答案】C

【解析】本题考查动词词汇。（A）Accepting 接受；（B）Admiring 崇拜；（C）Respecting 尊敬；（D）Praising 夸赞。根据句意，应为"尊敬老人"，故选（C）。

【翻译】尊敬老人是中华民族的传统美德。

【词汇积累】virtue 美德

(8)【答案】B

【解析】本题考查形容词词汇。（A）political 政治的；（B）financial 财务的；（C）fiscal 财政的；（D）monetary 货币的。根据句意，应为"公司的财务丑闻"，故选（B）。

【翻译】记者正在调查这家公司的几起财务丑闻。

【词汇积累】probe 调查

(9)【答案】A

【解析】本题考查动词词汇。（A）performed 执行；（B）prepared 准备；（C）

executed 执行；（D）started 开始。根据句意，应为"做手术"，而且perform operation为固定搭配，意为"做手术"，故选（A）。

【翻译】外科医生今天连续做了十三个手术。

【词汇积累】surgeon 外科医生

（10）【答案】D

【解析】本题考查形容词词汇。（A）hazardous 危险的；（B）horrible 恐怖的；（C）safe 安全的；（D）dangerous 危险的。根据句意，应为"火灾时乘电梯是危险的"，而且dangerous可以表示各种类型的危险。故选（D）。

【翻译】在火灾中选择乘电梯是非常危险的。

【词汇积累】elevator 电梯

Day 10

1. 扫码听写（根据所听音频写出本单元对应单词）

(1) strange	(2) temporary	(3) advanced	(4) product	(5) traditional
(6) mall	(7) critic	(8) persuade	(9) delivery	(10) record
(11) reduce	(12) recycle	(13) replace	(14) detail	(15) form
(16) mind	(17) model	(18) sculpture	(19) location	(20) belong
(21) demand	(22) song	(23) hate	(24) introduce	(25) individual
(26) facility	(27) coffee	(28) massive	(29) street	(30) interest
(31) honest	(32) observe	(33) remote	(34) disappoint	(35) convince
(36) enrol	(37) establish	(38) hand	(39) escape	(40) kitchen

2. 实战演练（选出最符合句意的选项）

（1）【答案】C

【解析】本题考查形容词词汇。（A）dirty 脏的；（B）familiar 熟悉的；（C）remote 偏远的；（D）distant 遥远的。根据句意，应为"偏远的农村地区"，故选（C）。

【翻译】偏远的农村地区需要引入电和自来水。

【词汇积累】rural 农村

（2）【答案】B

【解析】本题考查形容词词汇。（A）vile 邪恶的；（B）honest 诚实的；（C）calm 冷静的；（D）creative 有创意的。根据句意，应为"诚实的人"，故选（B）。

【翻译】他是个诚实的人，讨厌用卑鄙的谎言欺骗别人。

【词汇积累】deceive 欺骗

（3）【答案】C

【解析】本题考查形容词词汇。（A）different 不同的；（B）individual 独特的；（C）characteristic 独特的；（D）common 共同的。根据句意与逻辑，应为"独特的景观"，而且characteristic指鲜明体现某事物特点、本质的。故选（C）。

【翻译】金色的沙滩是马尔代夫岛的特色景观。

【词汇积累】feature 特征

（4）【答案】D

【解析】本题考查动词词汇。（A）quit 退出；（B）leave 离开；（C）flee 逃离；（D）escape 逃脱。根据句意，应为"逃脱惩罚"，而且escape the punishment为固定搭配，意为"逃脱惩罚"，故选（D）。

【翻译】罪犯是不可能逃脱法律的严惩的。

【词汇积累】criminal 罪犯

（5）【答案】C

【解析】本题考查动词词汇。（A）sent 发送；（B）passed 传递；（C）handed 提交；（D）submitted 提交。根据句意，应为"把证据交给警察局"，而且hand over为固定搭配，意为"移交"，故选（C）。

【翻译】调查人员把他收集到的证据移交给了警察局。

【词汇积累】investigator 调查人员

（6）【答案】B

【解析】本题考查名词词汇。（A）road 道路；（B）path 小路；（C）tree 树；（D）grass 草。根据句意和常识，应为"开辟一条小路上山"，故选（B）。

【翻译】由于山洪暴发，士兵们不得不开辟一条上山的小路以节省时间。

【词汇积累】soldier 士兵

（7）【答案】A

【解析】本题考查名词词汇。（A）kitchen 厨房；（B）garage 车库；（C）toilet 厕所；（D）basement 地下室。根据句意和常识，应为"去厨房取餐巾纸"，故选（A）。

【翻译】女主人到厨房去给客人取餐巾纸。

【词汇积累】napkin 餐巾纸

(8)【答案】C

【解析】本题考查动词词汇。(A) restored 恢复；(B) resigned 辞职；(C) recycled 回收；(D) responded 回应。根据句意，应为"不能回收或不能降解的材料"，故选（C）。

【翻译】我们应该拒绝那些不能回收或不能降解的材料。

【词汇积累】degrade 降解

(9)【答案】D

【解析】本题考查形容词词汇。(A) eccentric 古怪的；(B) delightful 令人高兴的；(C) interesting 有趣的；(D) strange 奇怪的。根据句意，应为"真奇怪"，而且strange为常用词，含义广泛，形容奇怪或不自然的事，eccentric指偏离常规的怪异或怪癖。故选（D）。

【翻译】真奇怪，本来这个周末开演的歌剧被取消了。

【词汇积累】opera 歌剧

（10）【答案】D

【解析】本题考查动词词汇。(A) enlist 使参军；(B) attend 参加；(C) recruit 招聘；(D) enrol 招收入学。根据句意，应为"招收三个高级技能班"，故选（D）。

【翻译】我们可以再招收三个高级技能班，每班15名学生。

【词汇积累】advanced 高级的

Day 11

1. 扫码听写（根据所听音频写出本单元对应单词）

(1) adopt	(2) community	(3) employ	(4) fight	(5) graduate
(6) price	(7) power	(8) force	(9) complain	(10) determine
(11) control	(12) contact	(13) inspire	(14) driver	(15) material
(16) date	(17) hide	(18) invent	(19) reflect	(20) traffic
(21) qualify	(22) paint	(23) village	(24) register	(25) suffer
(26) teenager	(27) solve	(28) appeal	(29) manager	(30) actor
(31) island	(32) attempt	(33) attention	(34) aeroplane	(35) marry
(36) audience	(37) behaviour	(38) ring	(39) safety	(40) body

2. 实战演练（选出最符合句意的选项）

（1）【答案】B

【解析】本题考查名词词汇。（A）plan 计划；（B）appeal 呼吁；（C）demand 需求；（D）solution 解决措施。根据句意和空格前的an，应为"发出呼吁"，故选（B）。

【翻译】警方发出呼吁，市民在遇到抢劫时应确保自身安全。

【词汇积累】robbery 抢劫

（2）【答案】C

【解析】本题考查名词词汇。（A）audiences 观众；（B）onlookers 旁观者；（C）spectators 观众；（D）coaches 教练。根据句意，应为"观众来现场看比赛并给球员加油"，而且spectator 多指体育比赛的观众，故选（C）。

【翻译】许多观众选择来现场观看棒球比赛并为球员加油。

【词汇积累】scene 现场

（3）【答案】D

【解析】本题考查名词词汇。（A）attitude 态度；（B）manner 行为；（C）mood 心情；（D）behaviour 行为。根据句意，应为"消费者在互联网上的行为信息"，而且consumer behaviour为固定搭配，意为"消费者行为"，故选（D）。

【翻译】企业可以通过技术手段获取消费者在互联网上的行为信息。

【词汇积累】means 手段

（4）【答案】A

【解析】本题考查名词词汇。（A）safety 安全；（B）danger 危险；（C）language 语言；（D）mode 模式。根据句意与逻辑，应为"交通安全"，故选（A）。

【翻译】教给孩子们交通安全知识是非常重要的。

【词汇积累】knowledge 知识

（5）【答案】C

【解析】本题考查动词词汇。（A）absorb 吸收；（B）introduce 介绍；（C）adopt 采用；（D）adapt 适应。根据句意，应为"采取物资管制措施"，故选（C）。

【翻译】几乎所有国家在战时都采取物资管制措施。

【词汇积累】material 物资

（6）【答案】A

【解析】本题考查动词词汇。（A）fight 战斗；（B）put 安置；（C）take 携带；（D）depend 依赖。根据句意，应为"坚定了继续战斗的决心"，故选（A）。

【翻译】敌人顽固不化的态度坚定了他继续战斗的决心。

【词汇积累】unrepentant 顽固不化的

(7)【答案】B

【解析】本题考查动词词汇。（A）assigned 安排；（B）complained 抱怨；（C）praised 夸赞；（D）attempted 尝试。根据句意，应为"抱怨受到不公平待遇"，故选（B）。

【翻译】哈里森抱怨说他在购物中心受到了不公平的对待。

【词汇积累】unfairly 不公平地

(8)【答案】D

【解析】本题考查名词词汇。（A）money 钱；（B）price 价格；（C）tip 小费；（D）fare 交通费用。根据句意和逻辑，应为"出差所产生的交通费用由公司承担"，故选（D）。

【翻译】员工出差所产生的交通费用由公司承担。

【词汇积累】incur 带来（成本、花费等）

(9)【答案】C

【解析】本题考查动词词汇。（A）rule 统治；（B）remove 移开；（C）control 控制；（D）dispose 处理。根据句意，应为"控制自己的情绪"，故选（C）。

【翻译】他努力控制自己的情绪，以免被对手抓住弱点。

【词汇积累】opponent 敌人 seize 抓住

(10)【答案】B

【解析】本题考查名词词汇。（A）code 密码；（B）contact 联络；（C）communication 沟通；（D）signal 信号。根据句意，应为"与总部失去联系"，故选（B）。

【翻译】由于雷达故障，这支部队与总部失去了联系。

【词汇积累】headquarter 总部 radar 雷达

Day 12

1. 扫码听写（根据所听音频写出本单元对应单词）

(1) communication	(2) owner	(3) series	(4) elementary	(5) option

(6) ability	(7) dish	(8) factor	(9) luggage	(10) leisure
(11) menu	(12) employee	(13) plant	(14) address	(15) door
(16) air	(17) degree	(18) pilot	(19) band	(20) exhibition
(21) nature	(22) image	(23) collection	(24) star	(25) issue
(26) collection	(27) science	(28) passenger	(29) lack	(30) goal
(31) applicant	(32) river	(33) journalist	(34) colleague	(35) process
(36) mistake	(37) treat	(38) front	(39) adult	(40) position

2. 实战演练（选出最符合句意的选项）

(1)【答案】A

【解析】本题考查固定搭配。a wide range of表示"各种各样的，广泛的"，故选（A）。

【翻译】声称能提高儿童智力的教育玩具、录像带和各种各样的婴儿用品涌入了市场。

【词汇积累】device 设备

(2)【答案】A

【解析】本题考查名词词汇。四个选项的意思都为"选择"，（A）options 指可选择的事物、选择、选择权、选择的自由；（B）choices 侧重指自由选择的权利或特权；（C）alternatives 指在相互排斥的两者之间作严格的选择，也可指在两者以上中进行选择；（D）selections 侧重品鉴能力的选择，故选（A）。

【翻译】比起其他超市，它有更广泛的购物选择。

【词汇积累】supermarket 超市

(3)【答案】A

【解析】本题考查固定搭配。pride oneself on sth.表示"以……为傲"，故选（A）。

【翻译】他以把人的名字和脸相匹配的能力为傲。

【词汇积累】match…with 把……相匹配

(4)【答案】B

【解析】本题考查动词词汇。（A）emphasized 强调；（B）addressed 解决；（C）dealt 处理；（D）given 给予。根据句意，应为"解决问题"，故选（B）。

【翻译】需要解决的问题是交际缺陷，而不是物理缺陷。

【词汇积累】communicative 交际的

(5)【答案】A

【解析】本题考查冠词。题目中没有特指哪个申请者，故选（A）。

【翻译】测试的结果会告诉HR很多关于应聘者性格的事。

【词汇积累】character 性格

(6)【答案】C

【解析】本题考查名词词汇。（A）point 点；（B）degree 程度；（C）scale 规模；（D）grade 等级。根据句意，应为"局面的规模"，故选（C）。

【翻译】很难说下个月我们将面临什么样的局面。

【词汇积累】situation 情况，局面

(7)【答案】B

【解析】本题考查名词词汇及固定搭配。play a role in表示"起作用于"。根据句意，应为"医生在社会上起到的作用"，故选（B）。

【翻译】最近，社会上越来越多人关注医生在社会上起到的作用。

【词汇积累】society 社会

(8)【答案】C

【解析】本题考查固定搭配。in advance表示"提前"，故选（C）。

【翻译】你必须至少提前一周预订参观这个地方的票。

【词汇积累】ticket 票

(9)【答案】C

【解析】本题考查名词词汇及固定搭配。train of thought意为"思绪的过程"，故选（C）。

【翻译】刺耳的门铃突然打断了我的思绪。

【词汇积累】interrupt 打断

(10)【答案】A

【解析】本题考查名词词汇。（A）lack 缺乏；（B）shortage 缺点，短缺；（C）absence 缺席；（D）loss 损失。根据句意，应为"缺乏证据"，故选（A）。

【翻译】老师把这个故事描述为一个神话，尽管缺乏证据，但住在这里的人仍然坚持这个故事。

【词汇积累】myth 神话

1. 扫码听写（根据所听音频写出本单元对应单词）

(1) pound	(2) race	(3) stage	(4) term	(5) action
(6) award	(7) bag	(8) bank	(9) luggage	(10) beginner
(11) century	(12) context	(13) editor	(14) effort	(15) luxury
(16) list	(17) image	(18) direction	(19) pool	(20) knowledge
(21) fashion	(22) factory	(23) temperature	(24) face	(25) care
(26) matter	(27) decision	(28) assistant	(29) bar	(30) baby
(31) supermarket	(32) access	(33) tool	(34) tip	(35) species
(36) selection	(37) round	(38) practice	(39) disadvantage	(40) match

2. 实战演练（选出最符合句意的选项）

(1)【答案】A

【解析】本题考查固定搭配。make efforts to do sth.表示"努力做某事"，故选（A）。

【翻译】他大力鼓励人们读书。

【词汇积累】encourage 鼓励

(2)【答案】B

【解析】本题考查名词词汇。（A）slides 幻灯片；（B）bars 酒吧、小吃店；（C）ban 禁止；（D）obstruction 阻塞，故选（B）。

【翻译】这有许多休闲酒吧和餐馆。

【词汇积累】restaurant 饭店

(3)【答案】D

【解析】本题考查名词词汇。四个选项的意思都为"缺点、错误"，（A）disadvantages 指引起问题、妨碍某人或某事成功或发挥作用的因素；（B）handicaps 指妨碍某人达成目标的因素；（C）errors 指错误；（D）drawbacks 指计划、产品等的不足之处，故选（D）。

【翻译】这个产品有很多缺陷需要我们改进。

【词汇积累】improve 改进

（4）【答案】D

【解析】本题考查动词词汇。（A）pursue 追求；（B）practice 练习；（C）know 知道；（D）train 训练。根据句意，应为"训练技能"，故选（D）。

【翻译】这门实用课程让人们有机会在现实生活中训练他们的技能。

【词汇积累】chance 机会

（5）【答案】A

【解析】本题考查名词词汇及固定搭配。be in two minds表示"拿不定主意"，故选（A）。

【翻译】对于这个职位是否适合我，我曾经左右为难，但我很高兴最后选择了它。

【词汇积累】decision 决定

（6）【答案】C

【解析】本题考查名词词汇。（A）behaviour 行为；（B）manner 方式；（C）action 动作；（D）fight 战斗。根据句意，应为"拍摄动作"，故选（C）。

【翻译】用于拍摄动作类的新方法是惊人的，我刚参加完这方面的课程回来。

【词汇积累】come back 回来

（7）【答案】D

【解析】本题考查名词词汇。（A）environment 环境；（B）implication 含义；（C）relevance 相关性；（D）context 语境。根据句意，应为"跨文化语境"，故选（D）。

【翻译】有些表达在跨文化语境中应该避免使用。

【词汇积累】expression 表达

（8）【答案】B

【解析】本题考查名词词汇。四个选项的意思都为"奖项、荣誉"，reward 指对品德高尚和勤劳的人所给予的奖励。也可指为某事付酬金；award 侧重指官方或经正式研究裁决后对有功者或竞赛优胜者所给予的奖励；honour 侧重指荣誉；prize 侧重指奖品，故选（B）。

【翻译】这家餐馆因对顾客的良好服务赢得了几次奖项。

【词汇积累】service 服务

（9）【答案】B

【解析】本题考查动词词汇及固定搭配。hand round意为"分发"，故选（B）。

【翻译】请将试卷分发给同学。

【词汇积累】classmate 同学

（10）【答案】B

【解析】本题考查动词词汇。（A）entry 入口；（B）access 接近/取得……的方法；（C）entrance 进入；（D）accep 接受。根据句意，应为"找到教材"，故选（B）。

【翻译】找到合适的课程教材并不容易。

【词汇积累】material 材料

Day 14

1. 扫码听写（根据所听音频写出本单元对应单词）

（1）background	（2）sense	（3）purpose	（4）thought	（5）object
（6）couple	（7）feature	（8）post	（9）performance	（10）complaint
（11）solution	（12）clinic	（13）pressure	（14）library	（15）impact
（16）wall	（17）relationship	（18）society	（19）technique	（20）doctor
（21）topic	（22）value	（23）sound	（24）title	（25）drive
（26）achievement	（27）advance	（28）attraction	（29）card	（30）insect
（31）camp	（32）education	（33）dream	（34）expectation	（35）discount
（36）atmosphere	（37）land	（38）industry	（39）energy	（40）majority

2. 实战演练（选出最符合句意的选项）

（1）【答案】C

【解析】本题考查名词词汇。（A）discount 折扣；（B）luck 运气；（C）prize 奖品，奖励；（D）sight 景象，故选（C）。

【翻译】海滩上的顶级酒店对于任何喜欢阳光的人来说都是一个很棒的奖励！

【词汇积累】sunshine 阳光

（2）【答案】A

【解析】本题考查名词词汇。（A）complaints 投诉；（B）letters 信；（C）references 引用；（D）notes 笔记，故选（A）。

【翻译】我们经常从居民那里得到关于街上堆积的垃圾的投诉。

【词汇积累】rubbish 垃圾

（3）【答案】C

【解析】本题考查名词词汇和固定搭配。leading doctor表示领班医生，故选（C）。

【翻译】领班医生认为，即使一个人一周只做一次运动，也能对他们的身体产生巨大的影响。

【词汇积累】extraordinary 特别的

(4)【答案】B

【解析】本题考查名词词汇。（A）skills 技能；（D）techniques 技术；（D）power 权力；（D）methods 方法，故选（B）。

【翻译】这门学科依赖于高度复杂的技术。

【词汇积累】rely on 依赖于

(5)【答案】A

【解析】本题考查名词词汇。（A）relationships 关系；（B）relatives 亲戚；（C）relates 有关；（D）regularity 规律，故选（A）。

【翻译】他们想和住在这里的人搞好关系。

【词汇积累】develop 发展

(6)【答案】A

【解析】本题考查冠词词汇。因为理解并不是特定的，故选（A）。

【翻译】通读全文，获得对主题和内容的大致理解。

【词汇积累】general 普遍的

(7)【答案】D

【解析】本题考查固定搭配。shed light on意为"阐明，解释"，故选（D）。

【翻译】这些结果阐明了幼儿通过捕捉他们没有直接参与的信息来获得动词意义特征的方式。

【词汇积累】toddler 初学走路的孩子

(8)【答案】D

【解析】本题考查名词词汇。（A）air 空气；（B）condition 条件；（C）place 表示地方；（D）atmosphere 表示氛围，故选（D）。

【翻译】这里有很多年轻人，所以气氛很活跃。

【词汇积累】service 服务

(9)【答案】A

【解析】本题考查名词词汇。（A）attraction 吸引力；（B）attractive 有吸引力的；（C）charm 魅力；（D）action 行动，故选（A）。

【翻译】对山姆来说最大的吸引之处是他可以在课上学到新技能。

【词汇积累】lesson 课程

（10）【答案】A

【解析】本题考查名词词汇和固定搭配，"summer camp"意为"夏令营"，故选（A）。

【翻译】暑假我们都去了夏令营。

【词汇积累】vacation 假期

Day 15

1. 扫码听写（根据所听音频写出本单元对应单词）

（1）experiment	（2）resident	（3）vegetable	（4）bottle	（5）chocolate
（6）display	（7）spread	（8）risk	（9）occasion	（10）album
（11）standard	（12）budget	（13）engineer	（14）coach	（15）wave
（16）rock	（17）connection	（18）medicine	（19）population	（20）capital
（21）taxi	（22）voyage	（23）lifestyle	（24）decade	（25）catalog
（26）ambition	（27）resource	（28）request	（29）loss	（30）paper
（31）hobby	（32）sauce	（33）cartoon	（34）screen	（35）impression
（36）proposal	（37）lung	（38）survey	（39）gallery	（40）colour

2. 实战演练（选出最符合句意的选项）

（1）【答案】A

【解析】本题考查名词词汇。residential school意为寄宿制学校，故选（A）。

【翻译】将寄宿制学校教育与主流学校教育相结合是一个很好的方法。

【词汇积累】mainstream 主流

（2）【答案】D

【解析】本题考查动词词汇。（A）developed 发展；（B）happened 发生；（C）appeared 出现；（D）displayed 显示，故选（D）。

【翻译】屏幕上时不时显示的文字是在解释故事。

【词汇积累】screen 屏幕

（3）【答案】B

【解析】本题考查动词词汇。（A）casting 投射；（B）spreading 传播扩散；

（C）providing 提供；（D）offering 主动提出，故选（B）。

【翻译】因为顾客的需求趋同，所以一定的同质化现象正在扩散。

【词汇积累】demand 需求

（4）【答案】A

【解析】本题考查名词词汇。（A）wave 波浪；（B）sea 海洋；（C）shutter 百叶窗；（D）gift 礼物，故选（A）。

【翻译】波浪可能会中断拍摄。

【词汇积累】interrupt 打断

（5）【答案】D

【解析】本题考查名词词汇。（A）learning 学习；（B）paper 论文；（C）goods 货物；（D）survey 调查，故选（D）。

【翻译】我们对村里人们的经历和意见进行了一次调查。

【词汇积累】experience 经历

（6）【答案】B

【解析】本题考查动词词汇。（A）lost 遗失；（B）loss 损失；（C）disappear 消失；（D）losing 输掉；habitat loss意为"栖息地丢失"，故选（B）。

【翻译】由于气候变化、栖息地丢失等原因，他们的种群数量呈下降趋势。

【词汇积累】decline 下降

（7）【答案】A

【解析】本题考查动词词汇。（A）requested 要求；（B）imposed 实施；（C）offered 提供；（D）believed 认为，故选（A）。

【翻译】所有乘客都被要求到船上办公室领取登录卡。

【词汇积累】office 办公室

（8）【答案】D

【解析】本题考查名词词汇。（A）idea 想法；（B）development 发展；（C）understanding 理解；（D）ambition 野心，故选（D）。

【翻译】她有一个去探索新想法的野心。

【词汇积累】explore 探索

（9）【答案】C

【解析】本题考查名词词汇。（A）ship （大）船；（B）boat 小船；（C）voyage 航行；（D）旅行。其中，voyage表示在船上的旅行，故选（C）。

【翻译】任何进一步的延误将在航行期间通知。

【词汇积累】announce 宣称

（10）【答案】D

【解析】本题考查名词词汇，（A）moment 时刻，（B）chance 机会，（C）times 时间，次数，（D）occasions 场合，故选（D）。

【翻译】由于雨量少，植物生长缓慢，很少开花。

【词汇积累】rainfall 降雨量

Day 16

1. 扫码听写（根据所听音频写出本单元对应单词）

(1) wedding	(2) character	(3) envelope	(4) pleasure	(5) refugee
(6) vehicle	(7) recipe	(8) tent	(9) tradition	(10) contrast
(11) forecast	(12) pollution	(13) respect	(14) theater	(15) habitat
(16) wood	(17) surroundings	(18) stimulate	(19) apartment	(20) priority
(21) prize	(22) branch	(23) price	(24) quality	(25) specialize
(26) passport	(27) distance	(28) argument	(29) store	(30) secret
(31) cruise	(32) support	(33) progress	(34) ingredient	(35) dinosaur
(36) adventure	(37) size	(38) reflect	(39) satisfy	(40) waste

2. 实战演练（选出最符合句意的选项）

（1）【答案】A

【解析】本题考查固定搭配。It's my pleasure意为"这是我的荣幸"，是对感谢的固定回答，故选（A）。

【翻译】——你真是太好了！谢谢你接受我们的邀请。

——这是我的荣幸。

【词汇积累】kind 宽容的，体贴的

（2）【答案】B

【解析】本题考查名词词汇。（A）lorries 货车；（B）vehicles 车辆；（C）trucks 卡车；（D）cars 汽车，故选（B）。

【翻译】司机不允许待在他们的车里。

【词汇积累】driver 司机

（3）【答案】D

【解析】本题考查固定搭配。out of character 不适合，和……不相称；out of appearance 不是固定搭配；out of regard 出于考虑；out of respect 出于尊重，故选（D）。

【翻译】出于尊重，她不想谈论别人。

【词汇积累】discuss 谈论

（4）【答案】A

【解析】本题考查名词词汇。natural habitat表示自然栖息地，故选（A）。

【翻译】在自然栖息地观看野生动物总是一种美妙的经历。

【词汇积累】wild 野生的

（5）【答案】A

【解析】本题考查动词词汇。（A）stimulate 刺激；（B）reproduce 再生产；（C）duplicate 复制；（D）simulate 模拟，故选（A）。

【翻译】他们希望玩具能激发孩子们的智力，改善他们的情绪。

【词汇积累】emotion 情绪

（6）【答案】D

【解析】本题考查动词词汇。（A）relief 缓解；（B）remote 遥远的；（C）inflect 传染；（D）reflect 反映，故选（D）。

【翻译】她认为环境能反映一个人的性格。

【词汇积累】personality 性格

（7）【答案】A

【解析】本题考查名词词汇。（A）adventure 冒险；（B）experience 经历；（C）sense 感觉；（D）feeling 感觉，故选（A）。

【翻译】你需要一次去新地方冒险的经历。

【词汇积累】place 地方

（8）【答案】A

【解析】本题考查名词词汇。（A）progress 意为进展，（B）pursuit 意为追求，（C）move 意为动作，（D）development 意为发展，故选（A）。

【翻译】学校每学期发一份进度报告。

【词汇积累】term 学期

（9）【答案】A

【解析】本题考查名词词汇。（A）distance 距离；（B）distant 遥远的；（C）distinction 差别，区别；（D）distinct 清晰的，清楚的，故选（A）。

【翻译】这只狮子跑了150公里，同时还带着相机。

【词汇积累】kilometer 公里

（10）【答案】B

　　【解析】本题考查名词词汇，（A）branch 分店；（B）chain 连锁店；（C）row 排；（D）line 列，故选（B）。

　　【翻译】连锁店是由同一家公司拥有的一组商店或旅馆。

　　【词汇积累】company 公司

Day 17

1. 扫码听写（根据所听音频写出本单元对应单词）

(1) guarantee	(2) decorate	(3) fashionable	(4) separate	(5) assume
(6) cancel	(7) bake	(8) divide	(9) considerable	(10) domestic
(11) relevant	(12) sufficient	(13) attach	(14) ancient	(15) anxious
(16) false	(17) highlight	(18) familiar	(19) distinctive	(20) economic
(21) direct	(22) reliable	(23) climb	(24) annual	(25) potential
(26) demonstrate	(27) original	(28) administrative	(29) legal	(30) rough
(31) casual	(32) exotic	(33) bright	(34) romantic	(35) nervous
(36) aggressive	(37) handle	(38) flexible	(39) doubtful	(40) disabled

2. 实战演练（选出最符合句意的选项）

（1）【答案】A

　　【解析】本题考查动词词汇。（A）assume 假设，认为；（B）presume 推测；（C）assure 保证；（D）exclude 排除，故选（A）。

　　【翻译】许多人认为我的全部工作就是坐在电脑前尝试新游戏。

　　【词汇积累】game 游戏

（2）【答案】B

　　【解析】本题考查固定搭配。divide up into 意为把……分为，故选（B）。

　　【翻译】一周分为工作日和周末。

　　【词汇积累】weekday 工作日

（3）【答案】C

　　【解析】本题考查形容词词汇。（A）considerate 体贴的；（B）collective 共同

的；（C）considerable 相当多的；（D）sensible 明智的，故选（C）。

【翻译】这个节目会成功的，因为主持人有相当丰富的电视从业经验。

【词汇积累】presenter 主持人

（4）【答案】D

【解析】本题考查固定搭配。（A）associated 有关联的；（B）appealed 上诉引起的；（C）tied 系紧的；（D）attached 附属于，附上的，故选（D）。

【翻译】活动概要见附件。

【词汇积累】outline 概要

（5）【答案】A

【解析】本题考查形容词词汇。（A）doubtful 怀疑的；（B）good 好的；（C）wanted 被征求的；（D）uneasy 心神不安的，故选（A）。

【翻译】他对工程进展如此之快表示怀疑。

【词汇积累】quickly 很快地；立即

（6）【答案】B

【解析】本题考查形容词词汇。（A）invasive 入侵的；（B）aggressive 有攻击性的；（C）predominant 主要的；（D）stubborn 顽固的，故选（B）。

【翻译】你不能在教室里做出这些具有攻击性的行为。

【词汇积累】classroom 教室

（7）【答案】B

【解析】本题考查形容词词汇。（A）foreign 外国的；（B）exotic 异国他乡的；（C）royal 庄严的；（D）opposite 截然相反的，故选（B）。

【翻译】许多学生在毕业时就开始计划他们的异国之旅。

【词汇积累】journey 旅行

（8）【答案】A

【解析】本题考查形容词词汇。（A）legal 法律的；（B）authority 权威；（C）equitable 公平的；（D）legislative 立法的，故选（A）。

【翻译】白天，他写法律合同，而晚上，他花长达8小时画画。

【词汇积累】painting 绘画

（9）【答案】D

【解析】本题考查形容词词汇。（A）actual 实际的；（B）genuine 真实的；（C）real 现实的；（D）original 最初的，故选（D）。

【翻译】秘书不是她最初的职业选择。

【词汇积累】secretary 秘书

（10）【答案】A

　　【解析】本题考查形容词词汇。（A）reliable 形容词：可靠的；（B）rely 动词：依靠，信赖；（C）reliance 名词：依赖，依靠；（D）reliability 名词：可靠，可信赖，故选（A）。

　　【翻译】你的工作是要有说服力，听起来可靠，并要强调产品的价值。

　　【词汇积累】emphasize 强调

Day 18

1. 扫码听写（根据所听音频写出本单元对应单词）

（1）aesthetic	（2）assemble	（3）promote	（4）terrible	（5）wealthy
（6）private	（7）modify	（8）dirty	（9）investigate	（10）privileged
（11）affordable	（12）justify	（13）upload	（14）specific	（15）occupy
（16）sweet	（17）interrupt	（18）mention	（19）anticipate	（20）switch
（21）cruel	（22）eminent	（23）polite	（24）estimate	（25）ordinary
（26）vulnerable	（27）calculate	（28）anonymous	（29）shut	（30）damage
（31）abandon	（32）consist	（33）violent	（34）apologize	（35）combine
（36）unpredictable	（37）edible	（38）claim	（39）straight	（40）warn

2. 实战演练（选出最符合句意的选项）

（1）【答案】B

　　【解析】本题考查动词词汇。（A）compile 编译；（B）promote 促进，提升；（C）complicate 复杂化；（D）rise 上升，故选（B）。

　　【翻译】许多人积极支持或推动慈善事业发展。

　　【词汇积累】charity 慈善事业

（2）【答案】A

　　【解析】本题考查动词词汇。（A）modify 修改，改进；（B）change 改变；（C）alter 常指轻微改变，强调在保持原状的情况下进行局部改变；（D）adjust 调整，调节，故选（A）。

　　【翻译】他开始改变这种材料的颜色。

　　【词汇积累】material 材料

（3）【答案】A

【解析】本题考查形容词词汇。（A）affordable 负担得起的；（B）affirmative 肯定的；（C）reachable 可获得的；（D）approachable 平易近人的，故选（A）。

【翻译】这个菜单上的食物对我来说是负担得起的。

【词汇积累】menu 菜单

（4）【答案】C

【解析】本题考查动词词汇。（A）load 装上，装进；（B）participate 参加；（C）upload 上传；（D）uplight 向上照射的灯，故选（C）。

【翻译】请把我的文章上传到这个网站。

【词汇积累】passage 文章

（5）【答案】A

【解析】本题考查动词词汇。（A）anticipated 预想；（B）eradicated 消除；（C）predicted 预测；（D）corroborated 证实，故选（A）。

【翻译】找到丢失钥匙的主人比他想象的要花更多的时间。

【词汇积累】owner 主人

（6）【答案】C

【解析】本题考查动词词汇。（A）pose 造成，引起；（B）clam 抓蛤蜊；（C）claim 声称；（D）shout 叫嚷，大声说，故选（C）。

【翻译】健康专家声称世界各地人们的饮食习惯正在改变。

【词汇积累】specialist 专家

（7）【答案】D

【解析】本题考查动词词汇。（A）cooperate 合作；（B）undertake 承担，从事；（C）participate 参加；（D）combine 结合，联合，联合，故选（D）。

【翻译】每年那个时候，成千上万的人聚在一起赏月。

【词汇积累】thousand 千

（8）【答案】A

【解析】本题考查动词词汇。（A）abandoned 放弃；（B）avoided 避免；（C）explained 解释；（D）intended 打算，故选（A）。

【翻译】这一原则可因她的话而略为放弃。

【词汇积累】slightly 轻轻地

（9）【答案】B

【解析】本题考查形容词词汇。（A）harmful 有害的；（B）vulnerable 脆弱的；

（C）numerous 众多的；（D）difficult 困难的，故选（B）。

【翻译】今天游戏中的保障是脆弱的。

【词汇积累】safeguards 保障

（10）【答案】D

【解析】本题考查动词词汇。（A）expect 期待；（B）anticipate 期望，盼望；（C）foresee 预见，预知；（D）measure 判断，衡量，根据句意为"很快就能分辨出这些艺术家之间的差异"，故选（D）。

【翻译】你会提高对艺术品及其创作者的鉴赏力，很快就能分辨出这些艺术家之间的差异。

【词汇积累】appreciation 鉴赏力

Day 19

1. 扫码听写（根据所听音频写出本单元对应单词）

（1）government	（2）competitor	（3）military	（4）sensible	（5）oblige
（6）obsess	（7）district	（8）solid	（9）conclusion	（10）awareness
（11）feedback	（12）smooth	（13）frozen	（14）concept	（15）drama
（16）ban	（17）entertainment	（18）identical	（19）extinction	（20）dumpling
（21）reject	（22）launch	（23）decline	（24）agency	（25）possess
（26）generation	（27）certificate	（28）appreciation	（29）severe	（30）element
（31）guilty	（32）bargain	（33）addition	（34）remarkable	（35）inflatable
（36）congratulation	（37）field	（38）neutral	（39）gentle	（40）mixed

2. 实战演练（选出最符合句意的选项）

（1）【答案】A

【解析】本题考查形容词词汇。（A）sensible 明智的；（B）aware 知道的；（C）conscious 意识到的，神志清醒的；（D）reasonable 有道理的，合情理的，故选（A）。

【翻译】你自己做这件事是不明智的。

【词汇积累】yourself 你自己

（2）【答案】B

【解析】本题考查形容词词汇。（A）compelled 强迫的；（B）obliged 有义务的；（C）thanked (to) 多亏；（D）extended 延长了的，故选（B）。

【翻译】你觉得有必要物有所值，但这是有衡量的。

【词汇积累】value 价值

(3)【答案】C

【解析】本题考查名词词汇。（A）effect 效应，影响；（B）impression 印象，感想；（C）awareness 意识；（D）interpretation 解释，说明，故选（C）。

【翻译】广告不应造成误导。

【词汇积累】advertisement 广告

(4)【答案】B

【解析】本题考查名词词汇。（A）concepts 概念；（B）insights 见解；（C）perceptions 看法，认知；（D）judgements 意见，判断力，故选（B）。

【翻译】这件古董还可以为了解古代文化中的人们如何生活提供新的见解。

【词汇积累】antique 古董

(5)【答案】B

【解析】本题考查形容词词汇和固定搭配。be equivalent to 相当于……，等（同）于……；……be identical to 与……相同；matching 使……相配；be corresponding to 对应于，故选（B）。

【翻译】我一个月挣的差不多是500美元。

【词汇积累】earn 挣

(6)【答案】C

【解析】本题考查形容词词汇。（A）positive 积极乐观的；（B）negative 消极的；（C）neutral 中立的；（D）disinterested 公正的，故选（C）。

【翻译】他想以中立的方式传达必要的信息。

【词汇积累】manner 方式

(7)【答案】D

【解析】本题考查形容词词汇。（A）inflammable 易燃的；（B）inflammatory 炎症；（C）inflated 膨胀；（D）inflatable 充气的，故选（D）。

【翻译】他们用充气船在海上航行。

【词汇积累】boat 船

(8)【答案】A

【解析】本题考查名词词汇。（A）element 要素；（B）ornament 饰品；（C）essence 本质；（D）point 点，故选（A）。

【翻译】有了这类要素，这种语言对年轻人来说变得很酷。

【词汇积累】language 语言

（9）【答案】C

【解析】本题考查动词词汇。（A）possession 名词：占有，所有物；（B）own 动词：拥有，有（尤指买来的东西）；（C）possess 动词：拥有；（D）tangle 动词：使缠结，纠结，故选（C）。

【翻译】昆虫没有抗体。

【词汇积累】antibody 抗体

（10）【答案】A

【解析】本题考查动词词汇。（A）launched 上市，发行；（B）appeared 看来，好像；（C）happened 发生，出现；（D）pushed 推（进），按，故选（A）。

【翻译】这家公司去年才上市。

【词汇积累】last 上一个的

Day 20

1. 扫码听写（根据所听音频写出本单元对应单词）

（1）playground	（2）classmate	（3）overview	（4）grammar	（5）scratch
（6）spring	（7）analysis	（8）key	（9）vocabulary	（10）captain
（11）package	（12）reception	（13）channel	（14）judge	（15）picnic
（16）seal	（17）hometown	（18）measure	（19）participant	（20）reference
（21）taste	（22）belief	（23）mission	（24）silence	（25）charity
（26）aspiration	（27）workshop	（28）invitation	（29）video	（30）barrier
（31）ground	（32）signal	（33）chemical	（34）sentence	（35）interior
（36）merchandise	（37）reply	（38）balcony	（39）refund	（40）patient

2. 实战演练（选出最符合句意的选项）

（1）【答案】D

【解析】本题考查名词词汇。（A）outset 开始，开端；（B）scratching 划痕，划伤；（C）source 来源，出处；（D）beginning 开始，故选（D）。

【翻译】我不知道我做错了什么，所以我不得不从头再来一遍。

【词汇积累】wrong 错误的

（2）【答案】A

【解析】本题考查名词词汇。（A）spring 春天；（B）water 水；（C）season 季节；（D）jump 跳跃，故选（A）。

【翻译】这张花的照片是去年春天拍的。

【词汇积累】flower 花

（3）【答案】C

【解析】本题考查名词词汇。（A）treasure 财宝；（B）objects 物体，物品；（C）package 包裹；（D）wrap 有包装的，故选（C）。

【翻译】你可以在任何服务台检查你的包裹，腾出更多的手臂空间来放更多的购物袋。

【词汇积累】shopping 购物

（4）【答案】B

【解析】本题考查名词词汇。（A）telling 讲述；（B）measure 措施；（C）way 方法；（D）pric 价格，故选（B）。

【翻译】你在考虑采取什么措施来禁止在公共场合使用手机吗？

【词汇积累】ban 禁止

（5）【答案】D

【解析】本题考查动词词汇。（A）buy 购买；（B）purchase 购买；（C）demand 强烈要求；（D）refund 退款，故选（D）。

【翻译】她准备把坏了的洗衣机退了。

【词汇积累】machine 机器

（6）【答案】C

【解析】本题考查动词词汇和固定搭配。（A）except 不包括；（B）answer 回答；（C）reply 回复；（D）maintain 维持，故选（C）。

【翻译】请尽快给我答复。

【词汇积累】quickly 快速地

（7）【答案】B

【解析】本题考查名词词汇。（A）performs 执行；（B）signals 信号；（C）leadings 引导；（D）infomation 消息，故选（B）。

【翻译】马对几乎看不见的信号做出启动和停止的反应。

【词汇积累】invisible 看不见的

（8）【答案】A

【解析】本题考查动词词汇。（A）tasted 品尝；（B）cooked 烹饪；（C）made 制作；（D）drew 绘画，故选（A）。

【翻译】你已经闻过、尝过新食物了。

【词汇积累】food 食物

（9）【答案】D

【解析】本题考查名词词汇。（A）task 任务；（B）target 目标；（C）work 工作；（D）mission 使命，故选（D）。

【翻译】我们要出国完成自己的使命。

【词汇积累】go abroad 出国

（10）【答案】C

【解析】本题考查动词词汇，（A）revolution 名词：革命；（B）result 导致；（C）judge 判决；（D）solution 名词：解决办法，故选（C）。

【翻译】裁判员做出了公正的判决。

【词汇积累】referee 裁判

Day 21

1. 扫码听写（根据所听音频写出本单元对应单词）

(1) volunteer	(2) dollar	(3) furniture	(4) knife	(5) memory
(6) juice	(7) climate	(8) snack	(9) structure	(10) dozen
(11) principle	(12) label	(13) comedy	(14) garage	(15) rule
(16) diet	(17) manufacturer	(18) episode	(19) infection	(20) manual
(21) root	(22) seminar	(23) release	(24) passion	(25) medium
(26) politician	(27) fruit	(28) motivation	(29) trick	(30) satellite
(31) deposit	(32) ocean	(33) sympathy	(34) invention	(35) proportion
(36) qualification	(37) craft	(38) sample	(39) file	(40) muscle

2. 实战演练（选出最符合句意的选项）

（1）【答案】A

【解析】本题考查动词词汇。（A）volunteer 自愿；（B）voluntary 自愿的；（C）oblige 迫使，责成；（D）prepare 准备，故选（A）。

【翻译】哈迪森先生希望学生们自愿为活动日做准备。

【词汇积累】activity 活动

（2）【答案】B

【解析】本题考查名词词汇。（A）root 根源；（B）principle 原则；（C）cause 原因；（D）footing 立场，故选（B）。

【翻译】画的风格在特定时期有其原则。

【词汇积累】painting 绘画

（3）【答案】C

【解析】本题考查名词词汇。（A）film 影片；（B）series 系列节目；（C）comedy 喜剧；（D）opera 歌剧，故选（C）。

【翻译】男人喜欢喜剧而不喜欢悲剧。

【词汇积累】tragedy 悲剧

（4）【答案】B

【解析】本题考查名词词汇。（A）infective 感染性的；（B）infection 感染；（C）infectious 传染的；（D）infected 为动词感染的过去形式，故选（B）。

【翻译】春天的时候，我得了肺部感染。

【词汇积累】spring 春天

（5）【答案】C

【解析】本题考查名词词汇。（A）paper 纸张；（B）core 核心；（C）file 存档；（D）table 桌子，故选（C）。

【翻译】我会把你的报告存档在我的电脑里。

【词汇积累】computer 电脑

（6）【答案】A

【解析】本题考查动词词汇。（A）deposit 存款；（B）refund 退款；（C）money 钱，钞票；（D）cash 现金，故选（A）。

【翻译】我们希望贵方在此期间至少存入250美元。

【词汇积累】period 时期

（7）【答案】A

【解析】本题考查名词词汇和固定搭配。（A）trick 把戏，技巧；（B）treat 款待，招待；（C）fraud 欺诈，骗局；（D）game 游戏，比赛，故选（A）。

【翻译】作为初学者，我不会玩这个把戏。

【词汇积累】beginner 初学者

(8)【答案】B

【解析】本题考查名词词汇。(A) adaptation 适应；(B) motivation 动力；(C) application 申请；(D) competition 竞争，比赛，故选 (B)。

【翻译】申请人缺乏动力，所以他工作起来似乎缺乏激情。

【词汇积累】applicant 申请人

(9)【答案】D

【解析】本题考查名词词汇。(A) optimism 乐观；(B) caution 小心；(C) deliberation 考虑；(D) passion 热情，故选 (D)。

【翻译】由于她对创新风格的热情，她的电影获得了成功。

【词汇积累】innovative 创新的

(10)【答案】A

【解析】本题考查名词词汇。(A) seminar 研讨会；(B) school 学校；(C) fair 展览会；(D) company 公司，故选 (A)。

【翻译】这次研讨会的主题是讨论河流的污染问题。

【词汇积累】pollution 污染

单词话题归类

1. 服装与配饰

bag	perfect	small
clothes	popular	special
colour	recommend	suitable
dark	reflect	traditional
design	replace	typical
fashion	ring	unusual
fashionable	romantic	valuable
modern	separate	warm
new	short	watch
old	simple	wear
ordinary	size	

2. 通讯与科技

advanced	equipment	reliable
analysis	estimate	remote
camera	experiment	repair
channel	information	reply
chemical	invent	satellite
communication	invention	send
computer	investigate	system
control	launch	technique
decline	measure	technology
digital	mobile	useful
electronic	model	value
energy	receive	website
envelope	reference	

3. 学习与教育

academic	answer	belief
aesthetic	article	book

certificate	look	school
classmate	majority	science
concept	matter	seminar
context	mistake	sentence
course	motivation	solve
degree	opinion	specialize
education	overview	spell
enrol	package	start
episode	playground	story
graduate	point	student
grammar	practical	suggest
history	project	support
know	publish	talk
knowledge	question	teach
language	register	text
learn	remember	think
level	research	try
listen	review	vocabulary

4. 娱乐与传媒

advertisement	interview	release
art	leisure	remarkable
audience	magazine	signal social
concert	media	song
direct	perform	spread
entertainment	performance	stage
exhibition	photo	style
film	play popular	upload
highlight	post	video
image	programme	

5. 家人与朋友

adult	community	family
baby	connection	friend
child	couple	friendly

generation	personal	society
guest	relationship	sympathy
love	satisfy	talk
marry	secret	teenager
meet	sense	welcome
name	share	

6. 食物与饮料

bake	edible	restaurant
bottle	food	sauce
chocolate	fresh	snack
coffee	fruit	sweet
cook	ingredient	taste
delicious	juice	treat
diet	menu	vegetable
dish	mixed	
dumpling	picnic	
eat	recipe	

7. 健康与医学

body	infection	risk
break	lung	safety
clinic	medicine	serious
cold	mind	strong
dangerous	muscle	temperature
dirty	nervous	violent
doctor	patient	vulnerable
element	physical	warn
gym	pressure	worry
hand	problem	young

8. 爱好与休闲

adventure	bar	collect
atmosphere	camp	collection
award	cartoon	comedy
band	celebrate	craft

display	music	practice
drama	obsess	present
dream	organize	read
enjoy	paint	relax
hobby	party	sculpture
invitation	passion	sleep
life	plant	theater
member	pleasure	wedding

9. 家居生活

album	knife	screen
bed	kitchen	shut
care	lifestyle	switch
furniture	light	table
garden	live	tool
home	occupy	wall
key	resident	

10. 感受与观点

afraid	case	enormous
aggressive	casual	expectation
ambition	comfortable	exciting
anonymous	congratulation	experience
anticipate	considerable	factor
anxious	cruel	false
apologize	decision	funny
appreciation	deep	gentle
appropriate	disadvantage	goal
argument	distinctive	grateful
aspiration	difficult	great
attach	doubtful	guilty
awareness	dry	happy
boring	easy	high
brilliant	effort	hot
busy	eminent	image

impact	lack	polite
important	late	positive
impression	long	purpose
incredible	loss	ready
independent	low	sensible
interesting	lucky	successful
judge	necessary	suppose
keen	neutral	terrible
kind	object	thought

11. 建筑与地点

address	council	hotel
apartment	country	library
assemble	decorate	local
balcony	direction	location
bank	district	museum
beach	door	park
build	front	quiet
capital	gallery	street
centre	garage	village
city	hometown	workshop

12. 购物与服务

advance	discount	order
attraction	expensive	pay
bargain	facility	price
buy	feedback	prize
card	free	reception
change	label	reject
cheap	list	selection
choose	luxury	sell
compare	mall	service
complain	merchandise	shop
crash	money	standard
deposit	option	store

| supermarket | survey | tip |

13. 体育运动

action	climb	round
activity	fast	pool
cancel	match	volunteer
competitor	race	

14. 自然世界

air	habitat	sound
animal	insect	space
bear	island	species
beautiful	land	spring
branch	mountain	star
bright	natural	strange
climate	nature	summer
dinosaur	ocean	surroundings
environment	polar	underwater
exotic	pollution	unpredictable
explore	pound	view
extinction	recycle	water
field	river	wave
forecast	rock	weather
frozen	root	wild
global	rough	wind
ground	sea	wood
grow	seal	world

15. 时间与日期

ancient	decade	night
annual	hour	previous
birthday	last	recently
century	minute	time
daily	month	wait
date	next	weekend

16. 旅游与交通

aeroplane	inflatable	straight
captain	leave	taxi
cruise	luggage	tent
culture	move	traffic
delay	passenger	travel
distance	passport	vehicle
domestic	return	visit
drive	right	voyage
flight	ship	way
fly	sign	wide
foreign	stop	

17. 工作与就业

ability	conference	handle
achievement	contact	industry
actor	critic	inform
administrative	customer	job
affordable	delivery	journalist
agency	demand	letter
announcement	diagram	manager
applicant	driver	manual
apply	economic	manufacturer
assistant	editor	material
background	effective	message
budget	employ	mission
business	employee	modify
calculate	engineer	notice
career	establish	office
coach	factory	owner
colleague	file	pilot
commercial	financial	politician
company	form	position
complaint	government	process

product	qualify	staff
professional	reduce	task
promote	report	term
proposal	sample	writer
qualification	solution	

18. 其他名词

access	elementary	priority
addition	event	progress
advantage	face	proportion
advice	feature	quality
appeal	force	reason
attention	future	refugee
attitude	idea	refund
barrier	interest	resource
beginner	issue	result
behavior	medium	rule
catalog	memory	scratch
challenge	military	series
character	number	silence
charity	paper	skill
conclusion	participant	structure
condition	people	surface
contrast	plan	surprise
detail	population	trick
dollar	power	waste
dozen	principle	

19. 其他动词

abandon	agree	avoid
achieve	allow	believe
admire	arrange	belong
admit	ask	borrow
adopt	assume	bring
affect	attempt	claim

combine	find	keep
consist	finish	manage
convince	follow	mean
create	guarantee	mention
damage	happen	oblige
decide	hate	observe
demonstrate	hide	persuade
determine	identify	possess
disappoint	imagine	prepare
discuss	improve	prevent
divide	include	prove
encourage	increase	provide
escape	inspire	raise
expect	interrupt	realize
explain	introduce	request
express	justify	say

20. 其他形容词和副词

actually	extended	major
always	extra	massive
available	fair	obviously
average	familiar	original
basic	famous	possible
certainly	generally	potential
common	however	private
constant	identical	privileged
currently	immediately	properly
definitely	impossible	proud
different	individual	public
disabled	initial	quickly
especially	interior	quite
even	international	regular
eventually	legal	relevant
exactly	main	same

several	solid	sure
severe	specific	temporary
similar	still	top
single	suddenly	unique
smooth	sufficient	wealthy